THE HEART OF YOUR POWER

PLAYFUL GUIDELINES FOR AWAKENING YOUR
INNER WISDOM

LINDA NICHOLE CARRINGTON, PH.D.

My dearest Soul Sister,
I'm so very grateful to share
this journey with you.
My life is blessed by your
loving support in every
aspect of my life.
    Big hugs, much love and
cheers for all our successes
to come —
            Blessings of joy,
            Linda Nichole

Wellsourced Press

TABLE OF CONTENTS

*"There is a soul force in the universe,
which, if we permit it, will flow through us
and produce miraculous results."*
—Mahatma Gandhi

Printed in the United States of America

First printing 2018

Library of Congress Number: 2018905506

ISBN: 978-1-7320044-1-2

Limits of Liability and Disclaimer of Warranty:

The information in this book is not intended or implied to be a substitute for professional medical advice, diagnosis or treatment.

The names and identifying characteristics of individuals in stories, other than my own, have been changed to respect their privacy. In some cases, composite characters have been created to represent universal themes.

Published by: Wellsourced Press, Publishing division of Spirit's Wisdom.

717 Shasta Street, Roseville, CA 95678

www.Spiritswisdom.com

Cover Design: Deranged Doctor Design www.derangeddoctordesign.com

Editors: Anya Clowers and Lori Hermann

DEDICATION

TO YOU, DEAR READER

There is great wisdom and power within you just
waiting to be remembered.

ACKNOWLEDGMENTS

"If you light a lamp for somebody,
it will also brighten your path."
– Buddha

I had a village of kind eyes who offered their honest feedback in the making of this book. Many thanks for your contributions. You make me a better writer.

To my parents, Col. Milton H. Page and Glenna A. Page: You provided me with nutrient rich soil in which to grow, explore and be a citizen of the world. This was the perfect way to raise me. You were the perfect parents for me. Thank you for continuing to guide me from beyond this physical realm.

To my siblings, Kathy and Ken: Kathy, you saved my life by gently lifting my eyelids so I could see what I had so skillfully buried. We helped each other regain our power. Ken, you walk with power and humor, a rare combination. Your love, compassion and strength inspires me.

To each of my five children: You are the most beautiful human beings I could have ever hoped for: Shanon, Ryan, Melanie, Jennifer, and Heather. I'm so proud of each of you. Being your Mother is my greatest joy.

To my dear friend, Elizabeth: You inspire me. I love our time together. It is so nourishing to my heart and soul. You are a beautiful being of such radiance. I am often humbled by your honest love and unfailing quest to show up in your full presence.

To my dear friend, Delphia: Thank you for all the fun we had in Flagstaff. I grew because of your pure, loving heart and sense of fun. Thank you for doing the research needed to publish this book, being my friendly eyes for what works and what doesn't, and especially for being a life-long cherished soul-sister and friend.

To my dear friend, Bonnie Gallup: Together we've braved personal vulnerabilities to follow a path of self-awareness in service to the divine feminine. Your clear insights are always inspired, deeply appreciated and life changing. I always look forward to our Wednesday calls.

To my writing and developmental coach: Nancy Shanteau, your direction and humor inspired me in so many ways to be vulnerable with my story. You encouraged me, challenged me and kept my feet to the fire without burning them to a crisp.

To my Editors: Thank you Anya Clowers and Lori Hermann for your superb encouragement, shaping and editing. Your eye for detail, continuity, and structure has made me a better writer. Your fresh and friendly eyes helped to shape the book.

WHAT NICHOLE'S CLIENTS SAY
ABOUT HER

"When I first began coaching with Nichole I had lost my voice and my spirit. I didn't know who I was in this world. Through her supportive coaching, listening and guidance I rediscovered my voice and strengthened my spirit. I learned how to listen, feel and speak. I have become the person I have always wanted to be in my personal and professional life." – **Kerri, Manager**

"Your presentation last night was masterful in its content, its presentation, and its effectiveness. It was just a real masterpiece, a work of art, finely crafted, and finely done. The presentation, the exercises and the points around living one's color were superlative. It was absolutely inspirational and perfected. The point will be one that will NEVER be forgotten by any of those present." – **Keith M. CEO**

"I am still glowing. You restored my balance so I could move forward. Your non-judgmental wisdom makes it easy for me to trust my instincts. More importantly, you introduced me to everything I have longed for in life. You are a consistent, powerful and loving coach." – **Samantha S. Senior Manager**

"Nichole understands that the "self" you bring to work is part of a larger whole, and that understanding drives her coaching. She's helped me understand my own tendencies and motivations, where they work for me, and when I can steer them in other directions for better results - both at work and in my personal relationships. She's goal oriented and structures her work with clients around their stated goals, making very useful time of our coaching sessions. She's helped me immensely by pushing me out of my comfort zone and letting me know I can trust my own instincts and knowledge. I highly recommend Nichole!" – **Kathleen, Corporate Banking**

"On behalf of the entire Vocational Agency Network in Nevada County, we would like to express our deep appreciation for the excellent presentation you provided. We thank you not only for the information, insight and downright fun, but also for your patience in allowing us to complete the business portion of our meeting. Your presentation was a wonderful breath of fresh air for all of us. Thank you very, very much for your time, profession-alism and patience." – **Lin & Chris, Employment and Training Reps.**

"Last year two things were happening to me that didn't seem age related, but were a nuisance to deal with anyway: I started getting a sharp, pinpoint of pain on the inside of my right foot that felt like electrical current hitting it, and I would wake up with a persis-tent cough at night that was driving both me and my wife bonkers. I went to Nichole because I had heard of her energy clearing from a relative—that it worked wonders, and boy did it! Almost instantly all the pain in my foot just stopped, and my wife said I wasn't coughing at night anymore, but I didn't know that part because I've been sleeping soundly ever since! To this day, more than a year later, I have no coughing and no pain in my foot. Thanks, Nichole!" – **Ryan, Bestselling Author**

"I was so far on burnout with my 24/7 managerial role in a critical technical business I was losing my health. Nichole's coaching saved my life! Literally! I can breathe, my staff can breathe and strangely, we accomplish more and are having fun, if you can believe that. Invaluable! It is must for all high demand, high achieving leaders." – **Raymond, IT Professional**

"Kyle and I were blessed to find you, maybe divinely led to you and we can't thank you enough for what you have done for us to help us become our best selves. You have helped us to find inner peace and joy, you are an inspired angel that blesses the lives of others. We love you." – **Katrina, Real Estate**

"When people ask me about Nichole's 'energy work' I have a simple answer. "She has mastered the field of energy work in the quantum realm." The next question I'm asked is: Does it work? To which I have another simple answer. "Yes." I receive the proof I needed when I allowed her to connect and work with my energy fields. At times of extreme stress she has sent me calming and relaxing energy that arrived with unbelievable clarity of thought. At times of pain, she quickly dispatched energy solutions to completely resolve lifelong back issues and persistent knee pain. Most recently, I'm convinced, eliminated kidney stone pain by destroying the stone itself. Can I prove that one, no. But I can state that within an hour of asking for her assistance, the pain went away and has never returned. Scientific principles or not – you want to know and work with Nichole." – **Robert, Attorney**

"Every time I reach out to Nichole she provides the perfect insight for what I need for my life experience(s) at that particular time.

Her coaching provides the direction I need to obtain the most out of each experience. Because of her connection to the universe/angels/surrounding energy I'm able to approach life in a different light than was taught to me through the eyes of our old ways of the world. Nichole has a genuine ability, honest devotion and a network of coaching tools she utilizes to assist with my life experiences. Her guidance is unique and completely in tune each and every time. I truly am blessed not only to be able to benefit from her insight/coaching but also to be connected to such an inspiring and generous person!" – **Billy W. Real Estate Developer**

"You restored my balance so I could once again move forward. I see how you, being in your power, assists me in regaining my power...very clean, very clear." – **Mark T. Leadership Coach.**

PROLOGUE

Mirror, Mirror on the Wall
A Reflection of Power

Have you ever had something seemingly simple turn your world upside down? Today is Friday, date night with my husband, a night without the kids. How was I to know tonight would be one of those moments.

My husband and I went to dinner at our favorite restaurant. It felt good to take a break from family demands. I just wanted some time alone to reconnect with my busy husband. The dinner was mildly relaxing, but it didn't lift my mood or leave me feeling particularly valued or cherished. The date didn't nourish my heart. It turned out to be just a meal out and time away from the kids. That's okay, I thought. I was happy to dress up and be out, I consoled myself, which should be enough. What was I hoping for anyway, I silently asked myself?

We finished our meal, paid the bill, and left our table. I led the way, meandering through the tables toward the front door of the restaurant, when I saw the most beautiful woman I'd ever seen coming toward me. She had on a stunning white dress. Our eyes met as she and her date/husband walked toward me. In the space of a heartbeat, I sized her/them up. Everything was in slow motion, so I could capture every detail. Her beauty, confidence, and her radiant presence mesmerized me. She seemed to have everything I didn't have—a confidant, yet fluid, walk, a satisfying relationship and an ease in her body. The woman carried a quiet power that ran deep in her cells and, I surmised, her date/husband was a faithful and cherishing kind of man by nature.

I was totally captivated. It was love at first sight. Honestly, it was a miracle that I could even keep walking. She was everything I wasn't. In a flash, comparison cut through me like a knife. What seemed evident to me was that she had her life together in a way I could only hope for. How unlike my life, I thought. I felt small, unloved, uninspired, and insignificant compared to her. I wanted to keep her in my sights for as long as I could, absorbing her essence deeply into my cells. I silently prayed that her power and grace would take seed in my life.

Abruptly my awareness shifted. I don't know what happened, but it felt like time and space had shifted, yet I was still there in the restaurant, but in a different way. It felt a little bit like being on a carnival ride that had come to an abrupt stop, while adrenaline still created a belly sensation of forward movement. I was jolted awake only to realize I had actually been seeing *myself* reflected in the large mirrored wall of the restaurant. Yes, *I* was wearing my white dress. Yes, *my* husband was actually behind me. I blinked my eyes in disbelief. I was confused. Was this my doppelgänger? Or is it really me? Which one was the real me? Was I both women? I experienced a psychic shift of the *Twilight Zone* variety. I slowly realized the mirror reflection incident was a gift from my Soul, and I swear I heard my Soul say: *Why not try my version of you instead?*

Some of you may have had a similar experience. This is called Cognitive Dissonance–the gap between how we are now and how we want to experience ourselves. I would love to tell you I was able to claim this revelation corporeally, but I would be lying to you and to myself. The contrast was enormous, yet inspiring. At that time, my self-esteem was still lurking about like a nasty hangover from a difficult childhood. I didn't know I was born to be powerful. I had no idea there was a heart in power or that it could be playful. The most important questions we ask are: How do I see myself and who am I being?

Why I Wrote This Book

Like many sensitive and empathic people, I grappled with my identity. Sovereignty or agency, well, that just wasn't in my dictionary. This revelation gifted me with the first real possibility of living powerfully, from the inside out. My healing started with a fundamental truth: *I am how I see myself.* My daily question started with, *Who am I being?* That's what my vision offered: Powerful or powerless? We can choose either. My passion has always been to help others walk in their own power. I've been doing this professionally for 28+ years. I've actually been guiding others since I was Nine years old, I just didn't get paid. I wrote this book so you can access your spirit's wisdom and claim your inherent power.

As you begin any book of this nature, it's useful to name a specific intention, goal or purpose for reading. What brought you to this book? Put your own intention down on paper and let it be your bookmark as you read or get a notebook and put what you want from this book. That way, everything you learn will serve *your* intent, power and wisdom and will shape your listening.

DEFINITION OF TERMS

These are my definitions of words you will see as you read.

Soul: The enduring, nonphysical aspect of us that is the keeper of our collective life experiences. The indwelling spirit, higher self, and the little mind reside within the Soul. It has no personality; only Light, Love and Wisdom.

Higher Self: A wiser aspect of us that knows our divine plan, Earth's plan, all records of Earth and Human. It sees the Wholeness and Oneness in everything. Our Higher Self is the closest in proximity to us. If the term *Higher Self* isn't comfortable for you, substitute my *Wise Self*.

Spirit: Spirit is the pure energy of light and love that enlivens us, without which, we would not be alive. It inspires us and guides us. It is the unseen force of life in all things.

Whole Mind: Its nature is to seek connection rather than separation. It's our master computer for all things Physical and Spiritual. Contained within the whole mind is the subconscious mind. Our subconscious mind resides here and is our faithful servant for manifesting the reality we live in. This is the part of the Whole Mind which is 100% programmable.

Little mind: I use the term *little mind* as an endearing way to represent the ego or our limited ideas of self. Little mind focuses only within a tiny sliver of a huge bandwidth of what is possible. Little mind is useful, but it doesn't belong in the driver's seat of a high-performance car any more than a two-year-old does.

Free Will to choose for ourselves: This is the backbone of Earth's Mastery Academy. Nothing exists in your world without your permission and agreement. Therefore, there are no victims here; only Sovereign Beings who direct their energy through Free Will choice.

Sovereignty: You are the exclusive owner of your body and your life choices. You decide what is right for you. You are the cause rather than the effect, active rather than passive. It is the opposite of helplessness. Similar words for sovereignty are agency, self-empowerment, self-responsibility and self-respect. There are two expressions of sovereignty: Emotional and Spiritual. We need both to be fulfilled. Emotional sovereignty comes first: In **Emotional Sovereignty**, we take responsibility for our life, our choices, and their results, completely free from the need to make anyone or anything wrong, including ourselves. In **Spiritual Sovereignty**, we remember that we are grand Eternal Souls, sporting a totally amazing body with a very imaginative persona for this lifetime. We favor our Eternal Soul nature as the supportive landscape of our life, guiding us in unimaginable ways.

Our inherent power: This means we were each hardwired at birth with all the power and resources we need for this journey. We don't have to pay a fee in order to activate or use our power. We don't have to learn from scratch. Hardwired. Available. That simple.

Light: You are made of star-stuff. You are brilliant lights of the Divine Creator. Your Light is what you bring in service to Gaia, Mother Earth and her evolution into higher frequencies of Love.

Earth's Mastery Academy: This is how my guides invited me to look at the structure of the world. It is a structure within which we advance self-loving, into sovereign power, then into Self-Mastery. Self-love sometimes seems so far away, like it's the Grand Prize of Life. I prefer *self-loving* since it is an ongoing action of self-respect. The earth is not testing us nor do we get graded. Earth's Mastery Academy is a metaphor we can relate to.

INTRODUCTION

Who Am I to Be Your Guide

Many of you are meeting me for the first time, so in this brief section, I will hold open my door of vulnerability and invite you in. My path is to share and teach what I have lived through. I also believe we learn best from the stories of other's experience. My personal journey taught me this: Power must be occupied, not intellectualized. So, what qualifies me guide you into your sovereign power and awaken your spirit's wisdom?

Well, I know victimhood. I majored in victimhood. I was a master of self-blame and withholding. I was proud of my survivor armor, but owning my own power, in any form, was a surefire way to flirt with very real danger. On the other hand, I've had a beautiful relationship with my spirit guides and unseen spirit friends from a young age. Miracles have always followed me, and I've experienced plenty. I never had the experience of a stable hometown community of loving eyes that could consistently witness my blossoming.

I am an Air Force brat. Home was constantly changing. I was always starting fresh in a new place. I had to blend in with my new classmates, face rejection, while knowing I would be gone in a year or two, anyway. Coming from the family of Air Force, I felt the value of being a citizen of the world. I treasure the experiences gleaned from many different peoples, cultures, and religions. I appreciate the richness and beauty in diversity. I learned that we are more alike than we are different, and those differences are like fragrant spices enlivening the pallet of humanity.

I felt little safety or security in my home life, though. High alert was my normal gear. In addition to having a gypsy-like lifestyle, a hefty part of my youth at home included physical, emotional and sexual abuse. That was punctuated by torture, courtesy of the 1950s mind control program in Germany. In times of terror, safe became a place outside my body. In this timeless space, many Light Beings received me; they are the reason I never gave up. By the grace of God, I blocked the most violent memories until I was wise enough to process them with understanding and love. **You won't read any gory details about those experiences in this book. None.** This book chronicles my journey to sovereign power with these the 12 Keys. They led me out of those dark memories —completely.

I'm grateful for all my experiences. I made good use of them. I was able to restore my sense of wonder and play. Italian movie director, Frederico Fellini once said, "Never lose your childlike enthusiasm and things will come your way." Aren't we really longing to have a kind and loving, even playful regard for ourselves?

I promise you, my personal stories are uplifting and positive. I will also guide you through the stories of others, like you, who learned to walk in their own power. Will you trust me to be your Guide as you step into your power? If so, I offer you a foldout road map as we get started on our journey together. We all know a road map isn't actually the journey. A good map, however, gives us a broad view of the territory we will be traveling through. We can enjoy the journey when we know where the key landmarks are. It is equally important that you know the key to your freedom is in your pocket. You don't have to go find it or have a new key made. Everything is ready for you to walk in the heart of your power. There are sign posts along our path to power.

Each chapter begins with a **KEY** to awaken power.

- **A Universal Law:** The built-in, immutable structural elements for manifesting on Earth.
- **The Myth:** Something we *tell ourselves* is true, but is really just the smoke and mirrors of outdated beliefs and fears. The myth acts like a lock, disguising our power.
- **The Key:** A thought which, when occupied, liberates our power and frees our heart.
- **The Practice:** Practical actions which will shift the gears from powerlessness to POWERFUL.

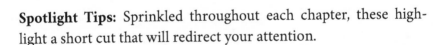

Spotlight Tips: Sprinkled throughout each chapter, these highlight a short cut that will redirect your attention.

I'll close each chapter with the following:

- **Playful Embodiment Experiments:** Embodying your power is key. Actions gather evidence of practical power. Evidence creates belief.
- **My Weekly Mantra:** this offers you a simple statement that will direct your energy. It can be an intention, if you prefer that term. It's potent.

The ultimate truth about any self-awareness book is that it's merely entertainment until *we decide to make it real.* You won't have to leap tall buildings or scale ragged cliffs for the prize. Awareness, action, focus, and gathering evidence will suffice.

Stories

The early readers of my book asked if my personal stories were really true. For the record, yes, all my personal stories did, in fact, happen as related. They are unembellished. Through them, you can witness my evolution to power.

The client stories I share are an amalgamation of common human themes to illustrate a specific principle within each Key. As I guide the clients through their process, I am also transmitting an energetic download to you, as if you are right here with me. Their successes were their own. Their healings were their own. Yours will be yours. These are stories of how each Key changed my life and the lives of thousands of men and women just like you.

Twenty Seconds

Did you know it takes less than twenty seconds for your Higher Self to reveal truth *for you,* if only you permit a pause—a mere twenty seconds—an exhale—before you press the start button on your analysis engine? Did you know that your body responds with your inner truth *before* your mind can engage and take you off path? I have an analytical mind, too. It's exciting to figure it all out. But, how do I know what is right for me, you may ask? The physical sensations you feel while reading are your body's way of confirming what's true for you. The analytical mind deftly bypasses the importance of these subtle body signals:

- A feeling of lightness with a phrase
- An involuntary muscle twitch or jump as you read a word or phrase

- An involuntary laugh out loud with delight at a thought
- A sigh and sitting back with an ah-ha awareness
- Goose-bumps or shivers on your skin
- Suddenly jumping up to walk around, letting an idea take root
- Something just relaxed in your body

Pausing.... gives favor to awakening your inner wisdom. Don't let the mental familiarity of each Key seduce you into half-heartedness. What you want is important, so be whole-hearted as you read. Otherwise, this is just a book rather than a personal journey.

The Key to Having Power

I always thought power had to be granted. I thought power had to be earned by bold actions. I thought some people had power and others, well, just didn't have it. Thankfully, my brother Ken set me straight.

He had followed in our father's footsteps and joined the Air Force. One day as we were talking, he shared his experience of becoming the new Commander of Hill Air Force Base in Utah. In the transfer of power ceremony, he said, he was *not* handed the key for leadership of the airbase. Why not? Because, power cannot be given.

The outgoing Commander held a large symbolic key in his hands; representing the key to the base my brother was about to command. The incoming Commander had to accept the power to lead within himself first. He had to know that his ability to lead and his commitment regarding the responsibility to command must be unwavering. Only then, could he authentically reach out and take the key from the hands of the outgoing Commander. Not until my brother actually took the key would the transfer of power be complete. It's the same for us. We must take hold of our own power. No one hands it to us.

True power is sovereign power: I alone direct and take responsibility for how my life is lived. Power exists in equal measure in all of us, no exceptions. Power isn't about gender, age, skin color, ethnicity, and position; nor is it about what we have accomplished or our status in our family, religion, or community. There is not my power or your power or their power. There is only one universal power to imagine and implement. This power remains potent whether we engage it or not. We aren't penalized if we pass on sovereign power this time around.

Power is how we walk in the world, not what we do. Power isn't about force or dominance. It is more about owning our own life and walking peacefully in all we do. No one has to change for you to hold your power; holding your power and keeping it fresh and clean is your business. Managing your energy is a vital key to walking in power. If you want a quick check for how you currently allocate your power, take this abbreviated version of the Energetic Power Survey *before* you get into the book. Record your numbers in your notebook or journal. This will give you a good baseline going forward and you can refer to it in each Key.

DISCLAIMER: This survey isn't about exactness. It is about expressing an emotional or instinctual percentage. It is not a factual percentage. There will be duplicate numbers. Each line represents 1-100%. So, if I were taking this survey, I might emotionally sense that I spend 80% of my time censoring what I say. So I put 80 on the first line. Perhaps I emotionally sense that I spend 78% defending myself. I would put that number on the second line. As you can see, just these two lines add up to 158%! That's because this survey reveals the amount of emotional energy you expend to avoid living in your power. The key to uncovering these energy thieves is to go with your initial gut response, not your rational mind. Are you ready to discover the energy thieves that rob you of your power?

Energetic Power Survey

I spend ____% Censoring what I say
I spend ____% Defending myself
I spend ____% Being nice, but not truthful
I spend ____% Having conversations in my head
I spend ____% Managing other's emotions
I spend ____% Reacting to what people said
I spend ____% Not asking for what I want
I spend ____% Lacking healthy boundaries
I spend ____% Dismissing compliments
I spend ____% Not asking for support
I spend ____% Not respecting my dreams
I spend ____% Downplaying my talents

Total _____%

Take a breath. Whew! That's the short list. We all do these to some degree or another, consciously or unconsciously. They may seem like habits or like second nature, so we are resigned to them or we complain about them. They steal your power, nevertheless.

Are you ready?

Come with me, for as St. Francis of Assisi said, *There are beautiful and wild forces within us still to be discovered.*

I AM A JOYFUL CHOOSER

KEY ONE

It is in your moments of decision that your destiny is shaped. —**Anthony Robbins**

- **The Law of Selection:** Selection focuses energy.
- **The Myth:** Uncontrollable circumstances shape my life.
- **The Key:** I deliberately choose how I will approach life.
- **The Practice:** What makes my heart happy? I'll go with that one!

THE WISDOM OF JELLYBEANS

We all have our way of looking at life. Selection is like having a super-duper big bag of jellybeans, and you want to eat only the green ones. That's not a bad thing, it's just one way to experience the jellybeans. Each color has a unique flavor all its own. Choosing the green ones is a conscious choice. You *love* green jellybeans! Tom may like only the red ones. Jennifer prefers orange ones.

When asked, why did you choose that color of jellybean, you may say because it's my favorite, or because I wondered what it tasted like. What if we chose that particular jellybean simply because *we can?*

No one forces us to choose the green ones. Even if our father liked the green ones or our mother liked the pink ones—we still get to choose what flavor and color calls to us. We *get* to choose our own color and flavor, including no jellybeans at all. Or do we? Do we choose out of habit or because we want what we want? Do we choose based on what we didn't get in childhood or, do we choose based on what enlivens us? The only real question here is this: Is this particular jellybean *my conscious choice,* or am I defaulting to what feels familiar? The act of *choosing* defines and structures our experiences.

Adapt Then Adopt

Right and wrong are the training wheels of childhood. This is how our family of origin's belief systems defined what's possible for us. We grew up with them, right? We learned to *adapt* to our caregiver's perspectives. They're the big people, right? They know right and wrong in the big world. Parents teach their children what's important based on their beliefs. Then we *adopt,* or borrow, their view of the world because we want to be accepted by our clan.

Perhaps Dad was a hard worker, so we pick the *hard-worker* jellybean because that's what success meant in our family. Hard work pays off. That's what you believed was true for you, too. These beliefs became our formulas for success and limits. This is also how we narrow down the universe's abundant supply. Part of becoming a healthy adult means we keep the childhood values that nourish us and leave the rest behind. There's no need to carry your childhood in your backpack. Let your life be freshly created. You want to leave your own fresh footprints in your family history.

∾

Spotlight Tip: The trouble is, if you don't direct your own choices, others will be happy to direct them for you.

There are many formulas for success and manifestation, but first, we all start with the legacy of our ancestors. It's important to note that our family, religion, cultural, gender, or societal values were often implied rather than spoken out loud, but since we grew up in that mix, this is just how life is. We all start out this way. I'll offer another slant on this subject in Key Four.

> *Getting over a painful experience is much like*
> *crossing monkey bars. You have to let go at*
> *some point in order to move forward.*
> Author unknown, but attributed to —**C.S. Lewis**

The good news is that the universal warehouse of supply is unlimited. Our right to choose for ourselves functions likes a magic wand. Selection and focus are the business of the joyful chooser's wand. Wishing belongs to doubt. Wishing isn't having, and to be clear, choosing isn't about explaining, justifying, adopting, or adapting. We could say we are deciders, but that has a hard edge on it with no soft insides. Still, sometimes we do have to make a hard decision in favor of our wellbeing. The magic wand we're talking about here isn't some kind of stagecraft with smoke and mirrors. This magic wand is about choosing in favor of the quality of life you want to experience. Respecting our own life is big, but each choices can still be made joyfully. Janette, in the following story, demonstrates what it's like to create from her magic wand of joyful choice.

Our anxiety does not come from thinking
about the future but from wanting to control it.
— **Kahlil Gibran**

Underwater and Floundering

Janette was struggling in her business. She realized something was stopping her from moving forward and being prosperous, and she really, really wanted to be prosperous. She could never get ahead of the bills. She often gave her services for a discounted rate because, as she said, "They can't afford it." (You can hear her lack of power, can't you? Not very joyful, right?) I asked her if she had a healthy cash reserve so that she could afford to discount her rates. She was quiet. Her spirit and her body wilted. She said, "No, not really," but she always felt compelled to give. Truthfully, she had no savings, and if customers didn't pay, she would sweat. She worked tirelessly while her bank account was begging to be nourished.

"Whose eyes are you looking through to define your success?" Janette thought for a moment and then almost whispered reverently, "It's my parents. They taught me that I should always give to those who couldn't afford things. They were like that, always giving."

"Growing up, did you feel like you had enough as a family so they could afford to be generous," I asked.

"Heck, no. We never had enough, but it was somehow noble to know that others could have what they needed." Janette's parent's valued service to others. They would give away their last dollar if someone else needed it. Selfless giving was big in her parents' value system. Most of us have some generosity in us anyway, but Janette's parents took it to the extreme and now she felt impoverished, perplexed, and powerless. "How do I change this so I can be successful and less stressed out?" she pleaded.

I asked Janette what would let her feel really good about her life and it didn't have anything to do with giving to others. From that question she was able to uncover her own values in just the right mix. Janette found ways to be self-defined and self-responsible. She discovered her unique value to her customers. These revelations revved her joyful chooser engine. Janette made a commitment for the next twelve months to charge full price, which would be a big leap, but she needed to build a reserve fund. She agreed to not take charity clients for a whole year. That choice was not a joyful one by any means. But, it was a necessary step. It was like the ultimate betrayal of her family values, and even through her tears, she firmly committed to stay with it. Joyful hadn't entered her picture yet.

She learned to envision ideal customers who didn't question her fees. She set her prices and stuck to them. She set up a business budget. She learned to listen to what her business needed so it could prosper. The thought that her business actually wanted to prosper revved Janette's joyful engine. Soon she was able to pay her bills on time, and later she was able to automate them. Eventually, Janette felt prosperous when she was able to deposit 10% of her monthly revenue into her reserve account.

Only after Janette had successfully made it through a full year, keeping her agreements to her business, could she then chose one charity to support. She learned to link the charity with her promotional events. Janette eventually elected to keep all her clients charity-free. Once she made the hard choice, she could joyfully and deliberately chart her heart-felt course of action.

We each live in our perspective bubbles. This simply means we each get to create our own reality. What we are comfortable with becomes our attraction factor, meaning we attract what we are kin to. Our social comfort zone determines our reality. It reflects what is familiar and recognizable to us. Our perspectives hold our habits and beliefs in place. As we explore other perspectives, we enlarge our attraction factor, thereby attracting new people and ideas. Eventually we no longer need a bubble.

Perspectives vs. Perceptions

There is a difference between perspective and perception. *Perspective* is a point of view; a lens, or a framework we use to look at life. They narrow our choices because we hone in on what we want to experience. *Perception,* on the other hand, is taking a step back to be aware of differing perspectives. Each new experience outside our social comfort zone gives us more choices about what is possible for us. When we expand our capacity, we have new insights, which then expands our comfort zone. *Perspectives* focus, whereas *Perception* synthesizes expansion.

Likewise, the word 'unlimited' means you get to decide everything. Yes, you read that right. Everything. It means you are a creative chooser machine, unstoppable and unlimited. Janette's choice had to a be a sharp right turn initially if she wanted her business to thrive. She showed us how we can love our past—but we aren't here to conform to another's way or want—unless it lights up our heart. Janette just needed a little altitude to see her own way.

"It is our choices that show what we truly are, far more than our abilities." —**JK Rowling**, (Dumbledore, from Harry Potter and the Chamber of Secrets)

Gain Altitude for a New Attitude

I remember the first time I flew in an airplane. I was five years old, and I would be starting school in a new place my dad called Germany. I had been in a car, but not in a flying car. My dad had taken me to see the planes on the airbase where he worked. He said he flew one, but I had not been inside one before and I had never seen anything from this height before. As I stretched up in my seat to look out the window on takeoff I saw the ground running very fast and my home became smaller by the minute as we got higher. And then—I was in the clouds! I had never met a cloud before. Since I had no reference for flying, I could only be amazed. With a bit of altitude, we discover a larger perspective about what is possible. Isn't that the real magic of life?

When we get some altitude from an experience, we can take in information from a broader perspective. For instance, when I have a problem or want something to change, I often imagine I am sitting on a fluffy cloud next to my guardian angel and we're snacking on bags of popcorn as we look at my life *down there* from the lens of a neutral observer. I can see everything clearly, all the players, the whole scene; how my younger self is being and the other's intent, whereas, when I'm on the playing field, I can see and react to what is in front of me or feel what I feel from only one vantage point. From my cloud perspective, I can see how my assumptions and actions impacted the outcome. This vantage point makes it easier to detect when we are in our power and when we experience a perceived loss of power.

∾

Spotlight Tip: It's easy from the cloud chair to whisper some advice in the ear of our grounded self. *Breathe easy; there's no fight here; make eye contact before you speak; ask for what you want in a* *friendly manner. I've got your back.* Altitude reveals the difference between an adventure and something to endure.

Joyful Choices = Joyful Body

Choices don't have to be made by denying ourselves anything. That's not joyful! On the other hand, too many choices clog our decision engine. That's not joyful, either. What if we choose based on what enlivens us over time?

Our experiences are meant to lead us to higher quality choices. And, we are always choosing, even if we are helplessly standing still, unable to decide where to start, we choose a pause. Let's expand our selection approach using eating metaphors: What if we could choose what to eat by not eliminating any food. What if we choose based on how we want to feel over time? This is a bite-size YES process.

Disclaimer: I'm not saying dismiss your doctor's advice or dump your prescriptions, only that you can deliberately hone in on what choice allows you to feel your very best *over time*, in any area of life. Choices are how we actively participate with life. Goals are choices for what we want to attain. Get your Goal, then create it with bite-size steps. We don't have to choose between right or wrong. Right and wrong are judgments, not choices. Don't concern yourself with what kind of foods you should eat to remain healthy (for this mental experiment). In terms of food, let's go bite by bite. Eleanor says it best.

> *The purpose of life is to live it, to taste experience*
> *to the utmost, to reach out eagerly and without*
> *fear for newer and richer experience.*
> **—Eleanor Roosevelt**

In my early days of professional training, I was often overwhelmed with information and full of other peoples' energy. When it was time for lunch, I could not process a menu at all, especially the big menu boards above the order counter in some establishments. I didn't know then that indecision is often related to an Empathic nature. When it came time to order, I would find myself ordering what the person ahead of me ordered, which didn't always sit well with me over the next hour. I eventually learned the art of asking my own body's wisdom what it would like through a sequence of simple refining questions. I would notice which one had a 'lightness response' to the question. For example: Hmm, meat or no meat? Okay, meat. (My body lit up with the idea of meat. I felt lightness.) Chicken or beef? Okay, chicken. Chicken or fish? Okay, chicken. Fried or roasted? Okay, roasted. Cooked vegetables or salad? Okay, salad. And so on. Step by step, imaginary bite by bite, I trained myself to listen for what my body wanted. I listened less and less to my stressed-out Empathic self.

> *Let yourself be open and life will be easier.*
> **—Buddha**

~

Spotlight Tip: Your magic wand is not just choice; it's about *joyful* choices. If a choice doesn't feel light or right, it's not the right choice for you at this time. Being a joyful chooser means we dump self-doubt and second-guessing in favor of continually feeling our best over time.

Our magic chooser wand isn't good for a limited number of choices and then it fizzles out. It's meant to be used over and over again. No batteries are required and there's no expiration date before for our chooser wand stops working. We often forget that we *can* choose something different. We *can* choose based on never letting ourselves down. All deliberate choices that honor our heart and Soul will lead us, joyful choosers, to a life we feel proud to live.

In relationships, for example, we fight over perspectives, not truths. We fight over the right way to roll out the toilet paper, and there is a right way! You know that, don't you? Do you take it from the top of the roll, or do you like it coming from the bottom of the roll? We may have borrowed the viewpoint from our family that the right way is from the top of the roll, of course. Yes, sadly, this is the stuff of marital fights. Dueling perspectives; fighting to be right. Will you die a horrible death if you roll from the bottom of the roll? I doubt it, but we do believe what we learned is the *right* way, don't we? We fight to be right, so we don't have to feel uncomfortable trying a different way.

You Can't Fix What Isn't Yours

When parents and significant others in our world expressed their frustration out-loud, it sure sounded a lot like they were blaming us, didn't it? Undoubtedly, we took their frustration personally, especially since they used the word *you*. You're so lazy. You're always late. You're shy, as if it's The Truth, but whose point of view is it, really? (*Hint*: if our mental chatter speaks to us as, *'you are...'* we are either not in our own life, or we are very telepathic! When we speak for ourselves, we use the word 'I'.) If you were 'shy', perhaps you were unknowingly empathically sensitive to your environment, needing time to acclimate to the energies in the room before you engaged. We have all felt the weight of innocently being or doing something that brought censure. We all know what it's like to be shut down or pigeonholed. Like Devon, in our next story, we might be trying to fix something that was never ours.

Devon, the team lead on an important company project, was chronically late. It adversely affected his team. His wife, he admitted, was beyond upset because of his chronic lateness. His friends and co-workers were frustrated with him all the time. They would jokingly say Devon's clock is broken. But, the cost to maintain being unreliable had become too high for him. He wasn't being considered for promotion. That is why I was called in. In his second coaching appointment, I asked Devon, "When did you first decide you were the one who was always late?"

He thought about it for several moments. It had been such a given in his life, so it took a while to surface the answer. He gave me some examples from his life that seemed to fit, but weren't the real source. I prompted him, "Who was always late when you were growing up?" He immediately said his Aunt Miki was always late. "Did Aunt Miki ever take care of you?" I asked.

Devon said his Aunt used to take care of him so his mother could go to work, and she was never on time to pick him up. It was a sore spot between his mother and her sister. I asked him what it was like for him when she was late.

"Well, she would come in and start yelling at me, telling me to put my toys away. I wasn't ready to stop playing, but she told me if I didn't stop playing with the toys we would be late for school and it would be my fault. She kept screaming at me and then she finally pulled me out of the house and shoved me into her car. She told me if I just minded better, we wouldn't be late. She made it seem like it was my fault, so I thought I was the one who was late," Devon said, surprising himself with this forgotten memory.

"So, what if being late was never really about you? What if being late belonged to your Aunt? [Pause] What if you were a little boy entertaining yourself until your Aunt Miki, the big person, could pick you up? What if you, an innocent child, didn't even know how to tell time or what schedules were?" He sat back in his chair, limp with the realization.

Devon slowly let his breath out and nodded with relief, his shoulders relaxing. This perspective had never occurred to him. It never occurred to him that tardiness was his Aunt's nature. Devon realized he was playing the role his Aunt had directed. He realized he didn't have to be late anymore. With a bit more work he began to dispel other superstitions about the idea of time.

Soon, Devon was able to make conscious choices about how and when he showed up. He found a peaceful power in that. This had lightened his heart. He explored the positive benefits of being on time. He opened to opportunities to feel good about how he showed up. This behavior was new to him as an adult. At first it was a balancing act to become aware of his time, but soon Devon was on solid ground and prided himself in being consistently on time. He didn't know he'd been carrying around Aunt Miki everywhere he went. Needless to say, his team changed their perception of him as manager. Leadership became more joyful for Devon, and his team flourished.

No perspective is wrong, but they are contextual. Some viewpoints simply work better than others to glide us along happily toward our goals. Devon found out that by being on time, he contributed more to his team. He began to respect himself and his leadership role. His confidence grew. Janette had agreed to the self-sacrificing lifestyle. Devon had agreed to be the problem for lateness. Neither of those agreements arose from independent thought or agency. We are all products of borrowed beliefs. As adults, we get to inhabit our own life. Comedian Lily Tomlin said, *I always knew I wanted to become somebody when I grew up. Now I realize I should have been more specific.*

I could tell you that you are the Creator of your own world, but that billboard may be too far away at this stage. It comes with such responsibility, right? Chill. Joyful choosing will get the job done with no fear. We feel anticipation when we respect the choices of our heart.

∽

Spotlight Tip: The little mind is always trying to keep us safe enough to fit in. What we try to protect keeps us small. It's not interested in you being *Alive*. Minimizing your life dismisses your sovereign power. It's healthy to question the desirability or the usefulness of our always-present assumptions *before* we act on them.

> *I never saw a wild thing sorry for itself.*
> *A small bird will drop frozen dead from a bough*
> *without ever having felt sorry for itself.*
> **—D. H. Lawrence**

The Comparison Lens

A flower never considers it should be tall like an oak tree, nor does a lion chastise itself for not being able to fly like the eagle. A flower is simply being a flower, doing its flower thing. A lion is doing its lion thing. Comparing one's self is a waste of good energy. It's simply not natural. It has to be taught. We were designed to be unlimited joyful creators, not imitators. Comparison is not a mirror you need to look in to see if you fit in. Simply being a joyful creator in your own right is enough to fuel your dreams.

However, if you've ever heard yourself saying, "I would *never* do what he/she did," then please know this: You are trying to find your value through the comparison lens of *being better than them*. That's faux-power. Please stay in your own skin and walk in your own power.

∽

Spotlight Tip: The rub of an identity based on what you wouldn't do is that you will always have to be around losers in some form, in order to identify yourself as *better than them*. Silly, huh? I thought so, too. You caught it in time.

Practically speaking, perspectives organize our thoughts, actions, and emotions as we frame *how* we want to experience our own life. As the saying goes, what you believe, you make true. What you look for, you get. As you think, so it is. What you notice grows. Perspectives are very powerful magic wands. They determine the artful quality of our life.

> *Between stimulus and response there is a space.*
> *In that space is our power to choose our response.*
> *In our response lies our growth and our freedom.*
> **—Victor E. Frankl**

The Creative Lens

It's been said that the meaning of art is in the eye of the beholder. Art invites our imagination. There's no right way to view art or life. In photography, for example, photographers look toward a broad vista for what interests them, and then they look through the camera's viewfinder to discover a perspective, a small section of the whole landscape which captivates their creative attention. They choose what mood inspires them, and then they take the shot. There's an interesting correlation between photography and how we experience life. The quality of our experience depends on where we focus our slice of attention and the mood we want to create. This is sovereign creativity. As a great co-creator with life, invite yourself to be a joyful chooser. If we don't feel alive doing something, it's probably someone else's dream. Get your own. Craft your beautiful life, your way. There's no limit to what's possible. Are you ready to make this Key REAL?

Playful Embodiment Experiments:

Pick one or two experiments to embody your power. You can also design your own experiment.

1. If I have always known that *my greatest power is being a joyful chooser,* how will this shape my day today?
2. Take a sheet of paper and draw a vertical line down the middle or fold the paper in half lengthwise so you have a crease down the long middle of the paper. On one side, jot down the viewpoints that limit you. On the other side of the paper jot down the viewpoints that let you feel alive and centered in your life. Which side gets the juice of your Magic Chooser wand?
3. Be aware today: Do you default to others' opinions, or do you respectfully express your own opinion?
4. Today imagine sitting on a fluffy white cloud with your Higher Self. Together take a look at yourself "down there" living your day. Watch the movie. What would you whisper to your grounded self that might make tomorrow even better?
5. It's safe for me to be powerful simply because I choose to develop better choices.

My Weekly Mantra: I create from my joy, and my best self is assured.

I AM THE AUTHOR OF MY OWN STORY

KEY TWO

The real voyage of discovery consists not in seeking new landscapes, but in having new eyes.
—**Marcel Proust**, French Novelist

- **The Law of Cause and Effect:** For every effect there is a definite cause. For every cause there is a definite effect.
- **The Myth:** I didn't ask for this.
- **The Key:** Life mirrors back my perspectives.
- **The Practice:** Give your story a new ending.

THE WISDOM OF THE CHERRY BLOSSOM

One of my *very* favorite movies is *The Last Samurai*, featuring Tom Cruise as the apprentice. Katsumoto, his teacher, we learn, is the ultimate, and sadly, the only remaining true Samurai warrior. Every great Samurai trains for precision, perfection and above all, honor. For Katsumoto, the driving force of perfection was inspired by his search for the perfect cherry blossom. As the movie unfolds, we see how the cherry blossoms and Katsumoto were intertwined in a lifelong dance of sought-after but never-found perfection. The true wisdom of the cherry blossom would not be revealed until the end of the movie. (Spoiler Alert if you haven't seen the movie) As Katsumoto falls in battle, mortally wounded and with death claiming him, he glances up only to see thousands of cherry blossoms drifting on a soft breeze wafting around him.

In that slow-motion moment, as his life force ebbs away, he realizes with clarity, the breathtaking truth that had eluded him until this, his final moment. With his last breath, we hear him softly utter his last words: "Perfect…. They are all perfect." This revelation came on his final exhale, dispelling the tenacious belief that there was only one perfect blossom and he was destined to find it.

Katsumoto found the elusive perfection in his last breath of life, but the miracle wasn't in the cherry blossoms. Neither was it in the last moment of his life. The real miracle occurred within the awakened heart of this great warrior. *He suddenly saw with new eyes.* Death's visit ended his quest for perfection. The ideal cherry blossom had been there all the time, he realized, each and every one as perfect as ever.

Perfection is always available in each and every moment, whether we recognize it or not. There's always a larger truth available within any conclusion. What shifts in us, as it did for Katsumoto, is how we see and experience life. Our perspective is best when it is clear and pure as Katsumoto's was in the end.

We certainly don't need to wait until the last moment of life to see things differently, although if often happens that way. We can start today to deliberately look with new eyes whenever we encounter the familiar stories we tell ourselves. You know, the less-than-attractive narratives: *I'm not good enough, I can't be successful, I can't seem to get what I want, prosperity eludes me, I'm lousy at relationships, I don't know enough, If only, etc.* These beliefs became the inner movies we run and rerun, over and over, with a different cast of characters, resulting in the same old conclusions, yet here we are, still hoping for a different ending. This is how we miss the moments to be as fully alive as Katsumoto was at the moment of his death.

> *When you get free from certain fixed concepts of*
> *the way the world is, you find it is far more subtle,*
> *and far more miraculous, than you thought it was.*
> —**Alan Watts**, American Zen Master

Martin Luther King, Jr., said, *"You cannot keep birds from flying over your head, but you can keep them from building a nest in your hair."* But that realization doesn't stop us from endlessly swatting at the buzzing noise of life. A man would seldom say to a woman with whom he was having a disagreement, "I am coming from the perspective that women are too sensitive." No, he just spats it out: "You're overly sensitive," as if it's a bad thing. An imperfect cherry blossom, he thinks. Sigh. The bird has nested. We say, "He has control issues." End of story. The bird has nested. Conclusions, like dirty birds, cannot be deterred from nesting in our hair until we are consciously present in the moment, with no expectation that people have be any different than they are for us to enjoy our life.

We are spectacular meaning makers, aren't we? That's what we do. All stories have one thing in common: every story has a *because* —spoken or unspoken. The stories became true because we gave our agreement to them. Perhaps it's time to donate those old stories to the Earth's Museum of Unnatural History. Will you accept a gentle invitation to consciously challenge your tried and trusted stories? Are you game? Can you choose a new narrative that doesn't have a make-wrong in it? Not everything is a genuine, bona fide problem.

~

Spotlight Tip: The 'problem' belongs to the person whose mouth is moving. This important distinction is useful: The person who is speaking *has the pain of an old hurt*; but is not the problem. The moving mouth signals this: What is being said *is not about you, the listener.* If your mouth is not moving, you don't have the problem, so chill. I'll remind you again in future Keys.

What others say needn't be considered an issue, a challenge, or a problem, but rather a gentle recognition that the speaker may still be carrying an old pain. There is nothing for you to fix. If we offer kind listening when someone is expressing a problem, even if it seems related to our actions, we remain in the heart of our own power. We compassionately listen only to be a gentle witness.

Note to Self: Don't chew on what isn't yours. It only leads to emotional indigestion. Everything after the word, 'because' only solidifies your perceived limitations.

Listening for our shared humanity reduces stress all the way around. Witnessing their bravery is a kind gift. Likewise, your story has nothing to do with the other person, even if it seems like it does. I know—you're sure it's the other person's fault, and he or she needs to change.

News Flash: The world was designed to act as a mirror. When we project our familiar complaints onto others, we remain power-less; at the mercy of circumstances. We project on others to see if *we* are in our own power or not. Keep it this simple.

Generally speaking, in terms of relationships, men love to solve problems and women need to be heard. Men love a challenge that allows them to be the hero by solving something difficult. For women, issues have a lot of moving parts in play before any satisfaction can occur. Issues, to men, imply there's no solvable end in sight. Men hate to be helpless. Men cannot solve issues, and women don't want to be a problem. Difficult times invite us to discover a new narrative. Put in simple men-women terms, when a woman knows her man will kindly listen until she is all talked out, her stress is reduced and her narrative about her man changes. Women need to empty out. Likewise, when men are allowed to be their woman's respected hero, appreciated, and valued, their stress is reduced and their narrative about their woman changes. Now we have happy lovebirds in the relationship nest.

Spotlight Tip: Being present in the moment is what reveals the perfection of life. In this presence, we aren't trying to make something happen. We're being natural.

When things go wrong, don't go with them.
—Elvis Presley

BLAH, BLAH, BLAH

I love the following phrase for complaint busting: "I'm making it up that you don't want me to ———." (Fill in the blank, for example: to be successful.) The *"I'm making it up that you..."* little phrase lets us keep our creative power and be responsible for the stories we project onto others. In my couples sessions I've been known to ask the spouses to honestly express their complaints to their partners. They are encouraged to speak freely, holding nothing back; just let it rip—uncensored and raw. (I know, sounds good, right, but it's very risky for sure, especially if you are on the receiving end!) However, my only rule is that they can only use one word: *blah*. They can load it up with tons of genuine emotion and really get into their feelings and let it rip, **but** they can only use the word *blah* to express their complaints.

The emotional intensity gets released along with old pain, and old story lines. "Blah, blah, blah, **BLAH, BLAH, BLAH,** blah, blah..." until there's nothing left to be expressed. With this nonverbal sleight of hand, they usually end up laughing and wonder where the problem went. They didn't know that emotions only needed to be released. Words amplify emotion. "Blah, blah, blah" minimizes the meaning and drains old emotions. This method let's us bypass the self-righteous mind.

Mama Bird Story

A perspective I inherited during my impressionable years from my military father and my family's religion was that women don't work. Period. Work was the man's job as the provider in those days. The woman's role was to nurture and support her husband and their children, take care of the home, and follow him wherever his assignments led him. That's the way it was. This story, as you can surmise, is only one of many stories about what it means to be a provider. When I became a single Mom, I was ushered into financially supporting five children. I had to triple my income so my children could have a home, food, clothing and a Mom present when they came home from school.

In the role of provider I thought I needed to be hard; you know, suck it up, stay the course, and bring home the bacon. I remember a telephone conversation with my mother during that time. My profession in those early years was Clinical Hypnotherapy, a title that scared her socks off, so I just stuck to saying I help people live happier lives. She told me I was really good at what I do, but said I shouldn't charge people money for it because it was a God-given gift I had. True, it was a gift, but my inner masculine side rose up, feeling challenged and a bit defiant. I managed to tone it down somewhat before I pushed back.

"Is it important that your grandchildren have food to eat, clothes to wear, and a roof over their head?" I asked, shifting my attitude from defiant to strategic. Pause. You know she said Yes. I self-righteously replied, "Then, I have to charge money because I'm the only breadwinner they have." My martyr side raised its chin, stuck out its chest, feeling justified and then changed the subject. It was then that I put my mother (and my inner feminine) in her place, or so I thought. I hadn't really met my power yet.

The subversive narrative lurking in the shadows was that I *shouldn't have to* support my kids financially. Their father *should* do that. He *should* be the provider. They were his children, too, I justified. Underlying that was the fact that I was never seen as an equal marriage partner; I was a trophy wife. I was upset about his perception of me. No wonder I was struggling and blaming! I decided to reframe these old story beliefs into something that acknowledged my feminine nature. Their father made a choice that was right for him. I have always wished him well, so now I'm the Mama Bird. My inner feminine puffed up her feathers with a dramatic flourish. *Oh yeah. I'm the Mama Bird. I nurture, feed, and provide a great life for my little birds until they leave the nest.* With this acknowledgment, I scripted a new story to live into. No one was wrong. I joyfully stepped into my providing power.

You are the only one powerful enough to stop you,
and you are the only one powerful enough to free you.
—**Gary Douglas**, founder of Access Consciousness®

Story Pearls

It's well established that we tell stories. That's what we great creative authors do. We string together meanings, like pearls on a string, to tell the story of our life. This is how we, step by step, shape our life. The spoken word is very powerful. We summon and command our creative forces every time we speak a story into existence. Either we freeze a story as the truth, redirect it as being in progress, or we lay down an inviting and lush garden path we want to continue to explore. Life is dynamic, always inviting us to favor emotional and spiritual maturity. Let's consider the oyster's gentle manner of dealing with disruption.

Spotlight Tip: We keep the old stories going because we already know how to handle them. We might not know how to handle something out of our comfort zone. Don't let that stop you.

The Oyster Knows

The oyster is praised for producing priceless pearls. Pearl divers gather what the oyster has perfected. Pearls, however, are a product of irritation. A grain of sand finds its way inside the soft, tender insides of the oyster. The oyster doesn't experience the sand as an intruder or get all huffy about the grain of sand. It doesn't do battle with the grain of sand. It doesn't run from the potential harm a grain of sand could cause. It doesn't try to convert it with sermons. The oyster doesn't shut down because something intruded on its sacred and tender insides. It doesn't make excuses for the grain of sand, either. The oyster didn't do anything wrong to attract a grain of sand into its shell. Instead, the wise oyster simply envelopes the innocent grain of sand, layer by layer with its soft inner body tissue until it produces a priceless pearl. It's the way of life for an oyster.

Masterful advancements aren't about getting rid of some nasty irritant. We can simply enfold the seeming irritant within the softness of compassion, forgiveness and love. We are continually being invited to be the priceless pearl rather than the irritant. Hurt will inevitably hurt back until it is finally loved. Instead, irritation is an invitation for pearl-making. Benevolent Love always invites us to see the truth, as Katsumoto did. There is perfection in all things, even if all we see is imperfection.

Spotlight Tip: Irritations are invitations, not life sentences. Opportunities for occupying our power come when we feel irritated, unappreciated, slighted, never right, shamed, rejected, controlling, or controlled. What's the use, we say and figure this is just the way things are. My friend, an oyster never makes that conclusion.

If you're going through Hell, keep going.
—Winston Churchill

Our Life's Theme

Our life's Theme is similar to a Ph.D. one might earn in higher studies. We selected our major focus and designed our path for this life, much like we would do with a college advisor. We each selected a Grain-of-sand focus for this life. It might be focused on love, service, creativity, abundance, freedom from constraints, or relationships, for example. When we get into the rhythm of pearl-making, everyone and everything in our life holds an opportunity for liberating the heart of our power. Our Theme (our pain story) signals us when the time is ripe for pearl-making and not before. When a irritant, a pattern of thought, or an old behavior is complete, we are then rerouted to higher levels of being. That's the name of the game in pearl- making; one layer at a time.

Abraham, channeled by Esther Hicks, says: *The basis of life is freedom. The purpose of life is joy. The result of life is growth.* Therefore, when your Theme comes up, don't confuse it with failure. Don't confuse it with something's wrong. Don't confuse it with your faulty upbringing. Trust that you are in the right place, right time, right situation, and with the right people. The issues or pains don't arise to be fixed or reworked so we can move forward. They arise because our heart knows a better way and *now we are ready* to free the inner pain with our love.

Here's the thing: Contrary to popular opinion, your Grain-of-Sand Theme of advancement isn't stuck in the ON position. It actually pulses on and off, off and on, and it can go long periods of time on neutral. When our Grain-of-Sand Theme *is* activated, it's downright uncomfortable. We get torqued, compressed, and drama-loaded with upset, grief or righteous anger. When our theme is activated, it signals that there is an innocent child within us that wishes to feel our loving heart before it exits. The Grain-of-Sand is a neutral agent of liberation. It is always in perfect timing. Don't blame the messenger. Just saying.

~

Spotlight Tip: When a pattern of thought or behavior is complete, we are rerouted to higher levels of being. You don't have to live your life on high alert waiting for the next shoe to drop, ever again. All themes invite us to step into a higher, truer version of ourselves.

Put Down the Cross

Your life script is not a cross you bear. Themes are not punishments from which you have to make your way back into God's good graces. Emotional pain only arises to help you stay in your own good graces. Our Theme, like a Ph.D. program, can span several lifetimes. Our grain of sand is the gym in which we build emotional and spiritual mastery muscles. We aren't here to learn lessons. We aren't here to be tested. We are here to joyfully walk in peaceful power, which advances our Mastery. We are here to perfect our themes and become Pearls of Wisdom. Terri, in our next story, will show us how we know when our Theme is activated.

Some stories don't have a clear beginning, middle, and end. Life is about not knowing, having to change, taking the moment and making the best of it, without knowing what's going to happen next. Delicious ambiguity..
—**Gilda Radner**, American comedian and actress

I Wanted This

Terri, by all accounts, is an accomplished technician. On the inside, however, she felt a bit lacking. She was always close to success but could never cross that line. Something was in the way, and she couldn't quite understand what she was doing wrong. She wanted to advance in her company, but there was a shadow that kept tripping her up, as she described it. (This is a great call for pearl-making, right?) I asked if she could give me an example.

"I work in a male-dominated environment and it's a good-old-boys club for sure. I can't seem to get recognized for what I bring to the table. The men are championed for sharing the same ideas or innovations I recommended! They get recognized for their contributions, but I get ignored. I feel invisible and often dismissed," she said. Terri went on to give other examples, which supported her theme of being ignored because she was a woman. Frustrating, right? You can recognize her Theme, can't you. That pattern won't advance her. It's just an irritant. It does, however, signal that right now is the perfect time for pearl-making. I invited her to affirm her sovereignty by speaking this out loud to her Soul, "I wanted this. Thank you! I'm ready, willing, and able to have a different outcome now." This verbalization signals that nothing's wrong. When we say *I wanted this*, we signal our Soul to level jump us. It engages our Whole Mind. *I wanted this* removes resistance and keeps us in our power.

"Well, that's different," she exclaimed.

"What opened up for you?" I asked.

"The possibility that this situation is a gift in some way. I feel energized about finding a different way to approach the situation. Still, something pulls me under when I think of the unfairness of the work environment, like I just can't get ahead. I'm really good but I get no recognition."

"Tell me more about these feelings; in what other situations have you feel similar feelings? They are familiar, aren't they?" I asked.

She nodded and named several earlier memories as a child, teenager, and as an adult. The theme in all of them was the same, she said. "I am not seen and not valued for my contribution; just shut out. I feel anger, lots of anger!"

Big anger is another signal that something is up for release. In each situation, she first felt empowered and then taken advantage of, and then ignored, and then dismissed. It was time to talk to the little one within. I invited her to connect with her inner disappointed self and to say with me, "I'm connecting with the one in me who feels invisible and taken advantage of, who has her ideas stolen or dismissed, and who has lost her way."

I paused, then asked her to say to the little disappointed self the following: "Thank you. I hear you. No one wants to be dismissed and not valued. I love you. I see your positive intentions. You've got spunk. You are amazing." I waited for Terri to digest that information and offer it to her inner child.

"Now, invite your healthy inner-child self to imagine a life where men are balanced. Real men. They value her contribution. They respect her. They're interested in what she has to say. There's genuine camaraderie in their presence, and she's also interested in what they have to say. And she grows up around these amazing men."

I waited while she assisted her little one. When she was finished, I asked how she experiences herself now when she thinks of going to work. She got up, walked around, and then paused to say, "I feel like an adult. What's *not* here is hoping to be recognized and accepted. I didn't realize how much I needed to be accepted. It was like the little one was asking for their approval. No wonder they dismissed me! I guess I really did want this after all!" she said. When we think it's about them, not us, we kick up a lot of self-righteous dust. This signals that an outdated aspect is *now* ready to leave. Terri had reached a place where her early pain was simply no longer needed, which is why it surfaced now. When she changed her energy, she could stay present, and one of two things would happen: 1. The team would begin to welcome and recognize her contributions, or…. 2. She would find another environment that welcomed her contributions. Either way, she owns her peaceful power.

No one ever finds life worth living—
one has to make it worth living.
—Winston Churchill

Updating our story never feels positive in the beginning. Whatever mess we are in, it just stinks, and we feel bad. Like any course of study, we can complain about every assignment and about the unfair instructors or we can just do the assignments, take the tests, and decide to graduate with integrity. We still need to do the work to get the degree. No one can do it for us if we are to generate priceless pearls. Remember, our Grain of Sand is a repetitive Theme. Once it can be named, we can begin a new relationship with our emerging power. Terri named her Theme: *Not Good Enough.* My theme was *Not Worth Loving.* Not Good Enough is a one-size fits-all Theme, if you can't pin yours down. Themes can play out in business, money or in relationships. Be the oyster—not the irritant.

Spotlight Tip: You're not going to be comfortable in your power until you stop hiding, blaming, or playing small. You're not going to be comfortable with yourself until you stop being afraid to be YOU.

The Wow of A Discovered Vow

It is helpful, when uncovering old patterns, to admit out loud: *I made a vow that I would never...* By starting a sentence this way, and by being curious, I was able to uncover a vow I had innocently made when I was too young to know the consequences that would follow. We all make vows as children. In my world, powerful people hurt innocent little people. I didn't want to be like them. I vowed with all my well-intended childhood willpower: "I will *never* be that powerful. I will never hurt anyone." That vow was meant to help me protect my future from further violence, or so my innocent self thought.

Power itself is a very good energizer to fuel our dreams and our heart's passion. I had unknowingly turned my power and my sexuality faucets OFF for anything that resembled powerful energy. Unknowingly, it insured I would withhold my natural power, even from myself. The truth is, we may have been victimized, but there are no victims in life. There are only people who couldn't prevent what happened. How could we ever learn about walking in our own power unless we had experienced the misuse of power?

My innocent vow kept me from accessing my dormant sensuality and authenticity. When I uncovered this vow, everything fell into place. I came to understand that I was the one who withheld my vulnerable self. I didn't need protection from ugly power. I only needed to be honest with myself. I took responsibility for being the punisher of men to protect my tender vulnerability.

Until I was able to own my part, it was very painful. I had been withholding my love, even from myself, by staying small, unforgiving, and wounded. In that moment of realization, my whole body was flooded with love and compassion for my innocent vow maker. I loved how she had served me for all those years. I felt an inner freedom.

What was done to me wasn't my business. It was done. The event had completed itself because I had survived. My business is what I did to myself as a result of the hurt. That old memory surfaced now because my innocent vow was no longer useful going forward. Whew! I was back in my Whole Mind.

Do you know your words are your best super-power? All of them. Good, bad or ugly, every spoken word is your creative super-power. Perhaps our stories aren't set in stone any more than our DNA is.

Designer Genes

We were taught in science class that we have a fixed biological and chemical nature based on the hand our DNA dealt us. We all accepted the idea of a fixed genetic inheritance. If our mother or father 'had *it*' we would most likely have '*it*.' If all the men in our family were over-weight, then we, too, would most likely be over-weight if we are a young male. And, we believe these myths because we want to fit in. If you are the skinny boy in a family of over-weight men, do you really fit in? That's the fixed DNA story. However, Dr. Bruce Lipton, contemporary scientist and author, says older science was based less on fact than it was on theoretical speculation. We accepted the speculation, as an advancement of science. We developed a shared consciousness in being genetically predetermined. But, are we, really? In his book, *The Biology of Belief*, Dr. Lipton said his repeated lab tests revealed that DNA, rather than being fixed, is actually being continually rewritten. As a scientist, he proved repeatedly that DNA is malleable, based on our attitudes about what we expected to happen. Our attitudes continually write and rewrite our DNA coding. We're really talking about your super-power: You've got Designer Genes.

Similarly, Dr. Masaru Emoto, author of *The Hidden Messages in Water* is a scientist who performed tests on water. He discovered that no matter what the quality of the water was, it could be molecularly influenced by the written word. He discovered if the word *love* was written on a piece of paper and attached to a test tube holding toxically polluted water, the water crystals literally conformed to the energy of the word *love* and formed perfect, beautiful snowflake-like patterns. Hateful words printed on paper and taped to a test tube of the most pristine water actually formed broken, damaged, and weak patterns. Why is this experiment relevant to this Key? Here's the deal: Adult humans are composed of

65% water and 80% water in children. Water is transformable based on a single word. Therefore, our words are energetic encoders, and as such, we are continually re-writing our cellular structure via the water in our body. How we speak about something shapes and continually reshapes our DNA via our attitudes. We get to re-write our genes by affirming our well being, by telling new and more interesting stories about what and how we experience life. Perhaps we aren't behind the DNA bars anymore.

Disclaimer: Don't stop your meds! The world hasn't built up a sufficiently dense enough morphic field—the glue that holds similar thoughts together—for intentionally changing DNA yet. It's still a relatively new discovery. It takes time for a new science idea to go viral in the educational system, so be smart. Don't think jumping off a tall building won't hurt you just because you think you can fly—it will *end* you. Just saying. There are layers and layers of hurt accrued from living. Being playful and knowing you are the ultimate author of your evolving story is much easier than mud wrestling pain to the ground.

This information made me wonder just how much of our accepted reality is nothing more than thoughts we historically gave our agreement to, as opposed to actual facts. Do the new stories we tell ourselves have that much power to shape our life and change our DNA? Oh, yes they do, and there are benevolent, courageous, bold, and daring new outcomes for every single story we've ever told ourselves. You don't know what you don't know, so flip the old story and see what appears.

Do the Opposite

Why not do the opposite of what you usually do? Once a week, why not declare an Opposites Day. Okay, if a whole day seems too far away, take an afternoon, or take a vacation where you allow yourself to do the opposite of what you usually do. Trust me, you will love this practice, so, start where you can, one choice at a time. For example:

- If you usually get frustrated with your boss, on Opposites Day, you get to choose the opposite. Perhaps you choose to find ways to align with the values or goals your boss is striving for.
- If you feel disappointed with your husband, do the opposite and genuinely appreciate what he does do for you.
- If you speak harshly to your children when you need them to do something, do the opposite, and praise the good values you've noticed them expressing.
- If you always eat at the same restaurant, choose a new place in a new area of town.
- If you always do the same thing on date night try something completely new to both of you.

Doing the opposite signals to our Soul that we're ready for new and better outcomes. It makes us more resilient, confidant, and refreshed. When we deliberately and frequently do the opposite, we literally change predictable outcomes. I overcame a lot of habits with this Key. We're familiar with our usual choices, so the opposite. Amazing new experiences are awaiting your attention.

One change to the system changes the system. Trust your best Self to know and do whatever it takes to deliver something significant to the world. It's time for you to take your place, so be brave and give life the best you've got. You've come so far, been through so much, and made it to this moment. You are a priceless pearl in the making; the perfect cherry blossom, after all. That's all the Grain of Sand Theme is about: shape-shifting your old story into a grand love story, revealing the best possible you, layer by loving layer. Are you ready to make this Key REAL?

Playful Embodiment Experiments

Pick one or two experiments to embody your power. You can also design your own experiment.

1. If I have always known that *I continually re-write my own story*, what wonderful new story will I write today?
2. Notice what Grain of Sand Theme plays over and over again in your life. Name the core complaint at the center of your stories. That's your main irritant. Now start your pearl-making.
3. Today have an Opposites Day. If you think today is going to be hard or difficult, what would be the opposite of that? Perhaps the story of today can be easy, where things just come together. Call that forth. What did you notice by the end of the day?
4. Today just notice when and how you minimize your power. Don't try to fix things in order to recoup power. Offer *the one in you who feels powerless* permission to fully feel that powerless feeling until there is nothing new to learn from it. Usually, it happens in a nanosecond.
5. Identify old beliefs that sponsor powerlessness in your life. Just identify them. Make a list. Take a breath. Drop into your heart. Do you want to choose a happier ending or take a new path? Can you envision this actually happening? Watch that movie—it's your next amazing story!
6. It's safe for me to be powerful because I'm the only one who authors my life story.

My Weekly Mantra: I write more joyful stories every time I speak favorably about my experiences.

I AM ALREADY WHOLE, PERFECT, AND COMPLETE

KEY THREE

Just sit there right now. Don't do a thing. Just rest.
For your separation from God is the hardest work
in this world. —**Hafiz,** Sufi poet

- **The Universal Law of Unity:** All parts express
  the whole.
- **The Myth:** We are separate.
- **The Key:** The Universe always expresses wholeness.
- **The Practice:** Hand on my heart, I remember my
  inherent wholeness.

THE WISDOM OF THE MISSING W

I met Frank Dukapoo, a Hopi elder, in 1982 as I was beginning my career in Flagstaff, Arizona. Frank is from a Navajo family of thirteen children. He was the eldest and the only one to graduate from high school and go on to college to earn his Doctorate degree. He was a highly recognized Ph.D. Geneticist. He was also quiet and unassuming. He never forgot his roots and was well versed in the ways of Hopi wisdom. At this time of his life, he wanted to pass on what he treasured most—the wise teachings of his people. Doing so would help him come home to himself, he said.

Frank came to one of my community classes held at the Northern Arizona University campus. My class that evening was on handwriting analysis. His quiet, calm presence filled the room. He'd ask a question now and then, but mostly he seemed to be soaking in the information. After class he asked if I would like to meet him the next day. You know that feeling when destiny taps you on your shoulder? Your body shivers with goose bumps. You have to respond with a brave Yes, and I did just that. This began our unspoken, yet assumed arrangement: I was Apprentice and he was Teacher. The first teaching he offered was this: "A sacred blanket of love is woven from our experiences in life, and it will be, in the end, our sacred offering back to Great Spirit. It is our thank you for the gift of life we were given."

Frank would frequently remind me that I lived in fear because I didn't walk in my power. I could agree. Still, I found his words lightly amusing until I really understood their depth and power. Frank would often point out, "That's your dress-up, Linda; your mask. Stop being afraid of your power! You're here to love all of you, without apology," he emphasized. The concept was Greek to me for a long time back then, but Frank was patient.

"In time, Linda, you will realize you are a hole-in-one; get it?" He laughed, as he continued, "You know, hole in one—the epitome of golf—except this is about your life, Linda, not golf." Frank let loose another boisterous laugh, the humor of which was known only to him. Me, I didn't golf, so I inwardly yawned and smirked. He's gone off the reservation, I thought to myself. He pressed on.

"You are whole, with a capital W-H-O-L-E. We are One with Great Spirit. Whole in One, you understand? The physical body resides in Wholeness. The identity resides in Wholeness. The mind resides in Wholeness. We are already Whole. We are already perfect. We are complete in our hearts because Great Spirit allows our identities to remember Him. We are faces of the Great Spirit. That fact cannot be changed. This is what white man forgot. We have Great Spirit living inside us." He gestured to his heart. "We are not separate beings. When you walk in your power, little one, you and Great Spirit move as *one*; breathe as *one*, and create as *one*, as we were meant to, as ONE. Circumstances only nudge us to remember the Great Spirit within us." This idea excited me.

Don't Drop the W!

When we drop the *w* in Whole, the little mind thinks only of *holes* it needs to fill in order to finally be Whole, as if Wholeness is a Five-Star resort destination. The Whole mind knows we are Whole. However, the little mind lays claim to a life based on maintaining a persona. It knows fitting in, protection, and safety. No one said the little mind was the real brains of the family. It hasn't met the inherent Wholeness residing within each of us.

We lose power when we run around looking out there for a superpower, an achievement or a person that will finally make us Whole. That's a whole lot of running blind hoping to be rescued from ourselves. We're are just looking for imperfect cherry blossoms. When we drop the *w*, the incantations of our little mind would have us believe we have to feed some hungry lack inside of us. Lack turns our faces away from the Divine within our pure heart.

Even with all that, can we soften for a moment and invite this thought to enter: "I'm always Whole, Perfect, and Complete, exactly as I am, even if my mind doesn't believe it."

The puzzle during your life is about how much of this truth of being part of the Creator you can accept. How far can you open the quantum door to see this truth, when you are alive! —**Kyron,** channeled through Lee Carroll

~

Spotlight Tip: The little mind has forgotten that it, too, resides within the Wholeness. There are no outsiders. Little mind has become an injustice collector. As we remember our inherent Wholeness, we claim our power.

Let's see how the dictionary defines whole, perfect, and complete. These definitions, together, give us our common sovereign power's default setting, if you will. I'll include Holy because we are what God is doing today.

- **Whole** *Undivided:* in one piece, not divided into parts or not regarded as consisting of separate parts.
- **Perfect** *Completeness;* completed; not defective or redundant; without flaw, fault, or blemish.
- **Complete** Quality or state of being without restriction, exception or qualification.
- **Holy** Having a divine quality of *holy love;* venerated, as if sacred. Belonging to, derived from, or associated with a divine power, sacred.

Drinking From The Straw of Wholeness

Wholeness offers a different approach to daily life. Wholeness has a seamless quality to it. In the act of drinking, for example, the liquid, the container, the hand, the mouth, and maybe a straw are often experienced together, as one *whole* experience we call drinking. We could have hot liquid or cold liquid. We can pull apart the pieces to study: hand, container, mouth, liquid or straw, but independently they don't constitute the act of drinking. Everything functions within a whole system, including us. Since we are contained within Wholeness, everything we will ever need to succeed is already hard wired inside of us. No resource is lacking. You didn't walk out of heaven and leave your briefcase by the tree of life.

Yes, but, you say. No, my friend, there is no exception. Wholeness is our prime nature. We may not choose to activate a particular quality, talent, or attitude, we may choose dark over light, but everything we need for success in every area of life was already hard wired into our life's Blueprint specifically for this adventure well before birth. We were designed for a holy purpose which contributes to the Whole. Our sacred Heart knows the Truth of our origins; therefore, we are already Whole, Perfect and Complete. This is our ethic background. No exceptions.

Each person comes in to this world with a specific destiny—he or she has something to fulfill, some message that has to be delivered, some work that has to be completed. You are not here accidentally— you are here meaningfully. There is a purpose behind you. The whole intends to do something through you.
—OSHO, Spiritual Guru

Wholeness is the big picture theme running throughout this book. Science and quantum physics are taking Wholeness to the cellular level. Neil de Grasse Tyson, American astrophysicist and author, made a bold statement as a guest on *CBS This Morning*: "One of the greatest secrets biologists don't share with you is that, because in spite of the diversity of life in the world, we all have DNA in common, so in fact, we are a sample of One."

We have become overly I-centric, as if one cell in our body decides it exists independently from the whole body of humanity. That's the flawed idea of a cancer cell, a rogue cell gone mad, separate from the Whole, it thinks. Our organs and cells operate from Wholeness, unless we retrain them otherwise, as we already learned. And, to be fair, some put deadly disease on their agenda for this lifetime, for their own purposes of advancement and it, too, is held within the Wholeness. Wholeness does not judge. We weren't designed for competition of the fittest, as Darwin suggested. Our cells are designed to work together cooperatively, in unity, within an inherent whole design of life. We were designed for cooperation to advance Humanity's consciousness. Competition really messed things up. Still, I like sports competitions.

Spotlight Tip: We were designed to create, not to be perfect. Every situation offers the same return path back to Wholeness, with no penalty fee attached. We were designed to have failures that lead to successes. Otherwise, where's the fun? We could have just stayed in heaven.

What if we didn't try to be perfect, to be right, or to be successful in each moment? What if we could step lightly, knowing the peace within and let the moment be good; let it be Whole, Perfect, and Complete as is. The Upanishads say, *Bright but hidden, the self dwells in the heart.* Exactly as you are, right now, as you read this, you are already Whole, Perfect, and Complete. Breathe it in, dear One. The Oneness of all life knows your name.

What's in A Name?

My mother always told me that a child with many names is a well-loved child. (Still, I hated it when she called me brat.) When I speak of the Oneness, I am including our collective sacred names for the Source of all life. I'll use several names throughout the book, including Benevolent Presence, Divine, Infinite Intelligence, God and others.

No matter what our religion, culture, or belief, we all have a name for the One who gives us the breath of life and inspires us beyond our circumstances. Man created religion, which is lovely, as long as it doesn't cloud the fact that religion is not a popularity contest.

The names we give this Benevolent Presence are like the many branches of the great Tree of Life, each unique and beautiful in its approach to embody the Great Mystery. Each name means HOME. We will realize our Wholeness when we understand there is not a separate human and a separate God. We will realize our Perfection when we understand we lack nothing. We will realize our Completeness when we become playful and lighthearted.

The Eyes Have It

Rumi says it this way: *The lamps are different, but the light is the same.* This understanding came through loud and clear in a workshop I took. In a group exercise, we were to visualize a familiar fearful moment arising from within our next guided meditation. During the meditation, I felt the fear of being trapped, hurt and controlled.

We were then asked in the meditation to notice the scene from different eyes. As something wordlessly and viscerally shifted in me, I blinked and looked again. All I saw was my face on every single human being the world over. The images all wore different clothing, but I saw my face on all people, and in that moment, all fear instantly vanished. There wasn't a 'them.' There was only the same face in different costumes doing different jobs. I think this is what Rumi meant in his poem.

The Light is the same in all our expressions because we are each a Whole expression of this Benevolent Presence. Resistance vanished. Only one face on billions of human forms remained, each with its own expressions, desires, careers, and purposes. The same Light animates each face. Isn't this how the Divine experiences us? This vision negated any ideas of competition, differences, or enemies. What remained for me, as the exercise closed, was the absence of fear. We are all ONE Humanity. What if we could meet each other with kindness? Namaste. The god in me greets the god in you.

All religions represent our earnest intent to connect with what is sacred within us. Yes, there are distortions, and that, too, still has the same face of the Divine, so don't get hung up on names or religions. When we come to know the Eternal Self that dwells in our hearts, we remember what it is to be Whole, Perfect and Complete. Competition ends. Cooperation begins. And we begin to walk in the Light of our own power.

"The same stream of life that runs through the world runs through my veins night and day and dances in rhythmic measure." —**Rabindranath Tagore**

The Kiva Beckons

The Great Source that gives us breath always awaits our exploration. As a psychic medium, intuitive, teacher, healer, and mystic, I travel the dimensions of time and space as we know it. I'm a multi-dimensional being. I'm at ease with it now. I got to see behind the curtain when I had my first spiritual awakening at the age of Nine, almost Ten-years-old.

One day while exploring ruins, my young self was taken by surprise. My family was on vacation to the breathtaking beauty of Mesa Verde, the Anasazi Indian ruins in Colorado. Here was real evidence of an ancient people who had carved their home right in the reddish-golden mountainside. Its beauty transfixed me. We had the place to ourselves this day. In the course of exploring the site, I wandered off by myself. I felt irresistibly pulled toward a round open hole in the ground about three to four feet deep and maybe five feet wide.

I later learned it was called a kiva. The ancient Anasazi made these pit-like areas, which the Hopi named kiva, meaning ceremonial room. Kivas were revered as sacred places where one communed with the ancestors and with the Great Spirit that made them. In their kivas the Native Americans may have held healing rituals or prayed for rain, good fortune in hunting, or abundant crops. This ground was the very same ground where ancient people went to sweat and pray. Of course, I didn't know any of this at the time. I merely followed the path that beckoned my Nine-year-olds attention.

Stepping into the kiva, I slid down onto the earthen floor, my small back resting against the cool earthen wall as I tucked my legs up against my chest, wrapping my arms around them like a seatbelt. My feet were solidly planted on the dirt floor. I was hidden from the world. This was my own private world. How heavenly! I softened and relaxed into this strangely familiar environment. My attention gently softened into a diffused state of daydreaming. A movie-like vision of my life as an Indian man living in this very place began to play out on a screen in my Whole Mind. I felt like I was him. I looked through his eyes and saw what he saw. I could feel the strength inside his/our body. He loved and provided for his family in this very place. My heart was full with the love he felt for his family and the pride he had for his tribe. I saw and smelled meals being prepared. I smelled and heard the crackling of the campfire. I heard the communal conversations through the ears of this male-me. I felt his joy with the laughter and play of the children. I felt his connection with all life, earth and sky. For him, life was a sacred privilege, filled with immense joy in being alive and one with all life.

In my innocent, childlike awareness I somehow knew I was witnessing another me in an earlier time. I don't know how I knew it, but I did. I didn't know this was the Whole Mind at work. This inner movie began to fade and an old Indian man's wrinkled face gradually began to occupy center stage in my vision. This wrinkled face, white hair and all, looked deeply into me with loving and deeply ancient eyes. I was startled, but felt no fear, only abiding love for me. He proceeded to tell me why I was here at this time of Earth's history and that my life was dedicated in service to the Great One and to the awakening of the human tribe. I was here to remind humanity that we came from the stars as great beings of infinite light and love.

What I irrevocably knew at that moment was that I was not my body. I wore this body, but I was so much more. There were more faces of me than just the one I wore, and I was here on purpose. Somehow I knew I had a larger, loving cosmic family I could feel and see. I belonged to a larger presence than I knew here. I was loved with pureness. This non-linear information quietly rooted in me.

During this awakening, I felt and knew a Wholeness I couldn't explain with words. This Oneness was alive and vibrating in every cell of life, but there was nothing I could point to or touch. I was enveloped, held, saturated, and caressed by a feeling of deep unconditional love and peace. I had no sense of me as an identity;

as a body. I had no sense of time as a thing. I felt only the bliss and perfection in all things. I felt at home.

I don't know how long the event actually played out. In other dimensions, the idea of time doesn't exist as it does here. I didn't have the words then to explain that there is something going on here, something beyond the world we see with our eyes, something that goes on while we are busy exploring ruins.

Based on my religious upbringing, I could only refer to my feeling as God, but this expansive and Loving Presence seemed way too BIG for such a small, three-letter word. My reverie broke when, from a distance, I heard my name being called. As I slowly and reluctantly scampered out of the kiva, everything in me was longing to stay in this wonderful feeling. I was momentarily torn between worlds. I wasn't at all sure I wanted to step back into the regular world and risk losing this expansive feeling. What I experienced was more real to me than my physical life was.

There is a whole lot more going on, and I am an intricate part of that Wholeness somehow, just as you are, just as we all are. I later learned that our infinite nature, the 90% we call our junk DNA is actually multidimensional, multifaceted, quantum and nonlinear. It radiates unconditional love for each and every one of us 24/7/365, even on leap year. Wholeness is non-linear and expansive.

Wholeness is not a club you join. It's not something to attain someday. We are already Premium Lifetime Members. As with Grace, we don't need to do anything to receive this perfection. We are it. Perfection is not the same as being perfect. It is about perfecting our connection with all life. It is about knowing there is a perfect design behind everything. It is original innocence. Like a new mother nurturing her precious little baby, our Infinite Nature is also constantly nurturing us. It's ironic that when we experienced any kind of childish frustration, such as fighting over toys or falling off our bike and getting scraped up we cried big tears.

We probably heard someone tell us, "Don't be such a baby." We thought it was an insult, right? But was it really?

> *The timeless in you is aware of life's timelessness.*
> **—Kahlil Gibran**

Original Innocence

Being a baby isn't a bad thing. Babies express Wholeness very well. Babies are pure and innocent. We grow up, and too soon, we lose our newborn innocence. Parents teach babies to separate themselves into parts; to name their parts is to learn their parts, right? How else will we know we have feet?

We had to learn mistrust. We learned as we grew up that the body is not safe because it bleeds, bones break, and we get sick. We learned to separate from our body in the face of trauma. We learn to please someone outside ourselves. We learn to identify with our mind and our persona.

Our religions confirm this separation as our fall from Grace. The doctors confirm this separation, too. It's our intestines, our heart, a failing kidney, and so on, with parts and parts and parts that seemingly betray us. Babies don't know any of this. Babies are naturally innocent. We can see timelessness in their eyes, can't we? We feel their purity. Perhaps when we speak of Wholeness we are really talking about our divine innocence. In Wholeness, we don't need to remember who we really are, we just need to un-learn that which keeps us separate from the intrinsic truth: I am Whole, Perfect and Complete. As is.

There are no separate wholes, like my whole career, or my whole life. Material is not separate from spiritual. Wealth is not separate from poverty. Dis-ease is not separate from health. Evil is not separate from love. Everything, even judgment and separation, are contained within the Whole. Light and dark are not separate from the whole. There is no *me* that is separate from the perfection of the divine within. We wear a body, but we are not our body. We have a name, but we are more than our name. We have an ego, but we are not an ego. We have a history, but we are not our history. We are infinite life, radiant and intelligent. We wear a body, but we are a Soul at play. We are a Soul with many life adventures already notched on our tree of life. When we drop the *w*, we no longer nourish our true power. Cindy will share how she recovered her dropped *w* in the next story.

> *Above all, to thine own self be true, and it*
> *must follow, as the night, the day, thou canst*
> *not then be false to any man.*
> —**William Shakespeare**, *Hamlet, Act 1, Scene 3*

Remembering Wholeness

Cindy, like many of us, suffered from amnesia. She was exhausted and yet she still had family care-taking responsibilities. She felt like her life was small and she didn't know how it got that way. She loved her husband and kids, but felt like something vital was missing. After we talked a bit, I decided to have her walk the line—her invisible timeline.

We used our imagination to define an imaginary line on the office floor from one end to the other. I marked Birth on a 5 x 7 white card and had her place it on the floor where it felt right. I then made another marked Childhood, one marked Teen-hood, one marked Adult, one marked Marriage and Family, and one marked Future, and she placed them on the imaginary line on my office floor.

I asked her where she wanted to start, and she picked Teen-hood. She stepped on that marker and closed her eyes. She felt herself as a teen who had lost her father, had moved, and had to start again in a new school in a new state. As you can imagine, she awakened a lot of suppressed emotions. She allowed herself to cry out any residual feelings.

I asked where she'd like to go next. She said she wanted to go back to birth and tell herself everything would be okay. I kept her on the timeline, and with my guiding hand, she walked backward until she stood slightly before the Birth marker. She wanted to tell her little self that everything would be okay. Plenty of tears flowed. When she opened her eyes, I asked if she wanted to continue forward, and she hesitated. I reminded her she wanted to be on Earth, in this family. She chose this life. She nodded, and I invited her to trust me and allow me to move her. After a moment, she said, "Yes, please."

I gently held her arm while she walked backward, well before her birth. I stopped when her body told me to and just let her be there. "This is well before birth, Cindy. This is you well before you entered your body. Just allow, notice and feel what's here." I stepped aside. I waited as tears released a deep wisdom. After a bit she was able to open her eyes and talk about her experience. I kept her there, on that spot as she spoke. Cindy shared her astonish-ment in meeting her *real self*, as she referred to her Infinite Self. She realized her timelessness, her immense love, and her radiance. She said it was the first time she ever felt Whole in every way. Cindy wanted to stay here forever.

We all know we can't stay in that space forever, because we came here for a body and for life's experiences, right? I asked Cindy if she would like to walk this feeling through her timeline, and she lit up like a Christmas tree. I helped her anchor her Wholeness feeling in her heart. She called the anchor her Golden Star, and she walked forward on her timeline as her Golden Star, pausing at all the places that whispered for her to linger and then moving when it felt right to do so. I steadied her so she could stay on her timeline and be present with her eyes closed, as she'd requested. When she stopped and opened her eyes, and when I knew she was ready to talk, I asked her if she would like to share what that experience was like.

"I felt pure love flow through me, moving through each cell, each experience I had planned for myself. In each I remembered the love I am, and everything seemed to take on a soft glow. I feel confident that I am in good hands, and more than that, I feel Whole inside, really whole and profoundly loved. I know everything is as it was supposed to be for me, to be in this moment, right here, so I could remember the truth of me. I am Whole in every way, always, no matter what emotions flow through me, I am an Eternal Soul."

We both felt the beauty of her energy. She stepped off her timeline when she was ready, and went back to her chair. I followed. Cindy said she felt complete; perfect exactly as she was. She remembered her Wholeness. She softly gave thanks and we closed the session. I would see her in a week, and I wondered what that future meeting would hold. I too, was deeply grateful for her experience. You see, when one person remembers his or her Wholeness, we are all, everywhere, forever changed and we each have a path back to Love, thanks to Cindy.

Stop Divorcing Your Authority

Note to self: You cannot outsource your Authority or your Authenticity, but we do. We hold others at fault because we did not choose well for ourselves.

Our primary relationship is with the wise Soul residing within us, giving us life. We are not here to settle into adulthood and grow old. No, we are always evolving, and that means we have to stop dragging around our past with us everywhere like a tattered childhood blanket.

Abandonment issues are prevalent because we believe other people shouldn't have abandoned or betrayed us. This kind of thinking means we are the one who dropped the *w*. The reality is they did the best they could in the moment, given their beliefs or their pain. Period. They left because it was time for them to leave. Their leaving had nothing to do with us. They simply left, but we, on the other hand, have been leaving ourselves every day since then. I know. I walked the treacherous line of self-abandonment most of my life. It's a bloody path with no victors.

Instead of measuring our progress by how far we've come from pain and hurt, perhaps we begin to measure ourselves by how honest, present, brave, happy or playful we are being. Harboring a hurt seduces us into divorcing our authentic self from taking responsibility for our own actions and misunderstandings. Feeling inadequate is how we abandon ourselves. Comparison is how we abandon ourselves. The people who inspire us and are successful are the same as us. They have developed their gifts and talents. People who are relaxed and confidant are the same as us. Inspiration doesn't have to mean comparison. Mark Twain said, *"The two most important days of your life are the day you were born and the day you find out why."*

Spotlight Tip: Whenever we withhold any part of ourselves, we will project abandonment or betrayal onto others. We do this so we can see what we have done to ourselves. Mirror, Mirror. Just saying. Please, offer yourself and them some Grace. Walk respectfully and kindly inside your own power.

The truth is that people know when we aren't being genuine. People know when we are being false or holding something back.

So why not be honestly honest? If you're angry, be angry as an honest expression, but then *let it be* once you've spoken it. Let it drain from your body. Put the fight down. Choose something different.

Leave the proverbial kitchen sink right where it is. Stay in the present moment. Breathe. It's natural to feel vulnerable until honesty becomes our preferred habit; until quiet vulnerability becomes our norm. Can we pause, stop the machine of the mind, and remember the innocent child within us who is full of curiosity and wonder? That's beginners mind, our Whole mind before we started conditioning it. Austin demonstrates this for us.

> *When you rest in quietness and your image of*
> *yourself fades, and your image of the world fades,*
> *and your ideas of others fade, what's left?*
> *A brightness, a radiant emptiness that is*
> *simply what you are.*
> —**Adyashanti**, The End of Your World

Spidey Senses

Rarely do we have a direct or unfiltered experience with the Wholeness of life. We're too busy trying to figure out how to get whole. This habitual thinking sucks the life out of our inner peace. To approach life with a beginner's mind requires us to release all preconceptions and just be, without trying to make the moment be something, without labeling anything.

Wholeness, when lived, means we don't have to struggle to figure things out. We only need to become curious with an approach akin to the wonder of a child. Presence is the beginner mind's path. It is the key to inhabiting the heart of our power.

Austin reminded me what an unfiltered, in-the-moment, freshness with life is all about, as only children can do.

My then Four-year-old grandson, Austin, found a spider on the driveway of his home one day. I was lost in watching him as I stood by my parked car. I remained still, feeling my happy love for him. I just observed, keeping my own energy snugly tucked away so as not to influence his experience. I witnessed unnoticed as he squatted down and gently rested his finger on the driveway so a spider could climb on. He was lost in softly marveling the spider.

I was watching an ancient and sacred dance of two creatures meeting one other in pure innocence. It was incredible and humbling to witness. He made no assumptions about the spider, as only an innocent child can do. His eyes were fresh. He didn't need words. When they finished communing, he gently set the spider down and watched it go back to its spider business. There was a profound and holy reverence enveloping him. He slowly looked up at me and sported an unassuming smile, waved, and went about his business. I had just witnessed a fully awakened human being, pure and innocent.

Little Austin had a direct experience with the spider, uncolored with beliefs about spiders' friendliness or unfriendliness. It wasn't intellectual. He didn't need to be taught about spiders. He assumed good will as he communed with the spider. If I had asked him afterward what that experience was like, he would have been taken out of his direct, wordless experience. I would have changed his experience. I would have caused him to put definition and meaning to a sacred communion. What occurred between them needed no definition and no words. It was the pure Wholeness of Being in action. It was Perfect and Complete in the moment. Be still, and know I am God, came to mind. It is in such reverent moments that our Divinity perfumes within us and we are serene. Lacking nothing. Wanting nothing. Oneness in action.

Bright but hidden, the self dwells in the heart.
—The Upanishads

You are Whole, Perfect, and Complete exactly as you are. Rest gently in this thought from **A Course in Miracles**, *We attend in silence and in joy. This is the day when healing comes to us. This is the day when separation ends, and we remember who we really are.* All is well. We reside in Wholeness. Are you ready to make this Key REAL?

Playful Embodiment Experiments
Pick one or two experiments to embody your power. You can also design your own experiment.

1. If I have always known that *I have everything within me for my success*, how would knowing this influence my actions today?
2. When you are tempted to feel scattered or down on yourself, remind yourself that you are being held lovingly in perfect Wholeness and all is well in your world. Bring yourself into that. Put your hand on your heart and gently breathe.
3. What perceived holes have you been trying to get others to fill for you so you can be whole? Take an honest assessment without judging others or yourself. Simply write down the holes you chase to fill.
4. Sit today in quietness for ten minutes. Be still. Breathe. Feel the Wholeness in the center of your being. Allow it to glow. Allow it to nourish every cell, every thought, with its wisdom of your perfection.
5. Walk slower today. Gift yourself some contemplative time. Open your curiosity aperture and allow yourself to

feel ONE with the air, trees, flowers, sounds of life, and the night sky with its vast array of magical stars.

6. It's safe for me to be powerful.

My Weekly Mantra: I am Whole, Perfect and Complete in action and in deed.

I AM ALWAYS IN RIGHT DIVINE FLOW

KEY FOUR

*Out beyond ideas of right doing and wrong doing
there is a field. I'll meet you there.* **—Rumi**

- **The Universal Law of Divine Order:** A perfect order is in play, even if we cannot see it.
- **The Myth:** Others can; I just can't.
- **The Key:** We are not flawed.
- **The Practice:** This must be the perfect time for this to happen, since it is happening now.

THE WISDOM OF FORGETTING

Almost a year before I went to Greece, I had participated in a group Shamanic Ceremony by a friend I had met while on a trip to

Mexico. During this ceremony, I was given the spiritual name of Aelethia (pronounced like _Aet_na, the Insurance company). It's beautiful and it felt familiar, but I wanted to know what it meant. Those around me didn't know and said it was for me to discover. From that day forward, I went on a quest to find the meaning of my sacred name. I searched everywhere, only to find nothing. When I quieted myself, I had an instinct that I would learn what Aelethia meant on my upcoming trip to Greece. I could, for the moment, relinquish my quest and be patient, not an easy task for me. Inquiring minds want to know!

Before long, I was in Greece with our small spiritual group. Oh, how I loved being in Greece! It's a land of such beauty, culture, and history. I knew I had walked this land before. Our tour guide was a beautiful young Greek woman. We loved her energy and attitude as she opened the doors of time for us. Our days were filled with the country's history and beautiful sites. Many of us on the tour had mystical experiences at the different sites we visited. I did as well, but I still knew nothing about the meaning of Aelethia.

Our three weeks timelessly flew by. It was the last day. The tour bus stopped to let our guide off before returning us to our hotel for the night. We were leaving for our respective homes the next morning. We had offered our guide a generous gratuity, sincerely thanked her, and said, "_Andio sas_," which she taught us meant good-bye in the Greek language. She pivoted and stepped off the bus. The trip was over. I slumped in my seat and rested my head against the glass window. I felt my heart sink. I thought with a sigh of resignation, _Well, that's that. I still don't know the meaning of Aelethia._ In a heartbeat, I heard a voice within softly say, "Trust your Divine flow."

Surrender Again

When we stop the hunt, we often find the treasure right under our feet, so I surrendered again, lifting my head off the bus window, letting out my breath and centered myself. In a nanosecond I surrendered everything in me. I surrendered not knowing. Just let it be, I whispered to my disappointed self. I had no choice but to trust.

As easily as our tour guide had stepped down, she took one step on the ground and then apparently pivoted and stepped back up onto the bus in a surreal kind of ballet. She planted herself on the top step and quite out of character, asked us a deliberate and rather blunt, insistent question.

"Do you know what our Greek word is for Truth?" Of course we didn't. She resumed, "Our Greek word for Truth is Aelethia. A means without, and Elethia means forgetting. Therefore," she said, "Truth means: without forgetting. When we no longer forget who we really are, in the larger sense, then we will know all Truth."

She then sputtered a bit of an apology as she backed down the steps. This perfectly describes the Whole Mind. My heart leapt and silent tears of truth slid down my cheeks. My Soul had delivered the answer through the words of our guide literally at the Eleventh hour and Fifty-Ninth second. I felt the power of divine flow lifting me into its Grace. I vowed to never forget who I truly am. I would remember. I am Aelethia, she who embodies the truth of the Divine Feminine heart. I am always in the right divine flow of my destiny.

Wisdom comes with the ability to be still.
— From the book *Stillness Speaks.* Copyright © 2003 by Eckhart Tolle. Reprinted with permission of New World Library, Novato, CA. www.newworldlibrary.com.

I know I am a joyful chooser, I know I author my own evolving love story, and I know I am Wholeness in action, exactly as I am. I don't believe in a random universe. As Earth is taking a giant step forward in its evolution, even amid all this conflict, I am here. So are you. We are here on purpose. Truth means *without forgetting* who you are and the power for good you carry within you. We all secretly yearn to be more expressive, more fully ourselves. We yearn for peace, harmony, and unconditional compassion. Be those qualities. Yearning for those qualities keeps us hungry, starving and sad.

All is well. Not everything is as it appears. We are in Earth's Mastery Academy, and we are beginning our graduation into more refined energies of Mastery. Together, we great Souls designed this Academy called Earth. This was our design. We were present to see Earth's creation, formed and reformed, until she met all the requirements for sustaining life. This great planetary Presence of Gaia, Mother Earth, knows what she is doing. This Academy was specifically designed to focus on the Mastery of Self-loving. Meaning, we are Love. We don't seek to be loved. Self-loving (not self-love) is Wholeness in action. Without mastering this essential element of co-creation, we could not move forward into other studies of creation. It's all right if you think only God created this Earth or if you think life was a random spin of the wheel that landed you here. You are still far more amazing than you can possibly imagine, and now we are here, together, so let's suit up.

Suit Up

We are fond of saying, without boasting too much, that we use 10% of our brain. What about the other 90%? Does that mean we placed only 10% of our vast infinite consciousness at the helm of this small, but exquisite physical form? Yes, indeed my friend. That was all you, Bold Creator. Does that mean we only have access to 10% of who we are? Nope. Not by a long shot. Within this amazing body lies our wisdom body, the 90% Infinite, multi-dimensional consciousness. This contains our personal Blueprint for this life.

Don't confuse this with a contract, though. God doesn't do contracts. Humans do.

We reside in a living flow of Divine Creative Energy. We can cooperatively work with our Higher Self to develop the wisdom planted within us. Our Higher Self is the memory bank for our life's plan and purpose for this life; it is part of the 90% of the unseen Soul. Our Higher Self is closest to our physical self and is still only a fraction of the vastness of our Soul. The Higher Self and the Soul (the Quantum self) know only Oneness. Together, they exist in the unseen Quantum environment of Earth's Mastery Academy.

We tend to think spiritual growth is about bringing the 90% unseen wisdom to the Earth (to create Heaven on Earth), but that isn't necessary. It is *ever* present. The body, however, is the one having the experience here, because it is made of Earth's matter. The physical matter of the body is advancing consciousness. The body is advancing its capacity to hold love and light. Self-loving, then, is all about consistently honoring the body's experience in the fields of matter. Our body loves it when we love it. Just kind thoughts, thanks and nurturing care are enough.

Eons ago, we chose to incarnate our particular point of Divine Light into Earth's Mastery Academy. Individual identity is not the same as separation, since there's only Wholeness, but then, the idea of separation is seductive. It keeps the game going, right? We are right where we wanted to be. We placed our feet into our own right divine flow of life the second we were conceived. The more we stay in our right divine flow, the more Alive we are. Divine flow knows our individual Blueprints and will always reroute us to our sovereignty.

～

Spotlight Tip: You are not an accident of creation. You were not cast out of heaven for breaking some injunction not to eat apples... as if God creates anything harmful. Nope, humans do that, not the Divine. Your body is not a burden; it is sacred, holy matter. You're in good hands. It's okay to still cherish the biblical story of creation. That, too, resides in the Divine.

> *For every physical adventure, there's the possibility of loss. That's what makes it an adventure. For every spiritual adventure, there's only gain. Which totally spoils the adventure, and is why you choose to forget that all physical adventures are really spiritual adventures. Everything makes you more.*
> — The Universe, ©**Mike Dooley,** www.tut.com

Flawless

There has never been a flaw anywhere in our being or in the design of life. Behind the scenes of everyday life, there is a divine flow. We don't have to wait for that perfect moment or that perfect circumstance to finally know sovereignty. This is not a random universe. We are each held within our own right divine flow of Infinite Intelligence. This is a very aware and interactive Academy, always evolving self-loving into Mastery. All is well.

Right divine flow means that if something uncomfortable is happening right now, it is the right time for it to happen. Otherwise, it wouldn't be happening, right? This is how we learn to trust life. Life is not our opponent. No one is randomly throwing chaos punches into our life. No matter what you have done or not done in your life, you are inherently flawless even if your little mind tells you otherwise. You may not know your life path or purpose, but your right divine flow does. Infinite Intelligence knows when we are ready for the next evolution of ourselves.

Our right divine flow is always unfolding our life's Blueprint.

Our right divine flow is in service to staying the course of our highest, most beautiful design. We cannot be infected by others juju when we attend to where our own river of love takes us.

If we can surrender to this larger perspective, we will radically reduce the wind resistance in our life. We are not flawed. The body is not our enemy. It doesn't keep us out of heaven. It is not out to sabotage us. We have no penance to perform to earn our way back to self-acceptance. Our body actually cooperates in awakening us to the heart of our peaceful power. Our body gives us signals when we are out of our own flow. Grace arranges synchronicity. Synchronicity shows us that there is something greater happening here than just being mere mortals. Synchronicity is your right divine flow in action. We are the living Grace we think we fell from.

The good news is that this Earth experiment, I lovingly named Earth's Mastery Academy, is wildly successful. This idea was given to me in a vision that helped me understand what's really going on with life. The Academy has been wildly successful by all galactic accounts. It's original intent, as a metaphor and a structure, is to serve one another, serve the advancement of consciousness, and to serve the Light of expanding Love. We walk in Sovereignty when we choose unconditional love for self and other. Still, you may ask: How can I unconditionally love and accept myself; I mean, I know me, right? I'm only human, we say. No, dear one, we are 10% human matter in the process of awakening to the 90% Divine consciousness residing in our very cellular structure. We are that amazing!

I love the words Don Miguel Ruiz wrote in his beautiful book, **The Mastery of Love**, "*You are Life passing through your body, passing through your mind, passing through your soul. You are the force that moves the wind and breathes through your body. The whole universe is a living being that is moved by that force, and that is what you are. You are Life.*" —From The Mastery of Love © 1999, Miguel Angel Ruiz,

I love this quote because, honestly, there are times I forget and think I am a tiny speck in this big world. I feel small and fearful. Sometimes I don't think past my body and its needs. This is the reason one of "My Rules for Me" is: *I am the vitality and ever-changing expansion of Love itself.* This is how I like to experience life. More fun with this idea is in Key 11.

We have never made a wrong choice because we were given Free Will to choose. Perhaps there is something to be learned by taking a different path. Our right divine flow already knows our Blueprint, so no need to beat ourselves up. We are always being re-routed to our highest destiny.

Free Will to choose/decide where we direct our energy is the foundation of this Academy. There's nothing that needs remodeling, except on HGTV, and you are definitely not a fixer-upper, though I do adore Chip and Joanna Gaines's work. Earth's Mastery Academy was deliberately designed as a **No-Fault Zone** from the very beginning. Even the turmoil on the Earth right now is still in right divine flow, awakening us to remember our sovereignty through accountability, compassion and love for humanity. This is the perfect time for that which was hidden to be revealed. Sovereign power will trump manipulative power. Mother Earth knows exactly what she is doing. We are collectively being rerouted to higher ground of self-sovereignty.

What is Wrong with You Anyway?

Still, we dread the implication of wrongness. What's wrong with you? Boy, that question/accusation takes us out of our right divine flow, doesn't it? Whether it's spoken out loud, implied in conversation, or habitual self-doubt, this question triggers the myth of powerlessness. What's wrong with you, anyway? My friend, you haven't missed the mark, you aren't left behind, nothing's wrong in the world, and nothing is wrong about you. You and the world are both evolving, even as we speak, no matter what it looks like.

Everything is in the hands of divine timing. There's no divine wrong flow. We may just be bumping up against the veil of forgetting—the truth about our magnificence is Wholeness. **Disclaimer**: The veil of forgetting. Yeah, we wrote that into the Academy's charter. Remember? We wanted a handicap to make life more interesting. Forgetting offers our inner champion a challenge to trust our right divine flow as we dive into the human experience. Of course you forgot that—as you were meant to.

Don't Go M.I.A

Simran Singh writes, *We are not meant to settle into adulthood. We are designed to experience and express on the playground of life as life's longing for itself...Divine Children. We are here to play full out, to not just live but to be fully alive.* (www.IamSimran.com) How alive do I feel at this moment? It's a great question to periodically visit.

On a scale of One to Ten, Ten being Fully Alive, *how alive do I feel*? Similar to the Emotional Energy Survey you took as you started this book, trust the first instinctual number that comes up for Aliveness from 1-100%. Don't argue with it; just feel the emotional number and say, thank you and move on. Don't ruminate. Don't be dismayed if you register Two on a 1-10o scale. Go on about your business. Ask this question periodically as a check in with your Higher Self. Be unattached to the number. Your Higher Self knows very well what you are aiming for. Simply by asking the question and getting a number is what begins the re-routing process of energetic alignment.

I used to define myself by my husband's reputation and his work. I used to define myself by how well my kids did in school, and I would feel a slight rush of hot shame when they goofed up in public. How alive I felt depended on other people's behavior. I used to be defined by the tenets of my church. I used to be defined by how I should be to fit in. I used to be defined by...well, you get the idea. I was M.I.A. (Missing in action) when it came to being authentic. I had a bad case of the *If only*... *If only* I had confidence. *If only*... You get it. This is the spinning nature of the little mind. It has no forward movement.

$$\sim$$

Spotlight Tip: You may already know that looking to others for your validation is futile. Identifying yourself by what's wrong and needs fixing is futile. Fitting in is futile. Comparison is futile. Only we can make our lives full of delight and alive with purpose. That's our job. We cannot make another person happy. That's their job. We didn't come here to get a Master's Degree in Futility.

Sensitive and Empaths, please pause and commit to staying in the right divine flow of *your own life*. HSP's (Highly Sensitive People) live to help others wake up, so we can finally relax into our own life. Did I say futile? We have already accomplished what we came here to offer. Now, it is time to be relaxed and inspired by *our* own life. Our Light shines the brightest when we are comfortable in our own body. The world needs our Love and Light, and that doesn't involve fixing anyone, including yourself. So, live inside your own life and let it be delightful. Let your Higher Self navigate the approach to your desires.

Life isn't about avoiding trouble; it's about being present in the tough moments so you don't miss the very thing you are trying not to lose: your self-respect, your innocence, and your healthy boundaries. This requires your attention and intention about what steers your creative interest. Let others live their life, their way.

Stay in your business. Being M.I.A. doesn't look good on you. Don't play small. You're far too grand for that.

> *Experience is not what happens to you;*
> *it is what you do with what happens to you.*
> **—Aldous Huxley**

Stay in Your Own Flow

Each of us has the last word when it comes to something that directly concerns our wellbeing. That's how we stay in our own right divine flow. We don't have to fight; we just need to speak *for* ourselves. We don't have to struggle with life. Life just is. Let it happen. Flow with it. Let Life soften your protective shell. Give yourself the moment—just BE. Put away your armor. The good news is that divine flow is always escorting us toward more aliveness, even if we get tangled in the eddy of someone else's thoughts about us. It's not an easy thing to stay in the heart of our own power, especially if we are highly sensitive. However, the more we mature our skills of tending to our own life, the more we rerouted to a higher version of ourselves. I was surprised right back into my own Flow.

I was sitting on my blue-flowered, 1980s love seat at the foot of my bed, staring at the view outside my bedroom window. It was 1:30 in the afternoon. I was tired of reading self-help books. It was exhausted trying to measure up so I could finally be enough for myself. I'll just sit for a moment, I thought. Still, I couldn't seem to relax. Something was going on. Abruptly, I felt the air in the room become strangely still around me, like a void in the time and space continuum had opened up. I could feel it in my ears. Strange, I thought. Then, I then heard a very loud *crack!* off to my right, above my dresser. It felt like the very fabric of my life had been literally split in two.

I felt a sweet rendering of unexpected freedom. In that moment, I knew I was finished chasing love and acceptance from anyone. As this realization inhabited me, the air became normal again, and I felt utterly free. Right divine flow had orchestrated my prison break from *trying* to be enough so I could be loved. It placed me firmly back in the heart of my own power. I am Love.

In that soft moment of truth, I realized the obvious. It is up to my husband, friends, or fans to love me or not love me. I have no control over someone's capacity to love. I didn't have to be different to be loved. Admittedly, I had a *lot* of practice pretzel-ing myself to suit the moods of others, but in that moment, with no tricks left in my bag, I said out loud: "I cannot outsource love. *I get* to love all of me." It wasn't really a decision I made on my own. It was a Soul gift. That's one way our right divine flow works. It helps us rub the sleep out of our eyes and wake up to our sovereign self. No more going M.I.A. Deal?

We Leave Our Right Divine Flow When...

- We try to control others to feel powerful
- We let others make decisions for us, then grumble
- We become overly helpful to gain appreciation
- We make others a project instead of enjoying them
- We don't tend to our energetic body's health
- We skate around the truth for fear of rejection
- We don't value our gifts, if we even recognize them
- We have weak self-respect boundaries
- We settle for unhealthy ways to fill ourselves

We can't hear *our* truth when we are in someone else's flow, unless that flow is compatible with our own desire.

Praise and blame, gain and loss, pleasure
and sorrow, come and go like the wind. To be
happy, rest like a giant tree in the midst
of them all. —**Buddha**

Hear Ye, Hear Ye...

A couple weeks after this re-routing, my husband and I tussled about something silly. He said what I was experiencing was like a square. Huh? This statement made no sense to me. I said it didn't feel like a square to me, and then I realized he was describing *his* impression of my experience, equating it to a square. Why was he messing with my contented flow, anyway? I didn't ask for his opinion. For me, it wasn't a competition of ideas. I was in my flow. Yet, this was the perfect moment for this to happen, because it was happening right now.

You see, after a major revelation or a new commitment to ourselves, we will likely have a Test of the Emergency Broadcast System: *Do you want to stay in your sovereign power, or do you want to continue your old behavior?* This only happens when we've had a breakthrough that required a hard right turn. Nothing is wrong. My Soul was just confirming the new direction. This experience was my test to see if I still wanted to walk in my own power; if I still wanted to be relaxed in my own skin.

My husband continued pressing home his point with vigor. In exasperation, he offered up the worst obscenity he could think of: *You should have been a lawyer!* Honestly, I knew how he meant it. He hated lawyers. Strangely enough, though, I felt calm, quietly relaxed in my body. This felt new to me. A silent space opened in me, like a garden fairy was holding the curtain open for me to see beyond a fight. I had a choice in how I responded! Trust me, this was a *very* new concept to me at the time. I took a few breaths and

I checked in with myself. Is this true for me? Hmm. Actually, I had been thinking of pursuing law as a career. I think I could be a great lawyer. More importantly, I realized *how* I hear something is my business. I could choose to hear his words as a compliment instead of a curse. That news was world shattering to me. Thankfully, I was able to set the fight down, and in a genuinely appreciative and peaceful manner, I sincerely said, "Thank you. I actually think I would make a great lawyer. Thank you for seeing that in me."

It's best not to bother about getting upset with people or situations. Without our reaction there is no fight. We do, however, get the last word when it comes to our own life. Any defensiveness we might have vaporizes when we choose to innocently respect our time and our path. Our right divine flow is always on the job. The heart of power has no need to push back. Let go of the reigns of retaliation. I love how Grandmother Carolyn taught me this lesson in our next story.

Spotlight Tip: It's easy to remain in our divine flow when we decide: I'm responsible for how I hear things. I hear others and myself with kindness. I speak for myself without judgment or fight.

Quit Horsing Around

Grandmother Carolyn was as close to a Hopi Elder as you could get. She was greatly revered in the Hopi nation as a wisdom carrier. She was a four-foot tall force of nature. I met her while living in Arizona. In the 1980s, a small group of us escorted Grandmother Caroline, Grandfather David, and Grandfather James to the United Nations. They were making their final plea for peace on behalf of Mother Earth and the peoples of the world.

They were invited to bring the sacred fire ritual to New York City's Central Park where they would offer a prayer for world peace the night before their appearance at the United Nations.

Traveling with them was an honor and an eye opener. They were wearing wrinkled skin, yet their eyes shone as bright as a full moon. Their energy carried a quiet peace. I hadn't really felt what it might be like to actually live in a divine flow until I met them. Being the empathic over-helper I was back then, I silently worried about their ability to travel. Soon, I became downright envious! They were stalwart. Their grace of presence was a miracle to witness. I was exhausted long before they were, and frankly, I never once saw any of them ever uncomfortable, exhausted or fretful in any way, at any time. *Ever.* Their composure radiated a consistent inner calm. It was uplifting to be in their presence. How do they do it, I wondered, and where can I get me some of that? I was utterly exhausted and they were serene and fully present.

Grandmother Carolyn would often share lessons with us from her Hopi perspective. Her stories weren't long unless we were talking ancestor stuff, but they were to the point. In response to some long-forgotten general complaint one member of our group had made, she responded, *"When the horse you're riding falls over dead, it's a good time to dismount."* We laughed as the teaching began to expand our understanding.

If the horse you're riding falls over dead, it's a good time to dismount. It's not time to feed it straw, kick it, love it more, or reason with it. There's no need to figure out what we did wrong that caused the horse to fall over dead. There'a no need to clear our karma with horses. There's no penance to pay. When the horse you're riding falls over dead, it's a good time to dismount and move on. Yet, how often do we carry dead horses around with us, certain they will revive if only we give in, love more, or try harder? Then, we can ride into the sunset of pseudo bliss, we think.

When things go off track and the energy no longer feels consistently life giving, it may be a signal to dismount. There are no brownie points for hanging on because you think someday he, she, or it might change. There is a time and a season for everything. When things unexpectedly change, we often feel thwarted. We think something needs to be fixed. Not true. Change is the name of the game here at the Academy and we are being re-routed. Emotional disappointment isn't tragic. It's our right divine flow asking us to respect ourselves and move on. Our experience in this situation is complete. There are greater things in store for us. Trust your right divine flow.

When we are ready to advance, we get rerouted. Nothing is wrong. We didn't flub up. We aren't being tested. What if we just let ourselves make new choices, think kinder thoughts about ourselves, or forgive ourselves for not being perfect? Life doesn't always feel good until we *know* we are always being re-routed to higher and higher expressions of self-loving. We won't really know the value of re-routing until some time has passed. For now, no matter what, know you are always in your right divine flow. Offer yourself some much-needed and well-deserved compassion. Something powerful happens when we simply declare out loud, so our cells can hear: *No one gets to be wrong, including me.* Your life just might be calling you to spread your wings and try something different.

Synchronicity is at work. When things get bumpy and scary, you are still on your right divine flow's conveyer belt. The universe is a naturally organizing system in spite of our misinterpretation of events. Yes, there are wrongs in the world, but fighting against them only leads to more fighting. Dismount and do some good wherever you can. Be an advocate for cooperation and harmony and start with yourself. Remember, Earth's Mastery Academy is a No-Fault Zone. Are you ready to make this Key REAL?

Playful Embodiment Experiments

Pick one or two experiments to embody your power. You can also design your own experiment.

1. If I've always known that *I am always in my right divine flow*, what relaxes inside me
2. Gift yourself with ten minutes of quiet silence to "just be" today; to just feel the energy of being in the experience you helped design. Nothing is wrong. Let your right divine flow visit your awareness.
3. If you declare today that you are always in your right divine flow, what natural qualities would arise?
4. Notice where you went M.I.A. (missing in action) in your own life? Whose flow were you in? What is one choice you will make today that keeps you happily in your own flow?
5. What metaphoric dead horse are you still riding? Name it. What would your life look like if you dismounted and consciously stepped back into your own right divine flow?
6. It's safe for me to be powerful since no one and nothing's wrong, no matter how it appears.

My Weekly Mantra: I am always in my right divine flow. Thank you!

I AM ALREADY PRE-APPROVED

KEY FIVE

*Just these two words he spoke changed my life,
'Enjoy me'.* —**St. Teresa of Avila**

- **The Universal Law of Deliberate Creation:** Whatever you put your thought and energy into grows choice by choice.
- **The Myth:** I have to prove myself.
- **The Key:** I'm already Pre-Approved for this life.
- **The Practice:** I approve of my choices. I can choose again, and again, and again.

THE WISDOM OF BILLBOARDS

I was traveling the California freeway from Stinson Beach back to Sacramento with my husband after a wonderful weekend adventure. I didn't know it, but I was about to have a revelatory moment when something larger than life pops in, like a cosmic peek-a-boo, to offer a fresh glimpse of what is possible. On the freeway, you ask? Yes. Awareness and enlightenment can happen anywhere, at any time, so stay awake, my friend!

My meditative question for that weekend had been about the nature of a true spiritual foundation. Suddenly, like writing in the sky, four simple words appeared, spelling out the answer for me. My eyes were instantly drawn to the right side of the freeway to a large billboard advertising a prominent bank. On a totally white background, a few words in bold red ink winked at every passing driver.

YOU WERE BORN PRE-APPROVED

I was captivated to my core. I soaked in the novel idea of being Pre-Approved. It was a new concept for me. I silently wanted my husband to turn the car around and go back so I could see the sign again. Obviously, such a maneuver was impossible on the freeway. In truth, I didn't need to see the sign again. My Soul had already tattooed its truth on my heart in a single instant. I let myself marinate in the words that would forever change the landscape of my life. *You Were Born Pre-Approved.* So, when did we stop approving of ourselves? Why do we still turn to others for their approval of us? Seeking second-hand approval is an emotionally expensive habit, for sure. It's a habit that divests us of our creative juices. It takes us right out of our own divine right flow.

When We Seek Outward Approval...

- We don't speak up for ourselves
- We don't trust our life
- We dismiss the nudges of our intuition
- We fuel the agendas of others

- We wait ages for permission
- We try to fit in where we don't belong
- We question our value

Truthfully, most of us dance around the theme of self-worth at one time or another. The early Greek playwrights coined the term *Harpies* to represent an essential ingredient in creating a good stage drama. The Harpies were mythical winged creatures who whispered in the hero's ear, harping on the hero's worst fate, heightening the risk of the hero's quest, and causing the hero to question their courage. The moment would come when all seemed lost. Will our hero reach their destiny or will they falter and fail? Will our hero boldly rise up and choose to be courageous and victorious in their quest?

The Harpies imply the question: *"Who do you think you are to...?"* Their job was to add creative tension by seducing the audience of the play to cheer the hero on to complete their quest. Our self-talk, lame excuses, constant complaints, setbacks, and lack of action are the Harpies in action. Without this creative tension, there is no real adventure.

A modern-day Harpy seduces us into thinking we aren't Whole, we aren't the author of our own story, we aren't a joyful chooser, and somehow we just aren't in the right flow of our life. The Harpies want us to believe we can't make our dreams real, as if others can make their dreams come true but we don't have what it takes. Get wise to these wily Harpies. Chill, Bold one. This is merely creative tension.

It plays out on the stage of life, whispering: You can't heal your past. You can't walk in your own power. You don't respect yourself. You never listen to your intuition. Within a short period of time, you, the Hero in this Academy of duality, begins to believe the Harpies: something really is at stake here, like life or death! Oh, my!

If we believe the Harpies, we don't create boldly. They only provide creative tension; they don't provide Truth. We have *already* been Pre-Approved for our Earth experience. If we fail to take this to heart we actually increase the tension in our lives, which makes those darn Harpies bust out a happy dance. Seriously, don't feed the Harpies!

You have brains in your head. You have feet in your shoes. You can steer yourself any direction you choose. —**Dr. Seuss** (Theodor Seuss Geisel), from, **Oh The Places You'll Go!**

I'm Alive!

Experiences aren't a life sentence; they don't brand us. They happen. They are the creative juice that moves energy from the low end of an energetic frequency to the higher end of the frequency bandwidth, based on how we respond. Every experience offers duality so we can work on our chosen spectrums of advancement. Some familiar low to high spectrums are: Sadness pairs with happiness. Anxiety pairs with choice. Fear pairs with courage. Nothing matters pairs with I matter. Powerlessness pairs with sovereignty. Poverty pairs with enough. Grief pairs with love. Pain pairs with aliveness, and so on. The lower frequency beckons our inner hero to valiantly move up the energetic spectrum, delivering us to our highest and finest expression. Charon, in the next story, illustrates the flapping of the Harpies preceding her Pre-Approved Hallelujah.

I was invited to teach a workshop about reclaiming the genuine self after trauma to a class of Hypnotherapy students. Many of the students had been dealing with the theme of childhood sexual abuse in their lives. Charon sat in her big cushioned armchair, swaddled in a wool blanket, legs tucked under her with her head listlessly to one side. It was her turn to speak. She lamented through her sobs, "I'm no good. I'm just crap. I died a long time ago, so why should I even try? I don't matter. Nothing matters." Can you hear the flapping of the Harpies' wings? Can you see how she names the spectrum she's exploring? (I don't matter/I matter) It felt like all the air had been sucked out of the room. Everyone was holding his or her breath.

I let the silence fill in, letting the moment call a truth into being. In a tender voice, I innocently asked her, "Charon, if you died, who is speaking to us now?" A different energetic signature began to permeate the silence in the room. She was momentarily too stunned to answer. I do love the power of a well-timed pause. That's when our indwelling spirit wafts in, pirouettes, and does its best work.

"I, uh, I don't know. Uh…Oh, OH!" she sputtered as new and higher possibilities gained traction. She straightened up in her chair, her feet purposely meeting the floor. She cast the blanket aside and stood tall.

"Oh my god! I didn't die! I'm alive! *I'm here!*" Her arms and hands were punching the air like an athlete who had just pushed to win the race, winner's tape flowing from her triumphant chest. Her body visibly softened into this inalienable truth as she released a long breath of stale air. Silent tears cascaded as her heart opened the door of truth. The group had been holding a safe space for her and we were thankful to finally breathe again. She seemed to relax even deeper before she exhaled.

"I guess I didn't die after all," she softly concluded. In the next moment, her whole body began to shake with big laughter, and the room burst into infectious laughter with the joy of her profound realization. Genuine laughter thoroughly dissolves old pain, faster than lightening can strike. Every single time.

While we are Pre-Approved, our most challenging undertaking is to approve of ourselves as Priceless Pearls in the making. If we continue to wound ourselves, we will have a difficult time with self-acceptance. No matter what life brings us, we can use our Free Will to choose something different. Therein lies the heart of our power. We each authored our own story. We can re-write it as we go, because we're already Whole, Perfect, and Complete. Charon had just been re-routed.

There is a divine flow ushering us to higher truths and deeper revelations whether we recognize it or not. Knowing we were born Pre-Approved is the gateway to sovereign power. A seed doesn't need to be taught how to become a tree, a flower, or a vegetable. Our body, if loved and respected, knows how to be a good and loving human. Our cells are rooted in a deep respect for life. They know what it is to be fully awake to the magic of life. Our worth in the world doesn't need to be justified or measured; it just is; like the color of your eyes.

Likewise, before spirituality or religion became concepts, we moved through our days, tilled our fields, fed our children, welcomed the sunrise and thanked the sunset, always quietly respecting the web of life. We sang to welcome our children to life, We drummed, to respect and honor death's passage. There's a quiet wildness within us. Trust that somehow, somewhere, your body remembers its loving place in Creation.

～

Spotlight Tip: Proving worth is not energy efficient; nor is it necessary. Loving your beautiful Being is enough. That's the real fuel of life.

If you're still looking for your purpose, know that looking for it is futile. If you are alive—then you are living your purpose, which was to incarnate here at the Earth's Mastery Academy. You're here now, so take the pressure off yourself. You don't have to prove yourself by having a purpose, as if having a purpose makes it okay for you to be here. Rainer Maria Rilke said, *"The future enters into us, in order to transform itself in us, long before it happens."*

The truth is, the only thing that's happening here are experiences, experiences, and even more experiences. Experiences don't determine worth. Many of us have energetic battle fatigue from proving ourselves in so many subtle ways. Perhaps personal sovereignty is, as yet, an unknown territory for you as it was for my daughter in our next story.

A Hairy Moment of Truth

One of my daughters was in her first year of junior high school when she came home one day, dumped her backpack on the floor, and asked me if she could change her hair color to blond and straighten her hair. I was inwardly taken aback. She has beautiful, naturally curly, long black hair. Before she was even conceived, she came to me in a vision wearing her curly black hair and sporting adorable hints of freckles. She reminded me in that vision that I had agreed she could come through me, so I knew this moment was pivotal in her life. It would be easy to just say *no*, and that was that. I'm the parent, right.

Yet, this was a pivotal juncture on her time and space continuum ... she was about to go M.I.A. from her life. Instead, I calmly answered, "Sure, no problem. We can get some hair dye and make it blond and we can have it professionally straightened. So.....what makes you want to go blond?" I quietly asked. She shyly tilted her head to the right and said she liked Kenny, a boy in her class. I asked if Kenny liked blond girls with straight hair, and she lit up. "Yes!"

"No problem," I nudged. "We can make sure you have straight blond hair." I paused for a moment. "And when he moves on, maybe you will like another boy, but not to worry. If he likes redheads, we can easily dye your hair red. [Pause] And after him, well, maybe the next boy will like you if you have a bold Mohawk haircut, but we can easily cut your hair into a Mohawk, and maybe even tip the ends purple. Or when he starts to like someone else, you..." I trailed off.

She exploded like dynamite, screaming at me, gesturing wildly as she stomped upstairs to her bedroom, mad as a hornet, screaming, *"You don't understand!"* Her bedroom door thundered shut and the walls of her esteem rattled. Well, I did understand. This was the first time she had been willing to change something about her so a boy would like her. Yes, I felt a little pang in my stomach. Did I go too far? My spirit reassured me, so I sat down and waited, pretending to read a magazine, keeping my breath as steady as I could.

After a while, she came down the stairs and firmly marched into the family room where she stood in front of me, her back ramrod straight, her head set firmly with a 'don't mess with me' attitude, while her eyes bored into me. Hands on her hips, she pronounced a vehement vow: "I'm not changing myself for anybody. If he doesn't like me the way I am, too bad for him." We both breathed a sigh of relief. Whew! That was close.

She is who she is, as you are who you are. Already Pre-Approved. If you've ever danced for the nod of acceptance or approval, take a breath, exhale, and bring yourself back inside your own skin, okay?

You are enough exactly as you are. People and events come and go. It's still hard to accept ourselves unconditionally, so please be gentle with yourself and others. We are all in the process of remembering our peaceful power; living in our sovereignty.

Our worth is not, nor has it never been, at stake—no matter what we were told, what we experienced, or who wants us to fit their ideal. You are worthy of your magnificence. You were born

Pre-Approved. You already have a seat at the table of life. Deal with it. You are here on purpose.

Permission is not Approval

Okay, let's take a reality check. Do we really have to learn to approve of ourselves, or do we only need to remember what's been inside us all along? As babies, approval was not the motivation for that first scream as we came to life. Babies naturally cry and fuss if their diaper needs to be changed, or if they are hungry. They never apologize for poop explosions. They don't beg our forgiveness for their neediness. They cry when they want human touch. They don't judge themselves for that explosive milk burp. They never require approval. They never ask for permission. They only look for connection in our soft, loving eyes. The baby never once questions whether it should be here or not. It never considers itself as being too selfish or of having too many unrealistic needs. Rolling over and standing up was an adventure, not a struggle; not one failure after another. It was the joyful triumph of a new vista. That's why we love babies and new toddlers. They don't seek approval until we teach them to do so. They are busy discovering the world around them. They only know loving connection. They smile and laugh for the sheer joy of being alive. We have to teach them to earn the right to have what they want and to seek our approval before we grant permission for what they want to do or be.

Permission doesn't trump Divine connection. Still, you may need to grant yourself permission to just be all of YOU. Maybe we're still waiting for someone to give us permission to bust out of our boxes, take center stage in our life, pursue our dream, or to shine like a star. Why not grant yourself the permission you've been waiting for right now? Who do you need permission from to fully be YOU? If you need God's permission, then write God on the first line. If you need a deceased Grandparent, or your parent's permission, then write that parent's name. Who are you waiting for to give you permission to be yourself?

Date: **Right Now**
I, _____, grant you full permission to unconditionally love, respect, and honor yourself in every way, in every situation, with every person, no matter how big or how selfish it may appears to others. You've already been Pre-Approved for this lifetime.
Signed _____ (your name).

We don't have to wait until we have achieved something before we can earn our own approval. All we need is to give ourselves permission to simply be enough. As adults, we have to deliberately unlearn our approval seeking addiction. Our innocent hearts aren't fulfilled by how many 'likes' we get on social media. That's fun, but it's faux-power. Power has to come from within. You've already been Pre-Approved for Earth. Deal with it, will ya!

Who Do You Think You Are?

Ultimately, we must give ourselves permission to BE ourselves, not in an arrogant manner, but from quietly knowing I am enough. I am lovable. We only need our heart's approval, so perhaps you put your name on both blank lines on the permission slip, if that feels right. Jeffery had to take a good, hard look at his photo ID in the following story.

Jeffery, a capable manager at a multimedia corporation, said he didn't feel like himself. He said he felt like he was back in time somewhere. He questioned his abilities. There had been some company restructuring, and he felt unsure of his position, like being back in fourth grade when kids didn't want to play with him, he said. He described his challenges and frustrations at work. When there was a natural pause, I asked, "Jeffery, do you have your wallet with you?" He stammered a yes, and said he always had his wallet on him. I asked him if he had his driver's license in his wallet and if I could see it. I'm sure he thought I was batty, but I wanted a practical way to restore his power. He took it out and handed it to me. I looked at his age.

"This says you are Fifty-Two. Is that right?" He looked at me like, 'duh,' but affirmed his age with a head nod.

"Jeffery, imagine carrying a photo ID in your wallet with a photo taken when you were shamed in the fourth grade. What would he look like if his photo is the one on your driver's license? [pause] Definitely not who you are today, right?" He agreed with a smirk and a nod. Handing him back his driver's license, I continued. "Now, if you were to pull out your metaphoric wallet, how old would you be in that photo ID?"

"I'm Seven, maybe, and I don't look happy at all. Kind of sad, no energy, discouraged." Jeffery looked a bit shocked at this revelation. After letting it rest, I continued the shift.

"Isn't it time to update it to reflect the successful, optimistic, capable, competent adult you are—right now?" He nodded his head and shifted into a more upright position in his chair.

"Sometimes we need to check our metaphoric wallets to make sure we have an up-to-date photo ID in our mind's eye. We want our emotional photo ID to match our current accomplishments and capabilities, right? Let's update this ID photo, okay? Using your imagination, remove that outdated photo. Give the little one a 'best effort' pat on the back with appreciation, and imagine putting that photo in an album of days long ago when you actually were Seven-years-old. That's right. Now recall as many of your accomplishments as you can. What are your successes, the growth opportunities you took on, and how you've grown and advanced from them... Imagine your capabilities and strengths." I waited while he rehearsed. "Those accomplishments feel good, right? Make sure they all represent your best so far. Let them merge into a single image of your capable, competent, and accomplished self. See it in Technicolor." I again paused while he envisioned.

"That's an up-to-date photo, right? Now, imagine taking out your driver's license, and seeing a current, up to date photo, one that actually matches who you are today at Fifty-Two, capable and confidant." Jeffery looked as if he had won the lottery. Now we could get to the issues at hand from a capable adult's perspective. As we come to trust our Pre-Approved status, the photo image we carry in our metaphoric wallet might need to be updated so it always reflects our very best self. As Dan would learn in our next story, we have a right to be here.

～

Spotlight Tip: When we approve of ourselves, we are providing nutrient-rich soil for our aliveness. Disappointment in any form doesn't equal disapproval. It signals an invitation to awaken the heart of our power, thereby, actively enhancing our life.

I'm Already a Winner!

Dan is a gifted engineer. His relationships outside of work, however, were pretty anemic, according to him. He didn't date, didn't go out, and gives up before he even starts to get to know a woman. He shared with me that long ago he had concluded he would only cause hurt and pain to everyone around him, so why try? I asked him if he physically hurts anyone or punches anyone on his way past them, or if he yells obscenities at people or calls them stupid names in anger. You should have seen his face! He was absolutely horrified I would even suggest such a thing.

"No! I would *never* hurt anyone." There seemed to be a contradiction here, one that Dan had been missing. We explored how he came to believe the idea that he could hurt anyone. He revealed that his mother had never been well after his birth and was constantly reminding him of her ailments. He was the reason she had so much illness, he concluded. If he hadn't been born, his mother would have had good health. I knew Dan was poised for a breakthrough. Reality trumps mind fiction every time.

"I know the truth lives in reality, Dan. If you consider the reality of our biology, for instance, you would have to conclude the obvious: that you are, in fact, here—in a body. Right? So you must have been destined to be here, or you wouldn't be here. Right?" This thought seemed to be new for him, so I let the moment marinate.

I invited Dan to consider how his life is when he believes the thought: "I am the cause of my mother's ill health." He slumped back in his chair.

"What if your mother just happened to mark her 'not-well' phase; using the proximity of your birth as the marker to attend to her own health? Perhaps those two events, your birth and her onset of illness, had nothing to do with you personally. What if it really marked the day she finally paid attention to her health? Perhaps, it was just the time for her illness to happen, just like it was also the time for your birth to happen. Nothing happens that isn't supposed to happen. We are always in our right divine flow of life. You have a body, so that means you were meant to be here. That's the reality of the situation."

Dan was pensive again. He was making minute nodding movements with his head as if listening to or watching some internal processor re-writing his inner code.

When he finished processing this, I asked him how different his life would be if he believed the thought that his mother was just marking the beginning of her illness by the proximity of his birth, and that the two events weren't related, even if she thought so. He let his breath out in a long exhale, as if the pressure of an inner balloon was finally being deflated. Dan said this felt right.

"In order to get a human body, Dan, you had to win the sperm race. I mean if you don't win the sperm race, you don't get a body, right? That's just basic biology. You're meant to be here because you're here. And, you're already a winner. Dan, *you won* the sperm race! Ta da!" I threw my hands in the air. We both laughed. He got it, just like you did.

We are already natural-born winners. We were meant to be here now. This is the perfect time for us. Why not donate *proving your worth* to Earth's Museum of Un-natural History and be done with it. Since we're already Pre-Approved for this life, why not approve of ourselves from top to bottom, no exceptions. When doubt shows up, we can proudly whip out our photo ID card: Pre-Approved for mission Earth. If your life doesn't feel refreshed, maybe all you need is a little imagination. Tobias knows how.

May the angel of wildness disturb the places
where your life is domesticated and safe.
—John O'Donohue

Just Imagine

Since we are already Pre-Approved, we can imagine ourselves whole, perfect and complete, joyful choosers, authors writing and re-writing a better future, always in our right divine flow, knowing we were Pre-Approved for this mission, no matter what's happening. Gratitude opens the door, but the real purpose for imagination is to infuse our energy with the feelings we will have when we imagine *having* what we want. Tobias, in a workshop, said his ideal future was to be surrounded by gorgeous blondes in a hot tub. He could envision it! Everyone at the workshop laughed, but he held true to the feeling he would have if that were true. Two years later, he married a beautiful woman who was a natural blonde. They went on to have three daughters, also natural blondes. He realized his earlier playful imagination had actually come true. It hit him with a wink and a smile as he and his precious family of gorgeous blondes were hanging out in their hot tub!

DISCLAIMER: I'm certain you already know this, but let me say it just to cover any misperceptions you might have, so I can rest easy.

You *do* know being Pre-Approved is not the same as a license to create mayhem in any form. It doesn't mean you are not responsible for your words and actions. You probably already know it's not about entitlement. You probably know it is not about unhealthy narcissism, which lacks empathy. You probably know it's not about being a Pollyanna, and you probably know it is not day dreaming, either. Just saying. Here are some benefits of your Pre-Approved status:

When You are Pre-Approved

- You follow the flow of your spirit
- You spontaneously appreciate yourself
- You speak with kindness and consideration
- You go for what is important to you
- You are effortlessly honest
- You actually enjoy your life
- You try on your dreams, for real
- You forget to take offense
- You make no apologies

People have asked me what we had to do to be Pre-Approved. Simple. You won the lottery for a body. Otherwise, you wouldn't be here. You are one of the bold ones who raised your hand in the air and said, *Pick Me!* Deal with it. Go do a happy dance. You are already a winner!

The Language of Mastery

Dr. Martin Luther King said, *Our lives begin to end the day we become silent about things that matter.* One of the most meaningful things we can do for ourselves is to stop managing the perceptions of others, and instead, respect our own life. We know when we didn't speak up, we didn't represent ourselves, we know when we went M.I.A. or when we aren't being honest with ourself. A mother will say to her upset Three-year-old, "Use your words, please." Perhaps we never knew the power of our words or the language of mastery, so we just kept quiet. Maybe no one taught us we already have a place at the table of Life.

We know the language of complaint, but perhaps not of Mastery. Passive words are habits of protection. Mastery words are neutrally purposeful, clear and collaboratively focused. I only knew the language of an oppressed and abused person. I had to learn this new language. Initially, I thought the mastery language was too harsh. I knew if I spoke like that, I'd get backhanded, guaranteed. I later discovered that I actually felt safe in the presence of someone who was clear, with no hidden agenda. I didn't know that language, but I really liked how I felt.

Mastery words keep us solidly grounded in our own power. I needed to learn this language because of my sensitive and empathic nature. Making sure others were okay, even if I wasn't, was a familiar habit. It can feel like dangerous business to walk and talk in our own power. Like brand new shoes, we need to break them in by walking in then. Check out these examples. You may want to practice with a friend who loves you, as I did, and who will kindly give you feedback about your believability and authenticity. We want them to withhold the thumbs-up *until* they know for certain, that we are 100% believable. Here are some examples:

Passive Words (Weak) **Mastery Words (*Strength*)**

I think..................... **I like the part of your idea about..**
I'll try this............... **What's the best outcome here?**
Maybe .... **I'll get back to you by noon**
I don't know .... **Here's what's important to me.**
I guess I could .... **Let's talk more about this**
I'm sorry.................. **Let me regroup**
I don't like that .... **What else is possible?**
I'm so stupid .... **I misunderstood**
It doesn't matter ...... **What if we tried this...?**
You hurt my feelings.. **Thanks for telling me ...**

Man-Made Concepts

Worth is not equated with competence or value. Competence can be learned and mastered; value is chosen, while worth is a given, like Grace, like our breath, like our heartbeat. We came in with it. Our Wholeness doesn't have a word for failure, approval, success, acceptance, or self-worth. These are all man-made concepts of the matrix. Remember, you only need your permission to be authentic: without apology, explanations, or justifications. This is peaceful power. Kind compassion for ourselves is the best fragrance we can wear.

Every point of contact either opens or closes a door; either distracts or clarifies, so be deliberate in your life. Don't wait for the wind to blow in the next opportunity. Commit to living boldly. You were Pre-Approved from birth so let your Higher Self glide you toward the flow of your destiny.

A great motto to write and tape to your mirror or where you can see it is this: *"I have nothing to prove to anyone, including myself."* Seriously, Inspector #29 from the G.O.D.com factory stamped you: "Approved according to the highest quality control standards." So, get over yourself! Life doesn't ask nature's trees, flowers, animals, or oceans to justify their existence. Like all nature, you don't have to justify your existence. You're a winner already. Now, get on with living your great adventure in time and space. Are you ready to make this Key REAL?

Playful Embodiment Experiments

Pick one or two experiments to embody your power. You can also design your own experiment.

1. If I have always known that *I was already Pre-Approved for this life*—what new adventure would I explore today.
2. Take several short, quiet moments each day to let your attention move inward, into the center where the Divine abides, and simply be with the timeless, Pre-Approved YOU.
3. Today give yourself permission to skip seeking approval. Take a breath and decide to just be present and enjoy a moment. You are enough.
4. Today give yourself written permission—like a school permission slip—to embrace being Pre-Approved. Put it in your physical wallet so you can check your ID as needed.
5. Today *act as if* you were indeed born Pre-Approved by

the highest authority. Feel it in your walk: Nothing to prove. Now go play!

6. It's safe for me to be powerful because I don't need anyone's approval but my own.

My Weekly Mantra: I am Pre-Approved for life. I belong here. I have a seat at the table and I'm a winner!

I AM THE ACTOR WHO PLAYS MANY ROLES

KEY SIX

We are in the world and of it and it is good that it is so.
The world is all right when we view it correctly.
—Science of Mind, May 2007

- **The Universal Law of Harmony:** The Universe is harmonious and perfectly balanced.
- **The Myth:** I'm a product of my circumstances.
- **The Key:** I'm more than the roles I play.
- **The Practice:** What is my real role in this situation?

THE WISDOM OF THE ACADEMY AWARD

One ordinary Thursday in 1985 will forever be etched in my DNA as another life-altering shift, courtesy of my Higher Self. After the echoes of getting my five kids off to school had finally faded, I plopped down on my sofa with a bone-deep sigh of fatigue. Ennui had been my resident visitor for several months. This particular morning, I could only stare blankly out my bedroom window, ignoring the tasks ahead of me for the day. I'll just sit for a moment, I thought. I had hoped somehow to find the energy to start my business day. Just a moment, I thought.

As I eased my back onto the cushions of my sofa, I let out a long sigh and my mind began to daydream. I was given a movie in my mind. I didn't write it. I just watched it, minus the popcorn and soda. In this vivid mind movie, I was apparently an actress attending the Academy Awards ceremony. I was a nominee for a recent movie in which I had starred. The house was packed with great actors, directors, producers, musicians, and artists of all kinds, all brilliant colleagues. Apparently, I was this actress. I *was* her, not just dreaming her.

In the movie, I felt hopeful that I might receive an award. The audience was filled with anticipation. Finally, the host announced the winner for the Best Leading Actress category. I heard my name called. Stunned and pleased, I glided to the stage, ushered by the applause, to receive my award. I was being given the Academy Award for my stunningly brilliant performances in my role as a victim. This was the latest role in a long career specializing in and perfecting the part of the victim. The crowd applauded and stood up to celebrate me. I was moved by their recognition of my performances. I stood tall and proud. I knew I had perfected the victim character with such artistic perfection that I had completely lost myself in the role. I was asked to say a few words to the Academy. I quickly shook off the role itself and spoke as the actress, the Best Leading Actress! I accepted the award and thanked those whose support contributed to our collective success.

Addressing the Academy and my fellow performers, I said I had focused on perfecting every nuance of the character of the victim and finally felt complete with it. I was now ready and eager to take on new roles and develop new characters that would equally inspire my beloved audience. Thunderous applause filled the room as the host turned toward me. Leaning into the microphone he said, "On behalf of us all, we eagerly await your next role. We're certain you will bring your natural gifts and brilliance to your next body of work." With wild applause from a standing ovation, the scene faded, faded, faded away.

I rubbed my eyes and stretched my body as I came out of this vision. I was stunned by what had just happened. What *had* just happened? I laughed. I love the humor of truth. I realized that I had fallen so deeply into the character of victim that I forgot I was the great Actress, not the role. I didn't know victim was even a role! Two thoughts arose: 1) I am not the role I play. 2) I can play *any* role that interests me. It's very seductive to think we have only one role, and that's our lot in life. Such thinking doesn't make us wrong; it makes us a polished Actor in a character role.

Waking Up the Actor

The truth is, I had only known the victim/shame role from the time I was Three-years old. The Academy Award vision had immediately shifted me out of victim thinking. I realized I was firmly attached to outcomes that were familiar, because I knew the script by heart. I didn't know victim was only a role! Until this vision, I didn't know what else was possible. How could I function past my script? How could I ever be that woman in my vision?

From this vision, I clearly realized there was a whole lot of speaking up I had secreted away out of fear of being shamed or disregarded. In my relationship, I was a silent sufferer. That day I decided to embrace the role of Speaking Up. Empathic and super-sensitive types are usually mute when it comes to our own needs, a fact that causes us to hold a lot of tension in our bodies. Our

Achilles Heel is self-worth and the endless doubt that comes with it. It was time for me to speak up.

When my husband and I had some quiet time, I shared with him, "I've held myself back. I see that I need to offer my voice, not just go along when I disagree or want collaboration. So as of today, I will share my thoughts. No matter what or how I say it, please know I am working with this. I'm letting you know because I'd like your support." He silently nodded, and with that, I started the journey to reclaim my authentic voice. Partnering was the role I needed to attend to. In the process, I became more resilient. There was a lot of wisdom, heart and power in me yet to be discovered. This was a big step but I was ready for it now.

> *Tension is who you think you should be.*
> *Relaxation is who you are.* —**Chinese Proverb**

Can I say I was a bit slow to understand that I needed to honestly represent myself? My body already knew this and had been giving me unmistakable messages. I frequently had a mouth full of canker sores, so many that my lips would literally seal shut, tighter than a vapor lock, during the night. To be able to speak or eat in the morning, I had to take a single-edge razor blade and slit my lips open. For real. How does it get any clearer than that for a freaking message? I didn't realize how easily I had dismissed my own thoughts and seldom said what I wanted, needed, or felt. I began to bargain with the canker sores as if they were my trusted consultants. "Okay, I will speak up. As I do, you, canker sore, will vanish, starting now. If I forget to speak up when I need to, please give me a canker sore, but as long as I speak up, my mouth remains canker free. Deal?" Metaphorically we shook hands.

My self-image began to shift as I spoke up for myself. My mouth healed the more I spoke up. I knew suppression and repression, but I was afraid of authentic expression. After my vision, I found I actually had a lot to contribute that might otherwise have slumbered had I not chosen to finally represent my thoughts, my ideas, and my desires.

I spoke up, not to be right, but to respect myself. I chose to be an equal partner, as much as was possible in my religion. More importantly, I began to restore power to my life. I'd had a whole childhood filled with others telling me what I wanted. My body and my choices had never been my own. *No* was never allowed. I knew submission and gradually, my own authentic voice went underground.

Wisdom slid into my awareness, as my Higher Self whispered in my ear: *Wake up, precious one. See life through my eyes. You can play any role that makes you happy as you expand your unique expression. The roles are as unlimited as I Am. You are me, playing in the field of density. I judge nothing, and I voted for you!*

∾

Spotlight Tip: Upsets and conflicts indicate a corrupted role. It signals we are off track. Every role has a unique function. Our life runs more smoothly when our roles are clean. With clear roles, we feel centered in our own life.

It's helpful to imagine our roles from the vantage point of a movie director. When we step back and sit in the director's chair, we objectively look at the actions of the Leading Actor (us), scrutinizing the scenes for believability. Is the Lead Actor congruent to their role? If the director catches other actors trying to deliver our lines, she blows the whistle. No actor gets to slip into another's role because they think they can do it better. That makes for a very messy movie. It's the same for us on the stage of life.

All the world's a stage, and all the men and
women merely players: they have their exits
and their entrances; and one man in his
time plays many parts... —**William Shakespeare**,
As You Like It, Act II, Scene VII

Every role we have ever played has contributed to our advancement in Mastery. In Key One, our role is to be joyful choosers. In Key Two, our role is to author our own story. In Key Three, our role is to remember we are Wholeness in action. In Key Four, our role is to stay in the right divine flow of our life. In Key Five, we learned we were already Pre-Approved to be here, so our role is to participate wholeheartedly. Now, in Key Six, we get to explore how to stay clean in each role we play. When we ask to remember who we are, beyond all roles, then our journey becomes interesting and full of surprises and synchronicities.

Mistaken Identity

I'm the smart one. I'm the responsible one. I'm just like my father. I'm an orphan. I was abused. I am a failure. Everybody takes advantage of me. I was born under a lucky star. I do the best I can. I'm better than those losers, etc. These aren't self-generated roles. Lots of daily drama signals mistaken identity.

There is something in every one of you that waits
and listens for the sound of the genuine in yourself.
It is the only true guide you will ever have.
And if you cannot hear it, you will, all of your life,
spend your days on the ends of strings that
somebody else pulls. — **Howard Thurman**,
American Theologian

Am I congruent with the function my role requires? What does that mean? Everyone is an actor on the stage of life and we all have a part to play in Earth's story. Let me offer some examples: It could be you've taken on the role of the parent to your spouse who is always critical, when your *rightful* role is that of a loving partner. Or, you may have taken on the role of judger instead of a contributing team member at work. Perhaps you've taken the role of royalty in your marriage and your spouse does all the heavy lifting to keep your ego afloat. Perhaps you took on the role of a critical manager when you were a staff member. Perhaps you took on the role of teacher; subtly correcting everyone's speaking. Perhaps you took on the role of scullery maid, cleaning up everyone's messes. You get the idea. If you are hired as a maid to clean up, and you do that beautifully, you are authentic to the function of your role. In the following story Sandy demonstrates how she used role identification to super-charge her business.

Who's Who in the Zoo?

Sandy owned her own business and was very successful making money. She was, however, less adept at directing, guiding, and holding her team accountable to the roles for which they were being paid. She thought if she just gave them a task, they should do it, and if they didn't, it meant they weren't right for the company and she'd fired them or they quit out of sheer frustration. She had a high staff turnover as you can imagine. In her deepest desire, she wanted to build a solid staff that could function so well that she could eventually take a sabbatical to pursue her philanthropic interests. She was ready for a different approach to her company role. On our second meeting, I asked, "Sandy, what's your real business role?"

"I hold the vision. I have to lead them to do their jobs, but they don't do them, so I have to do even more work," she said.

"That's what you *do*, but what is your business role?" I persisted.

Sandy was quiet for a bit. She fidgeted in her seat, touching her left ear lobe, searching for the right answer. "I don't know what you mean," she finally said.

"Well, let's look at reality. Truth. Whose business is this?" Sandy thought for a minute then answered. "It's all of ours. We work as a team," she replied with her palms up in explanation.

"Hmm. So, who is responsible for keeping the office leased, the lights on, and for authorizing the paychecks the employees get?" I gently pushed.

She emphatically said, "I am."

"So, this makes your role in the business...what?" I offered.

"I'm the owner. This is my business," she said with a firm voice as she sat up taller in her chair.

"Exactly. You have to be the owner if you own the business, right? That's your authentic role. Although you enjoy the team, you are not their peer, therapist, cheerleader or parent. Why? Because you pay the rent, utilities, taxes, salaries, and business expenses. The buck stops with you, right?" I allowed my voice to soften.

"So, what would your office look like, feel like, and sound like if you totally took on the role of the business owner? As a responsible owner, how would you show up for your team?" I asked her. She pondered a few long moments.

"Well, I would speak clearly and with more confidence. I would get to the point, but I would do it with more respect, for me and for them. I can feel my body standing taller." she excitedly said, as if this idea had been there all along, and she had merely misplaced it.

"Great, Sandy. Now this sounds like you are the owner and the leader. [Pause] And, when they don't handle their job the way you expect, what will you, the business owner and leader, do?" I asked.

"Oh, dear. I just felt my energy go flat. I get really uncomfortable asking them to do their job. What kind of leader does that make me?" She paused, shifting in her chair.

"Do they know what's expected of them? Is it written down anywhere? Do you have regular check-in and team report huddles?" I asked.

"I don't know. No. I think they should know what to do because they took the position. I still have to tell them what to do all the time. It's so much work."

"Can you notice how you slipped out of owner role just now? What role did you take on just now?" I asked.

"Let's see...I want them to like me. I guess I encourage them to share their work and personal problems so I can be sympathetic in the hopes that they will feel better, *then* they can do their jobs. Hmm. I've been in the role of counselor and the role of blamer. I also took on the role of a forgiving parent, but I'm really upset when they don't do their jobs well, I send them packing. Those aren't really my roles, are they?" she wisely concluded.

Sandy worked to keep her business role clean and clear. She chose to support her team as capable, competent people by asking them to be accountable to *their* roles. She began to see them as capable adults. She put systems of reporting and contributing at weekly meetings in place. Her team eventually became quite high functioning. In two years, Sandy was able to take a month off to pursue her nonprofit, volunteer interests because her team was high functioning. Her business continued to make money while she was tending to her philanthropy project. Identifying her role in a given context and respecting it became even more delightful to her year after year. She felt supported by a quality team who were responsible for their respective roles. Employee turnover ceased to be an issue.

The best way of successfully acting a part is to be it. —**Arthur Conan Doyle,** *The Adventure of the Dying Detective*

Each role is appropriate to some context. If we take time to do a reality check about what roles we are playing, and in what context, then we discover whether or not there is contextual integrity to the role. For example, if we correct other people's behavior, we have contextually taken a role that might not be ours to take, unless we are a prison guard, a sports coach, a military officer, a teacher, or a parent, for example. This is why correcting other's behavior backfires on us. We can only correct our own behavior. An environment of clean roles leads to successful endeavors.

We play many roles: daughter, son, father, mother, teacher, student, grandparent, lover, listener, blogger, developer, counselor, mechanic, nurse, pilot, and more. We cast the roles we play. We are, first and foremost, the Leading Actor in our own life. We are also the Director, so we can take a step back and make sure we are in character and we aren't in somebody else's business. That's why it's important to keep clean roles. We have the final say on how we live our life, but we are not the authority for how others' should live their lives. Perhaps your part is only a brief walk-on appearance to deliver a message, or to be a catalyst for another's growth. We are with others for a reason, a season, or a lifetime. Roles change as we mature. We can never achieve the success we hope for unless we faithfully accept and respect our roles. Christie discovered this concept in a different context in our next story.

Don't Role Over Me!

I met Christie at a conference. She confided in me about the trouble she had at home with her preteens. They were free spirits and she liked that about them, but they didn't mind well, as free spirits are apt to do. I asked her what role she was playing, meaning what was her role in these interactions, if it wasn't the role of their parent. "Wow, I guess…. I guess I feel like I'm their servant. No wonder I feel such a lack of parental power," she said.

"So, since you haven't been showing up as their parent, they probably assumed you were their servant, here to do their bidding, so to speak? Is that right? So, they just roll over your authority as parent. How does it feel to name it out loud?"

"Actually, it's such a relief. Wow! I'm not holding my breath! I am not here to be their servant, for sure, although I do want them to be who they were meant to be. How can I step in as their parent when they're used to me being their servant? Seriously, if you have the answer, I am prepared to hire you right now. I mean it. This is important to me," she said, as she pulled out her checkbook and calendar. We contracted to work together for one month. This evening would be the first session. I'll let you listen in for the beginning setup with Christie.

"You're the parent. That's your role. How do you know that? You birthed them, right? They chose you for their parents. How do we know that? You birthed them and not somebody else. That's the reality. When they were little, how did you parent them when they wanted something interesting but you didn't want them to touch it or to get hurt?" I asked.

"Well, when they became mobile, I would pick them up and get them interested in something else or I would move the object away, and I would tell them, 'No,' then I'd distract them. But they aren't little anymore. I see that."

"It's still the same principle. Your role hasn't changed. You are the parent and you want your kids to have their freedom, but as preteens, they must earn your *Yes* through a demonstration of healthy morals and trustworthiness. That's their correct role—to become trustworthy people. In your role of parent, you need to be assured that they have sufficiently embodied a healthy moral code and demonstrate a healthy value system. As their parent, you must help them earn the right to have your *Yes*. You aren't passing judgment as much as you are measuring their ascent into adulthood and reflecting it back to them in the form of a clean Yes." She nodded several times, soaking it in.

"It's not your job to say yes just because they ask, pressure, or demand. That's not how responsible parents behave, right? Perhaps it's time to develop and implement a *Say Yes!* program for them. What will you, their parents, need to see, hear, and feel from them that will let you know you can trust them out in the social and dating world?"

"Wow, I never thought of it in those terms," she said.

"That's your first assignment, then. Map out the values that signal maturity in your children. What do you and Ben need to witness in order to trust them to make good decisions? As they want more freedom, you need to know that they can be trusted in any situation because their values and moral pillars are healthy. This is your *Say Yes!*plan. This is a way to have freedom for all within a contextually healthy parent-child relationship. Isn't your heart's desire to parent your kids into young adults who are trustworthy?" She nodded affirmatively.

As we continued our coaching that month, Christie and Ben came up with new strategies for those times when they slipped out of their role as parents. After a month, Christie and Ben let me know they were upright in their role as parents. Their household had become happier. They needed to know they could trust their preteens to make decisions based on values. The kids have a stake in their parent's *Yes.*

The question is this: What is our correct role in situations where we experience frustrations, arguments, and lingering upsets? Like Sandy, Christie had experienced the frustrations that arise when there are fuzzy roles. Roles are channels of functional expression. It's about being whole in each contextual role we play until all roles function as healthy expressions of authenticity.

Organizations, whether family, business, or volunteers have many internal roles necessary for their organization to run smoothly. If we stay clean in our role and cooperatively interface with other roles, the organization can run economically and profitably. In the workplace, issues such as harassment, sexual misconduct, misappropriation of funds, unhealthy competition, lying, cheating, demanding managers, and low morale are all byproducts of contextually fuzzy roles, hidden agendas, and lack of respect. They promote lots of drama, but very little clarity, cooperation, or trust. Businesses run smoothly when the roles and the responsibilities are clearly laid out and respected.

Queen Of The Table

At home our roles must be equally clear as Christie and Ben discovered. I knew our roles could be playful at the same time. As a single parent, it's not always easy to maintain sanity with five kids who are all strong individuals. One summer day, I felt like I wasn't being heard after I had made a request. Each of my children had their attention on *not* doing their jobs, preferring instead to tussle and tease each other. I needed them to set the table and get ready for dinner. Mine was the last voice they were listening to. I'm just not a fan of nagging. Playful chaos reigned, so I climbed on the top of the kitchen table, hands on my hips in a defensive pose, I comically yelled, "I'm the Mother, damnit."

They literally dissolved into crazy laughter, holding their sides, finding my behavior hysterical. As they slowed their laughing, I stepped down and said, "Let's get this table set for dinner." And they did, still laughing about their crazy mother taking Custer's last stand on the kitchen table.

> *Instead of imagining we're all at the effect of a disconnected*
> *universe you can awaken to your role as co-creator*
> *with a sentient organic universe.*
> — **Mark Borax,** Soul Level Astrologer & songwriter.

Identifying our proper contextual roles can be a bit tricky if we are invested in being right. Look at these actual dynamics: If I am a parent, then that is my role until the child moves out of the home. This is where I started—I was the parent, not a nagger. To inspire other contextual roles, let's consider the following examples of fuzzy roles:

- Are you the husband who acts like a carefree adolescent instead of being the one who protects, provides for, and respects your wife?
- Are you the wife who acts more like a nagging mother than a lover?
- Are you a husband who dismisses your wife's complaints because you can't fix them?
- Are you the go-along to get-along silent partner?
- Are you still an inner five-year-old who thinks you're being scolded if someone asks you to step up?
- Are you the person who settles for what you can get so you don't have to take a risk speaking up?

Take a deep breath and exhale... That's a whole lot of fuzzy right there! Talk about energetic power drains. Exhausting, isn't it? And we wonder why we can't connect. Those were only a few examples of where a role had become corrupted. Under those circumstances, no one wins and no one can be trusted. When we are loyal to the correct function of our roles, we have energy, connection, and direction. Messy roles equal low energy, upsets, confusion, and depression. The good news is that you are your own solution. Ultimately, our job is to respect the role we play. Our life is the business we run. When we represent ourselves kindly and responsibly in our various roles, we are clean. While we all play our parts, we are, at the same time, so much more than the roles we play.

The deeper question is: Does our Soulful nature shine through all our roles? Elizabeth wanted an answer to the question, *who am I beyond the roles I take on?* This larger view organizes our roles and keeps them clean. Then, we have no use for competition, frustration or pettiness. She will show us how she found a higher vision.

Spotlight Tip: Our little mind habitually marches to its script day after day, faithful to our safety and security. It makes us think that the roles we play are who we really are. Our Soul knows we are joyful co-creators with Source.

I Am a Great Soul

My dear friend Elizabeth, co-author of *A Prayer of Two Women*, knew she was more than the roles she played. She had grown tired of the same old roles. When we met for dinner after work one evening, she said she had become frustrated with all the smaller pieces that needed to be fixed before she could feel loving and accepting toward herself.

"There are too many roles I'm playing. They're not me," she said. Elizabeth is a wonderfully conscious woman, and if you knew her, you would fall in love with her immediately. She's genuine, transparent and plays full out.

"Who am I really, beyond my roles? What can I bring to them that really reflects a richer quality of life?" This question, she said, required a direct conversation with her Higher Power in meditation. Her heart opened and she was shown her power. The following poem flowed through her, writing it in her journal as it was delivered. The response left her amazed beyond words because it felt true to her core. I asked if she would read it to me. I leaned back in my seat, ready to witness this beautiful woman.

After reading it out loud, she said, "This is all of who I am." She was radiant, and I was profoundly moved by her Essence and her words. I had tears in my eyes because I love Elizabeth. It's so easy to become absorbed in the roles we play and miss the bigger Self at play. I asked Elizabeth if she would allow me to share her message with you in this book. She said perhaps it would be an inspiration of what is revealed when we go to our Higher power for our true identity. This is Elizabeth's gift to us. This is her love story.

I am spirit-made woman, fully alive, at one with all.
I am the joy of the song, the grace of the dance.
I am a weaver of connection and love.
I hold sacred space for the symphony of all humanity.
I am the joy of the mystery, the silence in which all is revealed,
The breath of oneness,
The love through which all comes into being,
The All that is possible.
I am you. You are me. We are one.
I am holy, I am light,
I am Yes.
I am a celebration of life.
I am an Alleluia that sings the planet.
I am Elizabeth, God's Sacred Promise.

Broad strokes inspire our roles and keep them from hijacking our joy. Broad strokes also let us step into all our roles with heart, contextually appropriate to the role of the moment. The heart of our power is to be a bold Actor, unafraid to take on any role and contextually play it with brilliance, knowing we are already whole and complete. This eliminates drama and preserves good will. We are the great Actor, not the roles we play. Our power, however, is in keeping all our roles clean. Drama signals someone is out of their rightful, contextual roll. In our rightful roles, there is mutual respect or the conversation is over and we schedule another day to try again.

After the Applause

Imagine you and your fellow Actors, appreciating the rousing applause for a well-lived life. Imagine the curtain has closed. The theater cleaned. The crew has gone home. You and your fellow Actors have long since shed your costumes. As you look back on your life, all the roles you have played, all the plot lines you followed, you revel in the satisfaction of a wonderful journey. You gave your all in each and every part you ever played. You feel deeply satisfied. Looking off to the right, you may notice a tall Cherry wood and glass case displaying the many awards you've won for Best Actor, Best Supporting Actor, Best Director, and Best Screenplay. You did all that.

Who remains when all the awards have been accepted and stored away? Who is this amazing Actor? Allow yourself to be aware of the one who has played all your roles brilliantly. Imagine all the amazing stories you'll tell when you return to your pre-Earth Home again. "How brave you were," they will say, enthralled by your adventurous tales. Your life, dear one, is always a beautiful love story in the making. Are you ready to make this Key REAL?

Playful Embodiment Experiments
Pick one or two experiments to walk in your own power. You can also design your own experiment.

1. If I have always known that *I am an Academy Award winner for my role on the stage of life,* what role have I perfected and which role would I like to explore next?
2. Just for fun, list all the roles you play in the course of the day.
3. From that list, which ones do you play well and harmoniously? Give those a star. Put an asterisk by those that still frustrate you. With these, what is your responsibility for the smooth functioning of these roles? Pick one to set it right.
4. Identify one role in which you experience frustration or conflicts. Is your role appropriate to the relationship/situation? What kind, clear action will set you upright in your role?
5. Imagine yourself in the near future, being congruent and outstanding in all your roles. Notice how being true to your roles brings out the best in all. What would your fellow Actors say about you, great Actor?
6. Write your own inspired broad-stroke identity statement. Write it until it lights you up.

My Weekly Mantra: I am a wise soul, shining brightly through my many roles.

I AM EMPOWERED

KEY SEVEN

At this time in our history we should take nothing personally, least of all ourselves. Try to do whatever you do as an act of celebration. We are the ones we've been waiting for. —**Hopi Nation**, *Wisdom of the Elders*

The Universal Law of Perpetual Transmutation of Energy:
Change is constant.
The Myth: I'm not perfect.
The Key: Nothing's personal. I live life my way.
The Practice: Quit Taking It Personally.

THE WISDOM OF BLUE SKY NATURE

Frank, my Hopi teacher you met in Key 3, began another one of our teachings. It was on one of those Arizona early summer days I love so much, when I met up with Frank in the parking lot of the

San Francisco Peaks. These beautiful mountains are considered sacred to the Hopi. That day Frank and I hiked up to my favorite meadow, boasting a vista that takes your breath away and refreshes everything inside of you. The wild flowers were popping up their heads to drink in the warmth of the sun. The day was crisp and clear. The ground was dry enough to sit on without leaving a wet spot on the seat of our pants.

Finding our spot, we reclined on the grassy meadow, hands behind our heads, as we looked up. We joined the flowers, silently soaking in the warm day. I knew my training would begin when it would begin. Frank never rushed. After several long sighs of relaxation, I was feeling my body and Mother Earth's body becoming one when he finally spoke.

"Linda, what do you see when you look up?" I was used to his style of leading with a question. We didn't chit-chat.

"I see the sky, white clouds, and birds flying. I can see an airplane in the distance." There was a quiet pause.

"Linda, what do you see when you look up?" he softly repeated. Drats! I tried again since it was important in those days for me to get it right. My little mind went into overdrive, eager to flex its muscles for the teacher. "I see a cloud shaped like a rabbit, sort of, and one over there," pointing with my index finger, "there's one shaped like…" I spoke of several more cloud shapes I was imagining. More silence. Okay. I knew I was way off track. Even I could feel there was no heart in my speaking.

He then spoke. "That is the difference between my people and your people, Linda," he said as he turned his body toward me, propping himself up on his elbow.

"When your people look up they see the clouds and you identify with the clouds, always coming and going, never at peace. When my people look up we see the blue sky, we see our true nature. Serene, calm, eternal. Clouds are thoughts and feelings; they come and go on their journey. Thunderstorms come and go.

Soft puffy clouds come and go. Wind, rain, and snow come and go. My people know the changing weather is for our amusement or our learning, but we know we are not the clouds. Inside, we are as calm and steady in our nature as the Blue sky. We enjoy the clouds for what they are—cloud crossings. We don't fight with life; we are thankful for life. No cloud is ever powerful enough to disturb our Blue sky nature."

The illustrative cloud is any feeling, experience, opinion, situation, or belief that takes us out of being present in the flow of the moment. Sometimes, we decide to pause and explore a particular cloud's gift. Like feelings and emotions, clouds are transient by nature. If we judge or name a cloud, we stop its journey. Perhaps we think a cloud has the power to throw us off our game, disrupt our energy, or change the course of our happiness. Nope. Emotion is energy in motion: E + motion. We learned in Key Two that a feeling lasts a maximum of Ninety Seconds. Then, the cloud naturally moves on, unless we re-code it with a familiar story we tell ourself. If we want that feeling to stay for years, we keep telling the same story.

We have to go against nature to hold a feeling in place as The Truth. Emotions are meant to have movement, to come and to go. I previously thought I was the sum total of what had happened to me. I would get triggered when I allowed a cloud, in Frank's words, to push my buttons. Just the thought of a cloud pushing our buttons sounds silly, doesn't it? Frank lovingly dubbed me Little Cloud Chaser, and he was right. My identity was built on the fleeting clouds of my past experiences and of other people's energy and inner thoughts. I didn't know then that I was an Empath. I didn't know then that when I took on other people's unspoken thoughts as the truth of me, I would be ignoring my power. I didn't know then that I *decide* how I feel. Truth: Feelings are just clouds passing. I make them permanent or not by my attention.

Leave all thoughts of the world you knew before. Let your soul take you where you long to be.... close your eyes; Let your spirit start to soar and you'll live as you've never lived before.
—**Eric Fromm**, philosopher

I tried on the idea of having a Blue-sky backdrop on which my emotions traversed. I practiced not taking feelings or emotions personally. In the kiva of my youth, I had found a natural flow of life working itself effortlessly through me. I felt expanded, calm, peaceful and one with all life. It felt like home. I was definitely not that calm above ground in the peopled world. I took everything personally back then. Remaining centered and balanced is not an easy task for those who are HSP's. We are open to the world until we learn how to use our gifts.

Spotlight Tip: Emotions are indicators of how we are currently directing our energy. The good news is that we can always fly higher than the clouds. We can lift up above the minutia of the moment. We can have a neutral Blue-sky viewpoint. Decisions are better made from there.

Emotions or Feelings

Emotion is our bodies' natural response to external stimuli. "Oh, this energy feels so good." Energy and emotions are the soup we live in. "I don't feel good about this energy" is an *awareness* and a *sensing* that something feels different in our surroundings. It is an intuitive awareness of our environment.

Feelings are the conclusions we make. Energy in motion is a fluid state, whereas feelings are mental conclusions about familiar feelings. Sensing dishonesty, for example, can rev up the little mind if we live with manipulators. Then we might rationalize, *"They don't mean it. It's not that bad.*" Or, turn it inward, *I feel deprived. I feel sad.* These not intuition or emotion. These are conclusions; captive clouds, and I've had plenty.

Perhaps when an emotion comes up, all it really wants is to be received with a thank you, and then it will be on its way, like a cloud moving across the Blue Sky. 'Thank you for visiting,' our Blue-sky Nature says. We are unaffected by visiting clouds. Blue-sky Nature represents our quiet, peaceful power. It doesn't do cloud conclusions.

> *It's not trespassing to go beyond our own*
> *boundaries.* —**Dewitt Jones**

The Gain of Pain

I argued with myself about this cloud business because I felt justified in feeling traumatized by events and people in my life. I was singled out for abuse. How could that *not* be personal? You bet I took it personally! If I hadn't been a female, none of that would have happened. I didn't realize this conclusion would create a life of paying penance for being a female. As if I, the little child, had asked for the abuse because she didn't say *No* loud enough. A dark, stormy cloud persistently hung around me, justifying my pain. It was easy to punish myself thinking that my *no* had zero power. Once I really explored the abuse cloud, I knew that I *did* say no. Their, *Oh, yes you will,* was bigger than my *no,* but I had said "No!" I felt my inner wisdom emerging like sunshine through the clouds.

No emotion, no matter how painful it might be, can ever alter our inner Blue-sky nature unless we hold the emotion captive with a conclusion, and then gnaw on it like a dry bone. Blue-sky, by nature, is serene, vast, and neutral. It's always there. We never run to the window to see if the sky is still there. Really, I said to myself, what's my worry? I write my own stories. I was born pre-approved. I play many roles as a great actor. I'm whole, perfect, and complete. I have Free Will to choose. I am always in my right divine flow, so why not take off my armor and offer my best in each moment? Seriously, cloud experiences do not define us. Emotions and events do not define us. How we move through them defines us.

Sometimes we need to know when enough is enough. Enough stinky thinking. Enough taking things personally. Enough self-diminishment. ENOUGH! Time to do the opposite: I Am Enough! I am perfect as I am. I am what God desires. I, like many of us, carried around a big backpack stuffed full of old pain, shame, and guilt. I was ready to let it all go.

∼

Spotlight Tip: How do I know when a difficult experience has been completed? The answer is simple: You lived through it. You did not die. If you are still here, then the event was completed. Choose a different path.

Heart of Stones

In the process of remembering my inner Blue-sky nature, I came to the upsetting realization of just how extensive my collection of dark clouds was. It appeared that I was a collector of hurts rather than an experiencer of life. I didn't know that protecting myself had unintended consequences. I thought I was protecting my future. I asked Frank to teach me how to release my dark cloud collection.

"First, stop carrying dead things," he said. "Second, embrace only that which is Alive." This thought gave me a new way to consider the past shocks, traumas and hurts. I had lived through them, and I did not die. That was true. Frank liked to turn metaphors into literal experiences for me. I appreciated this, because I learn best from an exploratory approach. I couldn't wait until our next meeting.

A week after the Blue-sky teaching, we met again at a quiet spot in Sedona's Oak Creek Canyon to continue. This was the practical part of the teaching. Oak Creek Canyon is lush with beauty and one of my very favorite places to just Be. I love the red canyon walls, the lush greenery, and the clear water of the river that flows through the canyon. Frank found our spot and began the lesson. "What does it feel like when you know you have an inner Blue-sky Nature, little one?" He gestured to the expansive clear Blue sky above us, then to his heart.

I felt it immediately, and said I felt grounded, light, like I could do anything, free and expansive, untouchable. Frank then asked me to think on the heaviness of the dead things I had become accustomed to carrying. I didn't like that thought, not in this beautiful place. Nevertheless, he instructed me to let this heaviness guide me to practical freedom. I do like practical. My task was to collect river rocks that represented each heavy feeling I was still carrying. Some rocks can signify sadness, some can signify fear, some can signify entrapment. I was to feel an emotion and look for a rock that called to me, then write the feeling on the rock. We could be here all day, I thought sarcastically.

"If you hoard what has no life, your spirit (gesturing to his heart) gets heavy and you forget your True Nature. You carry deep heaviness in your body and heart, little one. You carry around everything you took personally. Your clouds have turned into rocks that weigh you down. Now, go. Collect rocks that speak of the dead things you carry." He gave me a well-worn backpack and a black permanent marker he had brought with him and I set about collecting rocks for each heavy feeling I still carried. Into the backpack they went. Meanwhile, Frank had stretched his body out beneath a shade tree near the river and closed his eyes.

The moment you love, you are unlimited.
—**Yogi Tea** bag label

The Release

I returned with my two-ton backpack to where Frank was resting. He instructed me to take out the rocks and place them in the shape of a heart in the sand next to the river. After I made my rock heart, I stepped back. I could feel my heart's anticipation for what was to come. My pain was a heart; no, my pain has a heart! I welled up with emotion.

We stepped to the center of the rock heart to dedicate this as sacred space with a smoke ceremony. We blessed the heart with salt sprinkles for purity. Frank lit his ceremonial pipe. Together we offered smoke prayers to the four directions. We sent the sacred smoke spiraling upward as a prayer, asking Great Spirit to take these clouds of dead weight and misunderstandings from my heart. I asked Great Spirit to purify my heart and mind to know that Great Spirit lives in me as my Blue-sky Nature.

As we completed our prayer to the four directions, I felt remarkably at peace, even excited. Frank said it was now time to free my heart. Trust me, I was *more* than ready.

"Life's experiences are meant to be welcomed fully in the moment, little one, then released in order to welcome a fresh moment. What was endured now wants to be free. That is the way of our peaceful Blue-sky Nature; to be with what life has to offer, without judgment, in the moment. Then we release the experience back into the great river of life. This activity keeps our energy clean, little one. Do it now. Free your heart."

As instructed, I took each rock in my hand, thanked it, blessed it, and then tossed it back into the river. I finally viscerally understood that I am Blue-sky by nature. I, like the Blue-sky, was meant to experience all kinds of clouds, all kinds of emotional weather, as they moved across my sky. I am not defined by my emotions unless I try to hold on to them and make sense of them so I can feel safe. That strategy had never worked. I never felt safe. Letting go is not painful; it is the tight-fisted holding on that causes our suffering. Clouds don't need us to respond or act out. They are simply moving across our horizon. The river of life always reminds us to stay in our right divine flow.

Spotlight Tip: Fighting with what has already happened doesn't make for a happier future. It doesn't make us a better person. Being right about being wronged keeps us out of the river of life. Feel, bless and release. That's our business.

Faux-Power

We take things personally, especially when the other person uses the *'you'* word. Let's clear up this whole taking-things-personally business, shall we? How do we know when something is personal? (This is a tool our younger self did not possess.) It's very simple. We met this idea in Key Four, so let's expand it here.

1) The person who is talking has the problem; they are not *the* problem. As long as *their* lips are moving, it is not our business. Zippo. Nada. Not ours. It isn't about us, so to repeat: If their lips are moving, nothing's personal to you.

Even if they reference something you did, their lips are still moving. *Their* pain is talking. *They* have personalized their world-view and it has nothing to do with us. Before we became pearl-makers, we had perfected our defensive skills. Defensive skills are not needed when someone else is talking. Ears and heart are. We can listen compassionately, if we've developed that skill, or we can recommend that they talk with someone qualified to offer advice, or if appropriate, we can say: I can hear your pain. Somewhere, sometime, you must have had to be very brave.

2) If you are the one speaking, your lips are moving. What you complain about has nothing to do with them, their behavior, or their opinions, even if you point out their poor behavior, even if you feel justified. Your pain is speaking because *now* is a perfect time to love and release your old hurts.

3) Excuses, lies, justifications, complaining, blaming or explaining signal we are flat out of power. Unaddressed, complaints form a fog of bitterness. We make excuses because we are afraid to take bold action in favor of an honest life for ourselves.

Complaining only means we aren't willing to take action just yet. We are afraid we will be asked to justify, show proof, or to defend ourselves. That doesn't have to happen. We can kindly answer before our pain slides into the driver's seat. We may say, "I am sharing my experience. I'm not asking for approval or direction. I'm asking for a kind witness so I can feel heard."

An inspired life requires tolerating uncertainty. This is a life that will always ask you to go beyond what you think you can do. Because that's how you meet your secret shaman, the part of you that surprises yourself with fresh capacities. Self-discovery is a process that never ends—if you're lucky. —**Tama Kieves**, from **Inspired & Unstoppable:** Wildly Succeeding in Your Life's Work!

Complaints and Empowerment are like oil and water. They don't go together. Trying is faux-power. That's the Harpies at play. As Guy Finley, author of **The Essential Laws of Fearless Living**, humorously writes, *"If movement actually meant getting somewhere, then your blender would be in France by now!"*

We think of faux-power as movement toward standing up for ourselves. Nope. Complainers think their life can't be different unless the other person, job, partner, parent, or system changes its behavior. We think complaining empowers us, trying is justifiable action; and that judging and being right make us strong. Nope. Not even close. Those are heavy rocks in your backpack.

Spotlight Tip: Complaining is just being afraid of uncertainty. Complaining is still hoping, wishing, minus the praying. You might want to head on down to the river with your rocks. Start owning your place in the world. You'll feel lighter.

From the spaciousness of our Blue-sky Nature perspective, the clouds of life being lived can simply parade on by, each one tipping its hat to us as it passes by. 'Thank you for visiting,' we might say, and let the clouds continue on their parade route. We are free to continually personalize our own world into a masterful expression of our own design.

We learn from each cloud how to choose better, to know what our limits are, to respect our life, to remember our peaceful nature, and to gain resiliency.

If we turn to the dictionary for commonly accepted definitions, we find there are two *very* different meanings of *personalize*. Sometimes, we don't know how to personalize our world. Maylene certainly didn't, as we'll discover in our upcoming story. First, let's be clear.

Personalize:

- To design or produce (something) to meet individual requirements, as in wedding invitations, unique to the maker.
- To cause something, especially an issue, argument, or debate, to become concerned with personalities or feelings rather than with general or abstract matters.

Partner to Empowerment

Maylene wasn't living in her power as a merchant. She designs and produces the most beautiful silk scarves. Undervaluing her work kept her a member of the starving artist club. She called for advice. Apparently a gentleman wanted to hire her to create a large hanging art piece made out of silk in custom colors for his home. Maylene hadn't made one on that scale before.

She was up for the challenge of making it, but was hesitating on her fee. I asked her what she wanted to charge him for the project. She said she wanted to charge him $75. She clearly didn't feel right with that fee and needed some help. I invited her to respect that this is a special-order project, which comes with a commission, not a fee. It would be the centerpiece that unified his home design. I suggested she partner with him on her commission by asking him what he felt something like this would be worth to him.

During her rehearsal I had invited her to pause before accepting the amount, whether the number felt right or even huge to her. She met with him the following week. While she was terrified to do so, she did what she had rehearsed, and asked him what he thought the project was worth, and then stood pensively facing the wall it would hang on. With some thought he turned toward her and said, "Seven hundred dollars." If she had asked outright for

$75, she would have undervalued her artistic work and prevented herself from living boldly. He would not have had the pleasure of knowing this was his one-of-a-kind art piece he had commissioned. He felt that he had bargained well, and she felt properly rewarded for her work. Win-Win. Her empowerment came by letting the client decide the worth to him. Empowerment requires our creative respect, because our signature brand personifies our joy. In the next story, Kate shows us another way to step into empowerment.

Respond to every call that excites your spirit.
—Rumi

Compliments to Empowerment

I asked Kate what her signature brand was. She thought for a moment. Her signature was a 'Thoughtful Complimentor.' She said it was her strength. She was great at complimenting others. I asked if doing that brought consistent joy to her inner landscape. While her brand was lovely, it wasn't a true energetic expression of personal empowerment.

As Kate paused for reflection, she noticed that her inner landscape had no sustained sunshine from complimenting others. Dark clouds formed fast if others didn't return her acknowledgement with like compliments. She frequently questioned her lovability. I asked what made her think they needed to give anything back to her. What made her think they had to acknowledge her before she would have value? She paused in thought. What she was doing was transactional giving, not empowerment. She was experiencing the Taking It Personal virus.

In additional sessions, Kate was able to look at how taking others' one-sided receiving had actually drained her power and left her with a sad heart. She was side-ways to her power and had a hungry heart. When the time was right, I reached for a Q-tip I had placed on my table; you know, a small white cosmetic paper stick with cotton nubs on both ends. I picked it up and handed it to Kate at an opportune moment. She curiously turned it over, not knowing what I expected her to do with it. "Q.T.I.P, Kate." I paused.

"**Quit Taking It Personally**," I said. She laughed because it was an easy reminder to stay in the right divine flow of her life. As Kate began to explore her career options, she realized what she really wanted was to be a Professional Personal Shopper. She felt empowered with this discovery. She knew what looked great on people, after all, she was always complimenting them. To be empowered, we have to be the highest version of ourselves in every opportunity: aligning fully with our heart's desires. No one in our world will really appreciate us until we fully appreciate ourselves.

> *What lies behind us and what lies before us*
> *are tiny matters compared to what lies within us.*
> **—Ralph Waldo Emerson**

We are here to personalize our life. Doing so empowers our actions and direction. Our brand becomes something unique and memorable about us. That's how we stay in the divine flow of our own life. We awaken the heart of our power when we are willing to take 100% responsibility for our happiness and even our over-giving compliments.

Spotlight Tip: It is not selfish to shine while there are still others who don't shine. Not shining doesn't make you a bigger person.

Authenticity and congruence sponsor sovereign power. Others can recognize us as a safe and kind place when we are in the heart of our power, doing what makes us happy.

As you masterfully choose, do so to personalize your life. Give up 'taking things personally' for Lent. Gary Douglas, founder of *Access Consciousness®* says, "*You are the only one powerful enough to stop you, and you are the only one powerful enough to free you.*"

Raise your sails, my friends. Stand tall in your life. Give all your rocks to the river. Occupy your delight. **Q-tip.** Just saying. Be bold and have fun with this wild life. Let others be. Just be about being YOU. Are you ready to make this Key REAL?

Playful Embodiment Experiments

Pick one or two experiments to embody your power. You can also design your own experiment.

1. If I have always known that *nothing is personal, but rather personalized*, how purposeful will I be today?
2. When you feel stuck, trapped, or small, let your attention fly above the clouds and feel your inherent expansiveness. How does expansiveness settle in you? What actions are possible now?
3. Imagine your Future Self, already having bypassed taking anything personally. Take one full day to behave as if nothing you hear is about you. Listen with compassion and follow your aspirations. There's nothing to debate. Keep track of your successes.
4. Find a creative way to make your own heart of stones and then release the "rocks in your backpack" to the river of life. Let it be a physical experience for the best benefit.

5. Put a Q-tip in your pocket or on your desk as a reminder to quit taking it personally.
6. It's safe for me to create my joy, because I don't take anything personally

My Weekly Mantra: I am empowered when I am faithful to my own life.

I AM ALWAYS SUPPORTED

KEY EIGHT

*The most important question a person can ask is,
'Is the universe a friendly place?* —**Albert Einstein**

- **The Universal Law of Polarity:** Everything is a vibrational continuum from low to high frequency.
- **The Myth:** No one supports me.
- **The Key:** My world is user-friendly by design.
- **The Practice:** What else is possible for me?

THE WISDOM OF BREAKING UP

1984 was the year I broke up with fear. Living in my power with any degree of competency, much less whole-heartedness was always a challenge for me. I was allowing my fears to keep me small, to keep me disengaged, and flat out of boldness. I was tired of feeling inadequate and giving in to the opinions of others. I was afraid something bad would happen at any moment. I felt like my fears were bullying me, and I'd had enough. *"Enough!"* I said. I had created the unfriendly environment I was fighting to exit. How could I possibly know I was always supported in the midst of all this fear? Survival strategies cannot see self-respect. It was time for a purge.

In January of that year I sat down and made a list of every single fear I had, that I knew about. I filled two full eight-by-ten-inch college-ruled pages with all my fears. I knew fear was useful in dangerous situation, but I wasn't in mortal danger any more. Still, I had social anxiety, PTSD, and I didn't value or trust myself. It was time I rose above my life. 1984 was the year I broke up with fear.

My first call to action happened the next month as I was on my way to a professional training in Phoenix, Arizona. I was driving on a long stretch of freeway with no cars around. I wasn't sleepy, but apparently I passed out and crashed into the right-side guardrail. Well, that woke me up! Strangely, I wasn't hurt, not a scratch or a bruise. I would have no residual accident-induced body glitches afterward, either. I immediately assessed the situation.

Well, I had an accident. Fact. It just happened, and I'm not hurt. Fact. Let's see, being stranded and changing a tire by myself were both on my fear list. I got out of the car and took a look at the tires. Two needed changing. One tire was turned completely side-ways. No way could I change that tire. Nope, can't cross that one off my list. My Mercedes was pretty well crunched into the guardrail. How would I get help? [This was in the pre-cell phone era!]

Well, I mentally looked over my fear list. I decided I could hitchhike (yikes!) and it was almost dusk (double yikes!). Okay. I bravely stood on the road near my crunched-up car. There were very few cars on the road, but my thumb was being faithful to my list. Vulnerability was giving way to tentative strength.

A car finally came along and pulled over next to me. My inner dialogue immediately ramped up: *"I could get raped. What if they beat me up and steal my money? Well, I'm still standing here, aren't I? Exhale. So far, so good."* The passenger window rolled down, as my anxiety heightened. A red-headed woman looked at me with a smile and a man, who was in was in the driver's seat, was leaning over to ask if I needed a ride into Phoenix. *They could kidnap me and do horrible things and my husband and kids would never see me again.* I did a quick check-in with my guidance and got a good feeling. I'm still okay. I said that would be wonderful. My suitcase and I climbed into the small space behind their seats.

Shame and I huddled together with our hands clutching my purse. I felt little, like I had done something wrong. I shouldn't have crashed my car. I silently said to this voice, "I love you. We're safe, little one. We're in good hands," and I tried to relax against the hard seat back.

The driver knew exactly where my hotel was located, as he had been there for seminars. He was happy he could be helpful. I also learned they were members of my former religion. I was in good hands. The couple happily drove me up to the front of my hotel and would not accept anything for their time and consideration. Whew! My first fear was checked off. I even felt a wee bit accomplished.

Fast-forward several hours. Interestingly, I later learned from the police that if I had had my accident the day before, I would have immediately plunged down the deep canyon ravine, and would surely be dead. The officer told me I was lucky because the old guardrail had been in bad disrepair. The highway department had literally replaced the old rail with a new, stronger one yesterday.

That's when I remembered with thanks; I am always protected no matter what. I had begun the process of letting my fears arise, like a flock of blackbirds, flying away once they felt the Light of my love. After all, I had lived through them all.

This experience was the first day I really challenged my fears in a big way. Coping with fears is not the same as challenging them. Fears are not personal. It's been said that all fear is the fear of rejection. Some say there are only two fears we are born with: fear of falling and noise. Empaths are aware of all fears—and none of them are personal! The Light in our sensitive energy field is designed to transmute them. No heavy lifting needed.

Spotlight Tip: You can't fix what's leaving you. If you're feeling fears, they are ready to vacate the premises, as we learned in Key 2. Every fear is recycled fear, wherever they come from; this lifetime or parallel lifetimes. Of course, *if* the danger is real, in real time— do what you need to do to stay safe; that goes without saying.

Life is For Me

It's certainly challenging to trust that life is *for* us in the midst of fears, real or regurgitated. Bertrand Russell wrote, *"Fear is the main source of superstition and one of the main sources of cruelty. To conquer fear is the beginning of wisdom."* I kept these words close to me as I approached each fear. I respectfully bowed to each fear as it vanished off my list. I lifted the curtain of the possibility of a friendly world for the first time. This *break-up with fear* task was bigger than it sounded, but if I wanted out of the house of fear, I had to stretch, trust, and keep meeting all my boogiemen.

Synchronicities flew in like hummingbirds diving in for the flower's nectar. I crossed off every fear I had listed, with the exception of scuba diving. I decided it's simply a preference, like seeing how many hot dogs I could eat in five minutes. I had zero interest in either. They never called to me. Looking back on that year, I could see how perfectly orchestrated the release of each fear was. I love how Rumi describes what that year felt like to me.

> *If God said, 'Rumi, pay homage to everything that has helped you enter my arms,' there would not be one experience of my life, not one thought, not one feeling, not any act I would not bow to.* — **Rumi**

Fear has many disguises: Criticism, Sarcasm, Indecision, Anxiety, Boredom, Anger, Racial bias, Judgments, Doubts, Indifference, Perfectionism and Fatigue to list but a few. I came to realize that what I was tackling was not really fear. It was my own conclusions, stated as a fact, as if I were not capable enough to handle what came my way. This was a conclusion, made by a very small child, in very horrific situations. I was justifiably terrified. That was natural, given that circumstances were beyond my control. I did not have the capacity to rescue myself as a child. Yet, I had lived. However, I had become numb. I didn't have healthy responses yet. Until I addressed the underbelly of fear, I wouldn't be free.

If I gave up my fears, what would happen to me? I knew how to function in fear but what else was possible? I slowly realized that detaching from fearful outcomes put me in a listening mode. There was a possibility of actually being inspired to new outcomes. During my eradication of fear year, I understood that while I had been victimized, it didn't have to mean I was, by nature, powerless. I credited myself for having made it out alive. I didn't give up on myself; I surrendered to a greater power than me to keep me safe. I didn't know my power actually had heart or wisdom. I learned surrender. That is worth celebrating! Otherwise, I wouldn't be here, right? Something kept me alive. I would eventually have to reconcile abandoning my body during the worst of it. That would come later. I was so busy trying to get past the past that I forgot *I had the power to survive* even in the worst situations, because I already did. Multiple times. I wouldn't learn until much later in my life that those terrifying experiences had played an important part in my life's work.

No experience is ever by accident; not in a friendly world. When Archangel Michael showed me a black and white scene of the torture experiences, I knew it was not my fate to be scarred by these events. It was my conscious, pre-birth plan to set an abuse frequency in my body. I would later use that frequency in service to ending the dark energies that have keep humanity enslaved. I found peace and comfort in this unexpected knowing. It is also important to realize that fear is a very low frequency; it's not our fate. We cut the power cord to that frequency when we choose to stand sovereignly in the heart of our own power.

You have to let it all go, Neo. Fear, doubt, disbelief. Free your mind.
—**Morpheus**, a character in the movie ***The Matrix.***

Quit Putting Fear Where it Doesn't Not Belong

If we look at life from the idea that something is wrong, we feel an immediate visceral tension in our body, right? That's evidence of an unfriendly world. With any kind of fear, our body tenses and our breath is held or exaggerated, and we begin to find reasons not to walk through the door of our shiny future. But, what if that fearful feeling we feel is disguised anticipation? Did you know the energetic sensations of fear and anticipation reside about a quarter of an inch apart in our belly area? True. It's really easy to get them confused.

Remember when we were a child and we were energized by walking along a tall wood or concrete ledge, arms out to balance. We ruled! Then, our mother saw us and yelled, *Be careful, you could fall!* She was really mad. Instantly, the anticipation of fun dropped a quarter of an inch into the fear of falling. Anticipation asks us to rearrange fear. It is said we are born with only two fears: the fear of falling and the fear of loud noises. What do we do about social or inherited fears? Remember when people began rearranging the meaning of the word FEAR? Words are creation's command frequencies. Some of these fun turnarounds will be familiar and others may be new. Let's have some fun shifting the gears back to anticipation:

- <u>Forgetting Everything's All Right.</u> *What if fear is meant to redirect our energy and to reveal our strengths?* Everything's all right in a friendly world. If a project doesn't scare us, it's not worthy of our time. When moving out of your comfort zone, step boldly! Everything's all right.

- <u>Future's Energized Aligned & Ready.</u> *What if this acronym for fear leads us back to joy?* What if fear doesn't show up unless you're on the brink of your dream? Keep imagining the best that could happen and get into strategic action. Be open to being guided the rest of the way.

- <u>Face Everything And Rise.</u> *What if fear is just in the air we breathe; like a pollutant?* Fear is not personal to us. It's a morphic field that's been around forever as a method of control. Fear keeps us from of knowing how capable and powerful we really are. If we give in to fear, we can be controlled and manipulated. Empaths feel the world's fear in order to heal it. Evil fears our sovereign Light because then, we are no longer malleable.

- <u>Feeling Excited And Refreshed</u>. *What if fear is* my *Consultant?* I lean toward fear being a friendly consultant. In the face of fear, we might ask our inner consultant, "What's the most loving message you have for me as I enter this path?" We may hear something like: *You have all the support you need to you move forward.* Now that's friendly, right? Our inner consultant may answer: *You're ready, and I've got your back.* When I met my dream monsters, I learned to boldly turn to face them. I would require them to reveal their true identity, which, as it turns out, was always benevolent.

~

Spotlight Tip: When we intend something wonderful, our Higher Self gets to work immediately lining things all up for a synchronistic delivery. The moment we let fear in the door, literally, *every* good thing gets put on hold. No kidding. So, imagine a year from now, and that (fear) never even happened. Just not there.

It's our job to transform fear back into anticipation to support for our dreams and goals. Our Higher Self loves to deliver whatever we want to experience. A fearful world says uncontrollable things randomly happen *to* us. We don't have to buy that old scary story. Fear is very afraid of our light, power, beauty and strength. In the face of a powerful, centered person of compassion and love, fear vaporizes. Poof!

Our soul knows the Blueprint for Earth's Mastery Academy. Everything is happening for our liberation from manipulative fear, even if it doesn't feel like it right now. Near the end of my year of breaking up with fear, I felt empowered, capable and free. Maybe salvation isn't the destination of fear. Maybe fear can be a spiritual path for the body's liberation.

*You gain strength, courage, and confidence
by every experience in which you really stop
to look fear in the face.* —**Eleanor Roosevelt**

It's Just a Decision

Einstein said, *The most important question a person can ask is, 'Is the universe a friendly place?* This is the headline quote for this Key because it is bedrock. It is not situational. It is a resolute Decision. It requires no reasons. Our Decision becomes the platform for how we greet life. The fact that we can't see the whole path doesn't mean it is going to be stormy or unfriendly.

Once we make the Decision to view the world as friendly, we don't ever have to think twice. It becomes reflexive, automatic, even if we can't make sense of what's happening, we can reframe the fear into something positive and optimistic. Life is for us. Will there still be storms? Yes, but we will make good use of them. When we need to step up in the face of blatant hatred or bias, Love will lead us to the right words and right actions to sponsor a friendlier world.

People often ask the polite question, *How are you?* It's a conversational starting point from which no one expects an answer. We are only looking for a connection. I had long since abandoned the obligatory and anemic response of "I'm fine." One day my grocery clerk asked me, "How are you?" She wasn't expecting anything other than the socially polite, fine, or good, how are you? That day I spontaneously responded rather enthusiastically with, "I'm fabulous!" The truth is, I am often surprised by what comes out of my mouth. I had turned my speaking over to my Higher Self a long time ago. My young grocery clerk paused as she was ringing up my purchases. "Fabulous," she mused out loud. I found myself softly saying, "It's only a decision." Truthfully, I had never considered that how I felt could actually be a simple decision. Neither had she. Usually we let emotions trump the decision maker. In our next story, John was about to feel the power of The Decision.

I was on the sidewalk heading toward the entrance of the law firm I was working with. We were well into a leadership training contract, and I was excited to continue with the next module. I paused on the sidewalk as John, an attorney at the firm, and I came up to the walkway at the same time. He paused to say good morning before he gestured for me to go ahead of him. We had both paused. I asked him, "How are you today, John?"

"I don't know. I'm getting by; there's a lot going on with me now, you know." Now that's a heck of a way to start his day. Where's the life in that? I looked into his eyes and in my kindest voice, I firmly said, *"John ... it's just a decision. That's all it ever is."*

He was thoughtful. He nodded, offered a rare smile, and said as he opened the door for us, "I guess it is. Well, then, I'm good." *Good* was a better starting place for John that day. A year after my contract had completed, John emailed me about the changes he had made as a result of that day on the sidewalk, when I told him, 'It's just a decision.' His life had changed radically. He said things had always been dependent on how he was feeling. What had happened at his former office and what others thought of him had driven his whole identity. He said he'd made a lot of new decisions and was very happy and well respected at another law firm.

Life is what you make it; always has been,
always will be. —**Grandma Moses**

Where to Start

When we make the friendly or not friendly decision, once and for all, then our life will line up to support that decision and we will begin to see how the puzzle pieces of our life fall into a perfect design or how they keep breaking apart. Default decisions are the starting place for how free we feel, how many risks we are willing to take, and what we will allow in our life. They determine how much fun we have, how many times we stay the course, and how many priceless pearls we mine from our life. So, what's your starting point? Friendly or unfriendly? In our next story I had an opportunity to speak with Mandy about her starting point. You'll see how her default decision was identified and favorably changed in an instant, with no heavy lifting.

I love Mandy. She has the best laugh, and she's a brilliant Licensed Clinical Social Worker. Her clients benefit from her loving guidance. Mandy wanted to weed out anything that kept her from being the clearest therapist possible. However, she has a closed loop perception called *"Nobody listens to me,"* which was not exactly an asset in Mandy's career, right. She collects evidence of its truth all the time, with no apparent exit in sight. It was on the loop of foregone conclusions.

She ran and reran this endless loop in every situation other than her work. No one listens to me. Her belief made her world an unfriendly and often lonely place to live, as you can imagine. She couldn't listen to herself, either. It took a lot of energy to keep this hidden. I asked how this played out for her. Mandy said she frequently spoke with an edge to her words, as if to command people to hear her. At other times her voice's volume would evaporate near the end of a thought, as if to say, my thoughts aren't that important.

One day in my office she reached a tender place inside her

heart and started crying with unrestrained gusto and volume. And I do mean with volume! After a few moments, she abruptly stopped herself, readjusted herself in the chair, wiped her eyes, blew her nose, and apologetically said she shouldn't be making so much noise, since my office neighbors could hear her. I paused a few seconds before my inner anarchist blurted with deadpan finality, "What difference does it make if you cry loudly or not? No one listens to you anyway." We both busted out laughing.

More importantly, I watched her energy field shift in a big way. When the laughing settled down, she said her new theme song should be, "I'll cry if I want to!" Oh yeah, more laughter for sure. And that's lovely because laughter is the magic eraser of old hurts. Guaranteed. She eventually found a new starting point, which led to better outcomes. When we know life is friendly, we know we are supported. We know and trust that everything happens as it is supposed to. This high-ground thinking opens the door of transformation from pain to power. Daniel and Lisa, in the next stories, will show us how they discovered how life was for them.

To Me or For Me?

Daniel is a senior manager of a media distribution company, but he always felt like he was swimming upstream. He couldn't please anyone—not his team and not his manager. Without knowing it, Daniel's thinking was creating his own resistance. Not having enough time; uncooperative, distant team members; unsupportive managers; and too many meetings were the problem, he'd say. Daniel believed the workplace was not friendly toward him. It wasn't him, he'd say; he was just trying to do a good job in a hostile work environment.

"What if all this is happening *for* you, not to you? What's the most loving reason this is happening *for* you, Daniel?" Since this was a new perspective for him, he paused to think about it. He said he wasn't sure, which was perfectly normal for those who are more accustomed to surviving than thriving. I asked him, "What does your life want for you in this leadership opportunity?" There was a lengthy three-minute pause.

"I don't know. I guess if it wants anything for me, it might be for me to stop being so unkind in how I think about my job and my staff. " he said, "I mean, I always look at how things don't work the way they should, and I get angry instead of finding what does work and emphasizing that point with my teams."

Daniel began to discover that even when things aren't going as he expected them to go, there is a hidden gift in the stress-mess. He liked the idea that things happen *for* him, not *to* him so much that he wrote the phrase on the whiteboard in his office so he could see it. He used this perspective to look for opportunities to step up as the competent leader he wanted to be. Others in his office became curious about his whiteboard message. He shared, when asked, how this one statement had released him from blaming others when things didn't go as he had expected.

Mysteriously the saying found its way onto the walls of more and more whiteboards. This thought went viral in his whole department. Daniel's workplace transformed in productivity and camaraderie with five words. *For* me, not *To* me. A *For me* decision means we know our best will eventually be revealed as we continue to trust in a friendly universe. A *To me* decision means we live in repetitive resistance to what's possible. When Lisa, in our next story, shifts her perspective, her dream came true.

> *To be yourself in a world that is constantly trying*
> *to make you something else is the greatest*
> *accomplishment.* —**Ralph Waldo Emerson**

I Didn't Ask for This!

Lisa, a partner in a venture capitalist firm I was coaching, was distraught that her relatively new boyfriend, Ben, wanted so much of her time. Lisa's thoughts toward Ben, she reluctantly admitted, had devolved into seeing him as a distraction rather than her boyfriend. She said she really liked him, but things had shifted somehow. She felt as if he was taking something away from her.

"He wants so much of my time. He doesn't understand how much I value what I do. I mean, I really like him, but..." she confessed, ending in a trailing sigh of resignation.

Lisa chose to mine her assumptions about men, love, support, competition, and work goals. She knew at some level that faulty assumptions were probably keeping her love in a prison of her own making. She really did want a healthy relationship and a profitable business. Uncovering her assumptions led to a larger, surprising awareness. She discovered she was living someone else's life.

She realized she was reenacting her mother's aborted-career drama. Yes, her mother had chosen to have children and to stay at home, while making it loudly known that she had unhappily given up her budding Ballet career to be their mother. Lisa remembered many times when her mother talked about what she could have done—if only. Lisa was too young to know that her mother made a choice in favor of marriage and nurturing a family. Lisa was too young to know this decision wasn't the way it was with all women who love their men.

Lisa saw how she was being competitive with Ben. She saw how she was the one being demanding. She realized she felt imposed upon when he was always asking for a date night.

"What's the diamond in all this angst? How is this an opportunity for you?" I asked. She said, after a pause, that she couldn't receive his love; no... she couldn't let herself feel his love, without pushing him away.

Receiving was something this hard-driving woman hadn't been able to do when it came to being supported. She realized this didn't have anything to do with Ben. He truly was one of the good guys. I asked her to consider taking the projected image of her mother's sad face off Ben's face for the next week. I mean, seriously, they don't even look alike.

I asked, "How would you experience Ben if your mother's image was taking a vacation on Venus for the next week?" She thought it was funny, but she was game.

The next week, Lisa related that a softening had occurred. During the week, when Ben was embracing her, he looked in her eyes and softly told her, "Look, Lisa, I love you, and I want to be with you. I'm not here to threaten your destiny. No one can do that. I would never do that anyway. I'm your lover, not your rival. I want your happiness as much as you do. I totally support you, babe. I just want us to set aside some downtime to enjoy each other." Lisa said she melted as his love filled her. She chuckled. Then, after a pause, she remembered a scene from six months earlier. While speaking with her girlfriends, she said she wanted to be with someone who was comfortable with her career and secure enough in himself to respect her passion and to follow his as well. Lisa laughed as she relayed this belated information. She said that perhaps this declaration had opened the way for Ben to come into her life.

When we try to squeeze this wild dance of the
Mother into orderly, tidy boxes, labeling everything
as good or bad, wanted or unwanted, this or that, we begin to experience
ourselves as fragmented. There's an ache inside: the ache of separation.
—Chameli Ardagh, awakeningwomen.com

This is a Free-Will Academy. That means you alone decide how you will live your life. It's YOUR life! No one decides for you. You can stand tall in your Mastery by partnering with a friendly universe. When things happen *for* us, there is no need for a rival in any way. Competition is the old way; co-operation is the new way, that's why life is *for* us and for whatever we want to create. When Lisa envisioned being with someone who was supportive and loving, she was directing her Higher Self: "I choose to have my career and love." A new kind of man had room to show up for her, just as she had asked. She didn't recognize him immediately because of her habitually fuzzy second-hand role: Living her mother's aborted career life.

~

Spotlight Tip: The truth is, whenever you withhold your love from a situation, the world *appears* unfriendly. Please read that sentence again. The world is how we see it. We are always supported. No matter what.

The Heart Knows

Which world do you live in, friendly or unfriendly? The heart knows. In this moment, gently place the palm of your hand on your heart and take a breath. Drop your shoulders as you exhale a soft "Thank you" and relax your belly. Notice how this simple movement shifts how your body feels. Allow yourself a delicious thought about loving your pet, your child, or your home. Feel this love increase with each natural breath.

Let this friendly world keep you in your divine right flow. No need to fear—you are already Pre-Approved, author of your own story, friendly or not. As you consistently remember you are already Whole, Perfect and Complete, exactly as you are now, the unfriendly world begins to fade away. You are a chooser by default in this Free Will Academy. You wanted it this way!

In a friendly world, your choices become joyous. In a friendly world you can be at ease. Your natural self is a Best Leading Actor, and you begin playing all your roles with clarity, compassion and honestly, defending nothing. Just honoring yourself. Just living your own business in a friendly world with other courageous actors on the stage of life. You put down the fight and remember, the heart of your power is to just be YOU in every way, every day. In a friendly world we go for our dreams, knowing we are fully supported and that life is the ultimate adventure.

Forget not that the earth delights to feel
your bare feet and the winds long to play with your hair.
—Kahlil Gibran

There's no need to struggle to make life work. That's old energy. In this Academy, we get to realize and utilize our support package instead of pushing life away or keeping our guard up. Everything that occurs in this Academy is for our advancement. We are always being re-routed to higher expressions of our true selves. Why not affirm: *"I relax and connect with my spirit's wisdom and my sovereign power. I live in peace knowing I am well-loved and well-supported."* All is well. Are you ready to make this Key REAL?

Playful Embodiment Experiments
Pick one or two experiments to embody your power. You can also design your own experiment.

1. If I have always known that *I live in a benevolent universe and I am always supported,* how would this influence your actions today?
2. If you forget something, and suddenly remember it, say

out loud, "Thank you for watching out *for* me," and see how that opens up a friendly world.

3. Perhaps you can put the pause button on an uncomfortable experience, and ask, "What's the most loving reason this is happening *for* me?" Then place your hand on your heart and receive the message.

4. Make a list of every fear you have. Take five fears and star (*) them. Ask your Soul to guide you in releasing them. When any success comes to you, attribute it to a friendly world and say, *Thank you, body, mind and spirit for releasing those old fears.*

5. Identify one or two things you are currently fighting for. What happens if you welcome the aspect of you who needs things to be different with some kind, unconditional love—not needing anything to be different in order for you to occupy and enjoy a friendly world?

6. It's safe for me to be powerful because this is a friendly universe by my decision.

My Weekly Mantra: Life is for me in every way, every day. I am totally supported.

I AM IRREPLACEABLE; ONE OF A KIND

KEY NINE

Today YOU are YOU that is truer than true.
There is no one alive who is You-er than YOU.
—Dr. Seuss, from **Happy Birthday To You!**

- **The Universal Law of Allowing:** I am who I am. I allow others to be who they are. I allow life to be what it is. I allow myself to be all I can be.
- **The Myth:** I have to be "normal" to fit in.
- **The Key:** I take actions that respect my values.
- **The Practice:** Ask BIG!

THE WISDOM OF UNMASKING

A startling discovery was made in Thailand (formerly Siam) in 1955. By all accounts, and there are many, this precious discovery had always been in plain sight. Its true identity was unknown for nearly 200 years. The monks residing at a monastery in Wat Traimit, Thailand, saw a revered clay statue of the Buddha every day. It was ten and a half feet tall and weighed well over two and a half tons. The statue was ready to be moved to a new location where it would have its own display room; however, the Buddha's real story began more than three hundred years earlier, with the invasion of the Burmese army in 1767.

The Siamese monks had a pure gold Buddha statue, more priceless than all the money it would bring if it were it to be sold, which was out of the question. In an attempt to protect this priceless Buddha from the plundering army, the monks ingeniously ensconced it with twelve inches of clay. The shape was still the same, but it became quite ordinary looking. The monks knew the invading army would think it worthless and pass it by. Sadly, all the monks were slaughtered in the invasion and the priceless clay Buddha went into obscurity for two centuries, never revealing its priceless nature.

If we time-travel forward to May 25, 1955, we see the monks arranging for the clay statue to be secured by ropes and then lifted from its pedestal by a crane to be transported to its new location. The ropes broke from the weight of the statue and sent it thundering to the ground. The monks didn't expect it to be so heavy. It was just clay, after all. They noticed the impact had cracked off some of the plaster.

Anticipating rain that night, the monks carefully covered the statue with tarps to keep it dry. In the dark of night, the concerned head monk took his flashlight and walked outside to see if the Buddha was still adequately covered. His flashlight beam revealed a bright, shiny glimmer huddling under a lifted edge of the tarp. He immediately set about carefully chiseling away the shards until the glimmer grew larger. By morning's light he had revealed a large portion of the Golden Buddha that now gloriously resides in the Wat Traimit Temple in Thailand.

We can take a lesson from the Golden Buddha account. First, the clay mask was intended to be temporary. It protected the precious golden truth from being revealed and subsequently plundered. Secondly, the mask was placed on with great love and respect. The Golden Buddha was not meant to live as a clay statue forever, and neither are we.

The truth is, we don't need to learn more before we can unmask. We only need to *subtract* the clay that disguises the unique Self we came here to be. Mastery requires us to lovingly release the need to hide our golden light in any form. Some say our first mask was when we took a body.

We've talked about life being for us. We've already been Pre-Approved. We are already Whole, Perfect, and Complete because the Divine occupies us. We are great actors advancing our capacity to love ourselves. We are always in right divine flow, even in the many roles we play. We are joyful choosers for sure. We are the author of our stories, and we are unconditionally supported, no matter what choices we make. Now we prepare to hang up our masks; the façades we use for faux-protection. In this Key, I will offer you the same energetic hygiene practices I use to clean up the dust of falling masks. This will be a longer Key because I want you to be centered and balanced in who you came here to be. You are totally amazing. No mask is needed. You're here to shine as yourself. So, let's get on with it!

Spotlight Tip: In this Mastery Academy's gym, there's no whining, no crying, no excuses, no blaming, no fighting, and no quitting. And still, these are choices. It's not as hard as you think to buff up your self-loving muscles and you won't even have to do a single abs crunch.

During the years when I was being abused, I buried my core self deep inside of me. Others could hurt my body, I told myself, but they would *never* have the most important part of me—my heart and soul, and for certain, they would *never* get my love. As a child, I thought this would protect my future from being plundered. We may have required a protective façade once, but eventually we all grow into capable adults, living miles away from Ground Zero's Trauma Zone. Our Radiance was meant to be experienced, not to be tucked away.

As we talked about in the last Key, there is a phantom-fear program lingering that still thinks we might compromise our emotionally safe places if we don't keep those masks in place. Hiding is an expensive coping habit. The truth is, we aren't broken any more than the Golden Buddha was when it fell. It out survived its mask. We will, too. We are resilient. The truth is we wear masks because our greatest fear is being sovereignly transparent. If we cannot see our inner beauty and our magnificence, we cannot claim our Mastery.

> *You, yourself, as much as anybody in the entire*
> *universe, deserve your love and affection.*
> **—Lord Buddha**

Our vulnerabilities will not be exposed, as we feared. What is revealed instead is our honesty, our kindness, our self-respect, our gifts and our bravery. There is more goodness in us than we can see through our masks. The flowers in a garden never think about whether they are beautiful enough or worthy enough to be here. They never judge themselves. What if we no longer needed to play it safe to avoid judgments or censure? It's important to remember that the monks who plastered on the clay mask to preserve the Golden

Buddha did so with sacred love, honor, and respect. So did you, dear one, the moment you innocently slipped your first mask on. What was put on with love can be released with love. You put your mask on; therefore only you have the loving authority to remove it. Don't listen to the Harpies. You can do this. Living un-masked and sovereign are the best stress reducers you will ever find.

Own Your Authentic Signature Brand

Authenticity is linked with being real, genuine, and unique, one of a kind. Living authentically is our signature brand. We can easily recognize name brands like Channel, Ralph Lauren, Oprah, Maserati, Apple, Disney, FedEx, Visa, or Nike. They are unmistakable. Their work is authenticated as an original. Our signature brand is our passion, our honesty, our transparency, and our presence. It's what we came here to express as only we can. We aren't meant to be or do the same thing in the same way as everyone else. Where's the sovereignty in that? Sometimes we think being authentic means we are 100% open, airing all our laundry, being rude or disrespectful just because we can. We're being real, right? Nope. That way is far too small for such a magnificent being such as yourself.

Creating drama doesn't honor us. As an example of an authentic and innocent response, imagine this scene: You are on a first date, and mid-conversation, your date brazenly asks you how much money you make. Can you feel a reaction rise in you, even now? Do you want to push back, shocked at how rude they are? Take a breath. Chill. What if you have no need to turn this question into a fight? You might honesty answer, "I don't know you well enough to answer that question." That's a fact. It's *only* a first date! There's nothing to defend. No one is stealing your wallet and leaving you bloody on the pavement. You don't have to push back.

No mask is needed. Just be *innocently* honest. Leave fighting for the boxing ring.

Authenticity doesn't mean exposure. It resides in the realization that we just told a fib, we just deflected, we just fled the scene, we just evaded, or we just now shoved our truth into our back pocket. Perhaps we felt a knee-jerk response to pull back or to push away. What if, instead, we push the pause button and rearrange ourselves. To be sure, such a pause and re-adjustment takes practice and a good coach, but its yield is priceless: being comfortable in our own skin.

What if your signature brand is Peaceful Power? Would it shape your words and actions similar to the compassion effused by the Dalai Lama? We don't have to be a devoted spiritual leader to have an influence in our world; we just need a worthy aspiration of our own.

Aspiration walks with authenticity. Aspiration means to aspire; to breathe life into an ideal achievement. Aspiration is the lifeblood of a cherished vision. Play encourages following our aspirations. When approaching a stuck place, start with play. Literally leave your home and go play. Take a walk in nature, play in the snow, sing, dance in mud puddles and have fun. Play releases the brake fear puts on our aspirations. Play resets our energy and increases our self-respect.

The greatest success you and I will ever have is breaking free from what constrains us. Come Alive with the joy of being comfortable in your skin. Let there be play!

Spotlight Tip: Authenticity is not consistent. Don't expect it to arrive as if it's a Five-Star destination. It can be wobbly from time to time as we learn to catch ourselves in the moment and stretch into unapologetic authenticity. Our inner shameful self is the only one who needs diversions and hiding. Our Soul does not. Our spirit does not. Our heart does not. As long as we feel a need for a façade, we will never be Authentic.

I like what Gilda Radner, American actress, said. *My life...is about not knowing, having to change, taking the moment and making the best of it, without knowing what's going to happen next.* I know, a little scary, right? We want certainty! We want to feel capable of handling things because we know those scripts. Yet, can we also feel the freedom, even playfulness of her bold statement?

We're so used to scripting conversations, scripting our future, scripting how others should be and scripting how we need to be to fit in. Where's the aliveness in that?

In business we navigate politics, multiple projects, we interface with other departments and this requires professionalism. Staying aligned to our objectives, their objectives, multiple outcomes requires staying present and in our role. How do I know when I'm fully present? Here are a few landmarks for you:

I'm Fully Present When...

- I can listen generously
- I have no hidden agenda
- My body is relaxed by default
- I am free because nothing is personal
- I make soft eye contact with others
- I listen for what has heart
- I have nothing to protect or to get
- I have a healthy respect for myself and others
- I judge nothing and evangelize nothing

Reset the Clock to Present Time

We live in a fast-paced world. It's easy to feel scattered. The following set of questions let's us quickly check in and reset if necessary in order to be present with no hidden distractions.

- **Where am I?** (Still at the last meeting, thinking about my vacation, or quietly present)
- **What time is it?** (Am I thinking about the past or the future, or am I Here Now)
- **How old am I?** (My scared six-year old inner child, a rebellious adolescent, or my capable current age)
- **What Am I pushing?** (Do I have a hidden agenda?)
- **Whose life am I living?** (Someone else's or mine?)
- **Who am I being?** (What is my role? Is it appropriate here?)

Can we just Be Here Now, with our kind attention, with nothing to fix, judge, or defend? What if we donated those to the Earth's Museum of Unnatural History? Being you is enough. Being honest is enough. Being totally present is enough. You're already a superstar because you made it to the Earth's Mastery Academy. You were Pre-Approved to be irreplaceable, one of a kind, so chill! The simple truth is that we always run the risk of being rejected when we veer off other people's agendas or when we seek their approval. What if the greater risk, though, is that our inner Golden Buddha will never be revealed? Don't be afraid to step off script to be genuine, even if you are the one who wrote the script.

Spotlight Tip: We can't solve a current problem by throwing in the proverbial kitchen sink full of complaints, spewing up all the wrongs ever done to us. We can only deal with what is happening here and now, in this moment, dealing with only one complaint. Be responsible for your actions and for the wake you leave.

To keep our authenticity in high form, I highly recommend cleaning off the dust of unmasking. In this section, we will learn Five Energetic Hygiene practices followed by Five Power Platforms, so we to can align with our Golden Self.

Disclaimer: Please do the following Energetic Hygiene practices *one at a time*. I'll give you step-by-step scenarios. Give yourself some time and space to let your power naturally root in your body. Don't rush it, because these exercises will rearrange you! Do one and put the book down, take a walk in nature if you can, and then come back for the next. You can thank me later.

Speed clearing is harder to assimilate. Let each step be well within you before you approach the next. There's no rush. In this Key, I will share two sequential processes I developed from my work: The *Authentic Soul Signature* and the *Energetic Hygiene Practice* ©*Spirit's Wisdom, 2001*. These are *essential* for sensitive, empathic folks and for all frenzied life styles. This might be a good time to look at your journal to refresh your memory of your results from the Energy Assessment you took at the beginning of the book. They reflect where you hide your power.

Keep it Clean

I use these Five Energetic Hygiene practices with myself and my clients to restore vital power. Energetic congestion happens throughout the day, and highly sensitive people get an extra serving. These are restorative, especially when you don't feel like yourself or you feel exhausted for no apparent reason. We may have someone else's energy hogging our inner space or an old mask might be ready to be dissolved. I like to do one of these hygiene cleanses at the end of each day. I have better dreams that way and with no emotional hangover in the morning. In the first energetic hygiene practice, I will set the stage with a personal unmasking experience. In the remaining hygiene clearings, we will follow Sandra's story as she shows us how she came to liberate her past and free the heart of her power. These are step-by-step 'live sessions' which I frequently use with clients when called for. Ready? Let's clean house!

Energetic Hygiene #1: Reveal a Fresh Face

During one of my professional trainings, Tom, one of our instructors, was sharing wisdom he gained from studying with an Indigenous tribe. He asked if we would like to be guided through an experience his teacher had taught him. Yes! We were game for anything out of the box. When we gentled our attention, he began.

He asked us to imagine wearing the mask of our pretend self, a self we use to hide our true feelings. We didn't need to identify what our mask was, because a mask is a mask. He invited us, with our eyes closed, to use our non-dominant hand to reach up toward our face, with our palm facing our nose and our fingers softly spread wide open. "Imagine," he said, "letting your fingertips gently discover the edges of the mask...now." He continued, "Carefully grip the mask and gently and slowly remove it. That's right... and with a breath, it easily releases... Now place the mask on an imaginary table in front of you. Just let it sit there and notice how you feel without it."

Wow, I felt the mask. I physically felt it, for real! That was a surprise, for sure. After a pause he invited us to bring our attention back into the room and softly look around with naked eyes. "How does this room feel to you without your mask?" he asked us. After a bit of silence, many comments arose from the group. They reflected the feeling of a quieter room. Respect was there, as well as honesty, less hiding, less avoiding, less pushing, genuine faces and spacious self-kindness. The group agreed; this feels like a more approachable and kinder room. I felt an internal sense of undefended openness as I looked around the room. I didn't have to avoid certain people or help others, please others, or know all the answers.

"How did you feel as you took off your mask?" he asked us. I felt peaceful, genuine, contained yet utterly free, so why was I so invested in wearing masks if I felt this good without them, I wondered. Are you ready to take off your mask and simply notice what's different for you, too? [Pause and discover.] Next, we'll meet Sandra as she shares how she learned to reclaim the heart of her power.

> *It's not who you are that holds you back; it's who you think you're not.* —**Anonymous**

Energetic Hygiene #2: Your Authentic Soul Signature.

Sandra was having trouble with her work performance. She felt pulled in too many directions. She kept going over and over all the possible outcomes to make sure her boss would be happy. She dreaded his being upset. She admitted her problem wasn't just with her boss. She never felt she could make a clear decision with her family either. The kids were always demanding her attention, and her husband said she was scattered, and never present.

She didn't want to let her family down, either. She admitted it had become easier to just go along. We can identify with her pain, can't we? This kind of situation always happens when we misplace our inner authority. We don't feel grounded without it. We can lose ourselves in an over-stimulated world. We can end up mourning the loss of our sovereignty, always making sure everyone else is happy. Sandra didn't like to rock the proverbial boat. She didn't want to be too demanding. I asked her, "Does it feel like there's a whole committee in your head debating about the right course of action?"

"Yes! I can't even think straight," she said, her arms gesturing in the air. "How do I make it stop?" she pleaded. I reassured her it could be done. It was time to evict the rowdy inner squatters. I asked Sandra if she would like to refresh her Authority Circle, meaning her ability to know what is right for her. Of course, she said yes. I invited her to remember a time in her life when she felt like she could do anything, be anything.

She recalled a time when she was Thirteen-years-old and had just hit a home run for her baseball team. Her team was screaming, yelling, and jumping up and down with big smiles and high-fives. Sandra's home run won the game for her team. When she paused, I asked her to hold that feeling and let it expand a little with each gentle breath. She relaxed. I asked her, "If this feeling has a color or colors, what color or colors would it be?"

"Mmm. It is like a big, bright morning sun," she said, with a satisfied smile.

"That's your Soul's signature color, Sandra. It's unique to you. This is how you recognize your Authentic Soul Signature from that of others. This is your starting point for all our work. You feel most like you in this big, bright morning sun energy," I said.

Sandra really liked having her Soul's signature color. She let out a sigh of contentment. Our energetic signature is distinct from the energetic signatures of others. It's how we recognize our Self. When we are in our color, our decisions become easier. Curiously, what's your Soul's signature color, dear Reader? How will you describe or draw it in your journal?

Spotlight Tip: Every one of us has exactly the same amount of self-directing authority. Self-authority means we honor our heart and spirit with fearless compassion. An open heart in power has nothing to defend. We respect our values and needs with full agency when in our color. This is how we become comfortable in our body. Okay, is a good time to take a break and let this marinate.

Energetic Hygiene #3: Return to Sender

We continued the following week. "Last week, you discovered your big, bright morning sun signature. Today simply notice— what is the color of your boss's energy? There's no right or wrong, just notice what color shows up."

"Oh, he's red, brownish-red," she reported with a bit of sass.

"Okay, and you want to do a good job, right, so…I wonder if you are inadvertently carrying any of that brownish-red in your body, as if you need it there to be prepared. Just check to see," I said, "I don't know if that's true for you or not." Sandy's hand reflexively covered her belly.

"There's some on my shoulders, on my back, and some, uh, a whole lot in my stomach." Surprised, she opened her eyes.

"Nice observation, Sandy. The brownish-red is not yours because your Soul color is big, bright morning sun, right? Let's do a little Elvis Presley's "Return to Sender" song. I laughingly sang the lyrics for her to get her in the vibe before we began. "Let's return that brownish-red energy back to its rightful owner. I'm sure you didn't mean to keep it. You're not a thief, so let's send it back to its rightful owner now," I said, assisting his energy to leave her nervous system and return it to him.

Spotlight Tip: Our nervous system is our immune system, and our immune system identifies us from other people. Just knowing this helped me heal my autoimmune disorder. Our nervous system responds best to pure vibration and color. Color frequency is the easiest vibrational information to firm up our true power.

After Sandra returned the brownish-red energy, I asked her to report any changes.

"Relieved! Lighter. I don't feel like I'm carrying such a weight," she said. I continued.

"Your job, Sandra, is to keep your energy clear and clean. This is why it's important to have a daily energetic hygiene system in place so we stay aligned with our Soul's Authentic Signature color. Notice how your big, bright morning sun naturally fills in the spaces where that brownish-red used to be. That's right. This keeps your Soul color true." After a pause I continued.

"As you think about speaking to your boss next time, how much big, bright morning sun energy is in your body?"

"Maybe fifty percent," she said with a look that conveyed disappointed hope for a higher number.

"Okay, so, this is what you do to stay safe, Sandra: you protect your energy. You pull your energy in close to your skin, thinking it will protect you. One-third out there and two-thirds tucked safely inside, right?" Sandra affirmatively nodded. "However, with two-thirds tucked away, you will still try to say what he wants to hear, right?"

She nodded. "This isn't a very effective strategy, is it," she remarked.

~

Spotlight Tip: The smaller we make ourselves; the more we have to protect ourselves, and the less risk we will take in the world. We don't have access to our own energy when we scrunch it down. Goes against our bold and expansive grain. Just saying.

I had Sandra stand up for this next part. "So, now imagine you are getting ready to go to his office because he called you there. Your business is not to know or anticipate why you were called in unless he told you the topic. Your business is to be 100% full of your big, bright morning sun energy. Just be fully inside your color, centered and attentive, fully present in yourself. Let your body fill up with 100% big, bright morning sun all the way up from a bottomless well of big, bright morning sun energy. That's right. Now let it form a circle around you, about three feet out all the way around your body. Imagine you are standing securely in the center of your Authority Circle. It moves as you move; always within this full circle of nourishing big, bright morning sun energy."

I had her walk around the room noticing and feeling her center consistently emanating three feet out, no matter how or where she moved. After her walk, she reported that her color wanted to be called Morning Sun. Her power now felt like second skin. Standing in her circle gave her greater access to clear thinking and clear expression. I waited for her to align energetically and then asked, "When you walk in his office with a healthy Authority Circle present, what feels different?"

Sandra was beaming. "I'm not afraid of him. I actually feel confident we will come to an agreement on how to proceed. I feel confident I can relay the necessary information to him to make a decision. I'm an important part of this team. Whatever he needs we can work together toward it," she said. "I know I'm really good at my job," she exclaimed, beaming her beautiful signature energy. It had definitely warmed the room as she returned to her chair to close the session. Her energy was so clear and energizing, we both needed to fan our faces as we laughed. We would revisit part two of her inner authority alignment the following week.

～

Spotlight Tip: If we aren't centered in our own life and in our own body, we become a white screen onto which others can and will project their movie.

Energetic Hygiene #4: Bringing our Innocents Home

Completing Sandra's inner authority alignment would involve calling her self-authority back home, inside her, where it belongs. Only then can she be truly present and in her peaceful power. We were dependent as children, so we innocently handed over our power to the big people; sometimes with a tug of war. Sandra came into my office the following week eager to continue calling her power back home. She'd reported great results in meetings with her boss. In this session we would begin the next level of energetic hygiene. Time to polish her Golden Buddha within.

As we began, I invited Sandra to reconnect with her Morning Sun energy. She said it was much easier to stay in her color. "Now I'd like to invite you to soften your vision, soften your breathing and imagine your parents, since they were the key people during your growing up." I paused while she did that. "Now simply and kindly notice how much of your Morning Sun energy you gave them to take care of you, to love you, to raise you right, and to keep you safe," I asked. She was thoughtful.

"My dad has the most, and my mother didn't seem to want anything to do with my color," she observed.

"All right, then let's start with Dad, okay?" She nodded, trusting the process. "You gave him your color and trusted him to take care of you, love you, and teach you about the world. Notice where he is still carrying your color," I directed. She said there was a lot of her Morning Sun energy in his heart, a lot around his head, and some in his hands. She smiled and became silent.

"Good noticing. Now, let's bring your energy home. Ready?" I asked, knowing there would be the inevitable objections. It always happens when we work with someone we love. I waited while she fidgeted.

"Yes. No. I mean…. if I take it all back, does that mean I won't have any connection with him ever again? Does it mean he won't feel my love? Does it mean I have to let him go?" she asked, clearly alarmed. This concern is normal when there are positive feelings in this process.

"Not at all, Sandra. In fact, I will show you a much better way to stay connected *and* have your Morning Sun power back. I promise, okay?" She nodded, and we proceeded.

"First, call all your Morning Sun energy home where it belongs —within you, its rightful home. We want the fullness of your color available to you. It's okay; now call your Morning Sun energy back home, clean and innocent in its pure state, bringing nothing back with it. Let it happen now with peace and kindness. Watch it all return to you, settling back into your body, knowing you will reconnect with Dad in a moment," I softly instructed and waited.

"Notice how it feels to have your color returned to your core and filling your body," I asked her. She said it felt wonderful and warm. As humans we are always making energy connections with others. That's what is delicious about life, but we also need to respect our inner Authority Circle if we want to be masterful and unique in our own life.

"Your energy's back home now, where it belongs, yes?" Sandra nodded, and I continued to guide her. "Now let's reconnect with dad in a more respectful and loving way. Imagine a beautiful pink thread of pure enduring love energy coming from his heart to yours and from your heart to his—pure love, pink thread. This thread is pliable and enduring and is now connected correctly heart to heart. Notice what feels different," I said. She quietly nodded, relaxing her body.

"Like it will last forever. It feels better than before. I actually feel like a grownup! I like this feeling so much better; it feels richer and deeper," she said. Adding to that, she said it felt perfect for her

Dad because she had always had a good relationship with him. Not so much with her distant and often critical mother, however. Sandra mused, "There's a lot I have to forgive her for, and I'm reluctant to do that." Her revelations bring us to an important forgiveness practice that may surprise you.

Energetic Hygiene #5: Activate Self-Forgiveness

First, let me provide a little background on this particular process of forgiveness. True forgiveness is when we take full responsibility for the choices *we* made *after* the offenses occurred. We are the ones who stopped trusting and began controlling. This was an innocent attempt to stay safe from further harm. But, that's not freedom. That's a clay prison. It took an autoimmune disease to teach me this principle. I was attacking myself by not forgiving myself. If you were one of the lucky ones and did not shut down during trauma of any kind, then forgiving the other is a beautiful gift that requires nothing from them or you. What the other did or didn't do is *their* business with their God and not our business. Only the one who took the hurtful action, because of their own pain, can forgive themselves. Sandra's continuing story will help us open to the grace of self-forgiveness.

∾

Spotlight Tip: Dear one, forgiveness is the grace you to give to yourself because *you* abandoned your connection with *your* loving nature. Read that again, please. People do what they do. Your business is to forgive yourself first for what you did, and continue to do, as a result of others' actions.

After Sandra sat down, I wanted her to know how to keep her inner authority in her body, especially around people with whom she felt powerless. "Sandra, let's give your body this direction. Let's say it together, okay. *'Take note, my beloved body. I intend to live my life fully in my Soul's Signature color. I accept nothing less now and forever. And so it is.'* I let her rest in this command, then we began the next step with her mother.

"Sandra, gently notice how you kept trying to please your Mother, trying to get her to notice you, and maybe even hoping she would be kind to you," I said. She nodded in agreement through painful tears.

"She carries all your 'wishing, hoping, praying, trying to be accepted and loved to-no-avail energy.' You gave your Authority away in an innocent attempt to feel hopeful that one day, if you were good enough, she would love you. You still silently hope she will accept you and love you, don't you, still to no avail?" I asked, to which she nodded. "It's time to call your inner authority home. If you leave it with your mother, you will forever continue to feel helpless, powerless, and unlovable."

Sandra slowly nodded. This had been her ever-present white noise. None of us can be present to our love until we end this pattern of looking outside ourselves for love, wealth, power, and peace. I continued, "It's important to know that your Mother's inadequacies in loving had nothing to do with your lovability." I slowly repeated this statement three times to saturate and nurture her rejected inner child. She nodded, soaking it in. Sitting up taller in her chair, she was ready to continue.

"Now peacefully call your Morning Sun energy back home from your Mother, like you would call your sweet child to a favorite bedtime story. Lovingly call your innocence home, inside your body, where it rightfully belongs. Everything that is not Morning Sun energy remains with Mother. Offer your innocent child a homecoming hug." I knew they would both gain from this experience. I waited and watched it happen until she finally nodded that it was all back. "Are you ready for the next step?" I asked.

But, I don't believe that life is supposed to make you feel good, or to make
you feel miserable either. Life is just supposed to make you feel.
—Gloria Naylor, novelist

A bit apprehensively, Sandra readied herself for the reconnection part. I asked her to create the same heart connection with the beautiful, pure, enduring pink love thread as she had done with her father, heart to heart. She took a deep breath of trust, let it out, nodded her head, and began. Soon soft tears fell as she reconnected to her mother in this new way. Heart to heart. After drying her eyes and waiting until she could compose herself, she shared, "I feel so present; full. I feel like I just came to life, somehow. Strangely, I can actually feel my mother's love for me, for the first time. I actually feel loved by her. I feel lighter and whole, as if I am being born again. This is amazing!"

Grace gently reminds us that if someone hurts us, there was someone who was hurt long before us, and that person is trying to mask their pain. If we pan the camera back, perhaps we can feel all our ancestors gathering around us, offering us their full support. They are asking, *Are you the one? Are you the one who will set us free? Are you the one who heals our timeline? Are you the one who remembers love?* It's okay to say, "Yes," then let it be.

Spotlight Tip: You alone have the authority to grant yourself forgiveness. Why? Because your loving energy is your business. It's a generous act of self-loving to keep your energy intact, fresh, and vital so you can be your best. Your energy is your business, so make it profitable, vibrant and loving.

Rest a moment with this process before you move to the Power Platforms, will you? Calling your innocents home is profound and life-changing. Just let it settle into your nervous system a bit. Get up, take a bit of a walk, hydrate yourself and let it be. Innocently notice what feels subtly different in your day. Just notice, "Hmm, the air feels softer." These five power platforms will give us easy ways to occupy our peaceful power. They will help us stand tall.

> *May your life be like a wild flower, growing*
> *freely in the beauty and joy of each day.*
> **—Native American Proverb**

Power Platform #1. Stand for Yourself

As the old country western song said, "If you don't stand for something, you'll fall for anything." True, right? What do you stand for? I know we are busy just trying to get through the day, but when we know what we stand for, it makes our decisions energy efficient. Personal values are our energetic backbone. We have a physical skeleton that holds our body upright and allows us to stand, walk, and move, but what makes up the skeleton of our joyous spiritual bodies? What values support confidence and self-respect?

Notice this Key isn't named Stand *up* for yourself. Respecting yourself means you speak for what is important to you, because to do otherwise feels like you are betraying yourself. We know when someone disrespects us. Just don't let that someone be You! We think we need to make a big, angry stand just to be heard, believed, or taken seriously, for heaven's sake! That behavior, my friend, spells T-R-O-U-B-L-E. We bottle it up and give in; we don't want to upset the apple cart of security. Sigh. We adjust our mask in the mirror of the other person's reflection. We just abandoned ourself.

When we barter self-respect to keep the peace, our resentment builds up like a steam teakettle full of unspoken thoughts on a hot stove. Eventually, we blow our top over some unrelated issue. It can feel like a righteous protest, but it's only empty steam. Steam isn't action. Steam isn't strength. Steam isn't power. Steam is just hot air. We either explode or we implode. Either way, we have totally ticked off our Authentic Self. We don't have to do it that way, my friends. We mistakenly believe it takes courage to give someone a piece of our mind. What if the real courage is to give them a *peace* of our heart? The truth is, we have little experience speaking authentically *for* ourselves in moments of upset. We have little experience being okay with our vulnerabilities. When our tender spots take a hit, it's an invitation to return to our self-respect and innocent vulnerability. Jamie learned to respect himself and help his brother.

Jamie's younger brother, Ben frequently cornered him to solve his problems. One day Jamie realized this was a waste of time since Ben never seemed to run out of problems he wanted his advice on. Jamie had had enough. When we talked, I asked him who would be a better fit to actually give Ben some answers. After thinking, he said, "A counselor, or maybe a minister. Certainly not me. I've been trying to be the answer man, which was flattering at first, you know, like he looked up to me, but now, jeez, I'm drowning in his messed up life."

"Which feels like the right fit for Ben, a counselor or a minister?" Jamie thought a minute. "A counselor, but I'm not sure he will buy that so maybe his minister, but that's iffy, too. I don't know. I just don't know," he said, raking his hands through his hair.

"Do you know why you don't know, Jamie?" I asked. He shook his head indicating no. "You don't know because it isn't about your life. It's about his life. You can't solve what isn't yours. One thing you know is that he doesn't take your advice, right?" He nodded his head. "At best you can let him know you aren't qualified to give what he needs. That's honest. Why not recommend that he contact a counselor or his minister. He'll decide what he needs for help or not."

We can't offer a solution to someone whose mind is stuffed full of helplessness. Jamie knew he would have to be persistent, so we rehearsed in his session. Jamie was relieved to discover he could stand for himself by admitting he wasn't qualified to solve Ben's problems. Jamie was able to hold that line until Ben stopped asking him. Later, Jamie said that one piece of wisdom I'd given him was a big turning point for him. He thought it meant that he didn't care about his brother if he refused to solve his problems. Standing on the self-respect platform holds real power. We can't speak from our heart without self-respect. What's that? I think I hear Aretha Franklin's soulful song playing in the airways... *"All I'm askin' for is a little respect."* Come on, sing it with me...R.E.S.P.E.C.T.

Spotlight Tip: You are here to respect and advance your unique life plan, thereby adding to the richness of our human fabric. You're not here to pretzel yourself into someone's ideal. You're here to own your agency. To own your life. To respect what lets you be your best.

Power Platform #2. R-E-S-P-E-C-T

You're one of a kind. Unique, just like everybody else, Virginia Satir, renowned family therapist, would say. Your uniqueness means you get to live your life in your way, on your own terms and others get to live their lives in their own way. Life isn't a contest of who lives the best. Just offer your best. Having healthy self-respect means you continue to stay loyal to what you promised yourself, long after the promise has transitioned into the business of the day.

Self-respect is much easier to start with than self-love, which often leaves us floundering. Self-respect is about living comfortably in your own skin. Only you know what is right for you. Honoring yourself first when something doesn't feel right is the key to the heart of your power. Self-respect is about being relaxed because you respect yourself in a healthy manner. It requires that you keep your word to yourself. Self-respect is very attractive. As Joseph Campbell said, *I don't believe people are looking for the meaning of life as much as they are looking for the experience of being alive.* We all want to feel alive in some way. We don't want to disappoint ourselves. The next platform will show us how to make this practical.

> *Don't worry about what the world needs.*
> *Ask what makes you come alive and go do it.*
> *Because what the world needs are people*
> *who have come alive.* **—Howard Thurman**,
> Theologian and civil rights activist

Power Platform #3. Fund your Deepest Desires

We are here as one of a kind, irreplaceable in every way. Often, we find ourselves funding other people's needs or dreams. Empaths and sensitives fall into this trap in the name of service. There's nothing wrong with that, as long as it also funds their own aspirations. Anais Nin wrote, *Life shrinks or expands accordingly to one's courage.* Courage is easier to access when we know our values. How do we want to be remembered long after we are gone? We begin to shape our values using this simple legacy formula:

- After I'm dead, I would like to be remembered for my
  _____.

- I want to be remembered as someone who exemplified
  _____.

Next, we convert our legacy into values we choose. They become living expressions of what we care about. They inspire our motivation. They make you be YOU. Some of my core values are: beauty, adventure, respect, learning and spiritual connection. Values inspire how we live each day so we are heart-fulfilled. If you want success, take purposeful action. If you want a deeply satisfying life, take purposeful actions infused with your highest values. They keep you connected with what is important to you and your best life.

Sam, a senior manager, after solidifying his top five values, took practical action. He took a Sharpie pen and printed his top Five values, one on each of the front of his five fingers, literally; words on five fingers so he could see them on both his hands. It inspired coworkers who were curious and asked what they meant. Words on fingers of coworkers began to show up everywhere. People were eager to share them with each other. Sam had unintentionally started a buzz in the workplace, and he was, as a result, asked to work with all the division managers to implement the company's values. This turned out to be a perfect fit for him and for the company. Jon, a member of the team couldn't readily identify his core values. What he could do was to write *respect* on one finger, *self* on the next finger, and he did so until all ten digits had either *respect* or *self* on them in ink. Self-respect. Even the smallest action, backed by a core value creates a life that becomes our signature brand. What are your top 5 core values for a well-loved life? Next, we can begin to activate our success formula:

**Vision + Values + Strategic plan +
Actions + Review + Re-vision + Action
+ Review = Accomplishment.**

Power Platform #4. Practical Passion
What's the *Big Why* that calls you to do what you do? It's more

than just getting out of bed in the morning, right. You know that. When we know our *Big Why*, our days will begin to fulfill us. Our dreams are worthy of a healthy goal structure, supported by inspiring values, and nurtured by practical actions. Stephen's values are: vision, contribution, teamwork, adventure, and the welfare of kids. His values were begging to be put into action. Stephen answered an inner call and created a compelling project goal that actualized each of his values. He wanted to live in a world that cared for our kids, something he didn't feel growing up (his *Big Why*). He wanted a project that stacked all his values with his personal goal of riding his motorcycle from northern Oregon to Mexico.

As an incentive, he decided to auction off the privilege of accompanying him to three participants, on their own motorcycles, of course, in exchange for a hefty donation to the project. The four motorcyclists would be adventuring on the open road and distributing clothing and school supplies to four Mexican orphanages he had already contacted. He organized fundraisers to gather needed supplies and funds. He put out a live blog, sharing his stories and photos of the trip to all who supported his successful charitable adventure. Some might call this passion, but it's simply pairing chosen values with practical actions. Keep it that simple. No need to hunt for your purpose. Values will deliver your purpose.

I'm not afraid. I was born to do this.
—**Joan of Arc** (1412-1431, Heroine of France)

Power Platform #5. Ask Big!

Nearly 800 years ago Rumi said, *You must ask for what you really want.* The whole idea of being irreplaceable and one of a kind, is to inhabit *your* body, *your* life, *your* choices, *your* voice, and *your* dreams, in *your* way. That's how we live from the heart of our power. That is how we live in our sovereign power. To do that, we must be comfortable with asking Big. Most people break into a sweat about now. Perhaps, in the past when we asked for what we wanted, we were shot down, shamed, humiliated or dismissed.

Most of us under-ask, and that's a great way to mask up. I was severely anemic in the Ask Boldly nutrient. Years ago, I was attending a Consciousness workshop. My most dreaded fear turned out to be our dinner-break assignment that very evening. "Ask for something and come back with Ten *No's*," the instructor said. I hate this! Maybe I could just leave now, as my inner escape artist began mentally strategizing all possible exits. That took Five minutes of wasted energy. I knew I would be shortchanging myself if I ran, and I had vowed not to run anymore. I needed to keep my promise to myself if I wanted to remain in my good graces.

I also knew that if I could master this herculean feat of asking, I would be open to possibilities I had only dreamed about. I had my assignment. The clock started ticking and I started sweating. My first ask was in the parking lot. A distance down the parking lot, I saw a man get out of his car. He was clearly in a hurry—a perfect target for a guaranteed *no*! I bolded myself up, stepped closer to block his hurried pace. I put my hand up to stop him and asked if he had a pen I could borrow. He patted his pockets front and back and found no pen there. (Yay! My first *no* coming right up!) He then said, "Wait a moment." He turned and sprinted back to his car to get himself and me a pen. He gave me one and thanked me for asking; otherwise he would have gone to his class with no pen. Tick-tock on the *no* clock.

I asked another man for a dollar (cringing inside; oh, how I *hate* this). He pulled out his wallet and gave me a Twenty-dollar bill and said, "Keep the change and pay it forward when you can." I felt guilty for asking, because I already had money in my wallet. Tick-tock, tick-tock. I had more asks to go, and no *no's* anywhere. I was due in the training room in Fifteen minutes. In desperation, I stopped a woman pushing her baby in a stroller. Surely she will say *no*. I honestly didn't know what to ask for, so I simply admired the cute little bears on her baby's blanket. She literally took the baby blanket off her baby and gave it to me, since I liked little bears! I felt like a moocher. Can't I just get a *no*? To my horror, she also took the baby's little pillowcase off, since it had bears on it as well, and gave it to me. "You should have a matching set," she said. What am I going to do with this, I thought, as she insisted I should have them. I graciously thanked her for her generosity. I knew I could give them to a new mother. Still no no's.

Later I realized that when we make it our task to ASK, the Divine will rush in, BIG time. Everyone gave happily, and even more than I had asked for. No one ever said *no*. That was new in my world at that time. As you can imagine, I discovered that people love to help one another. I discovered it was less about asking for me than it was about being able to receive the loving support of others. We don't ask because we can't receive. Why not start a daily practice of collecting Ten *no's* a day. I finally befriended Big Asking. You won't regret it.

Spotlight Tip: Don't be pushed by your problems. Be led by your boldness. Asking and receiving are the key to a rich and full life. Ask BIG for what you need or want.

This completes our five Power Platforms for occupying sovereign, practical power. It's safe to take off our social masks. This life is truly a 'Come as you are' party, not a 'Come already perfect' party. You were meant to take your place in this world. You were born to be powerful. Your destiny is assured, so relax; enjoy what inspires you. Life continually reroutes us to our highest good, so dust yourself off and stand tall exactly as you are. Let your Golden Self see the light of day. You'll be okay. Stand tall and meet the next moment relaxed about being you, one of a kind, irreplaceable and unique. Step lightly and let all your actions be bold. You needn't be visible on the world's stage to enact greatness. Life if more fun without a burdensome mask. Are you ready to make this Key REAL?

Playful Embodiment Experiments
Pick one or two experiments to embody your power. You can also design your own experiment.

1. If I have always known that *I'm irreplaceable, one of a kind* how would this influence my decisions today?
2. List the ways you hide your power. Choose one place to go mask-less. Be deliberate about this. How does it feel to be undefended? Repeat until the seed of honesty and authenticity have taken root.
3. Make a list: Today I will demonstrate self-respect by how much I _____ or by how little I _____.
4. Today I release others' energy with love. They live their life. I live mine. I stay in my Authority Circle.
5. Work your way up to collect at least Ten *no*'s today. Ask Big! Get comfortable with receiving.
6. It's safe for me to be myself. I will walk in the delight of myself today.

My Weekly Mantra: I am Irreplaceable; one of a kind, and I respect that about myself.

I AM ALWAYS GUIDED

KEY TEN

"Every blade of grass has its angel that bends over it and whispers, 'Grow, grow. —**The Talmud**

- **The Universal Law of Divine Guidance:** Ask, and it is given. Guidance is always available.
- **The Myth:** I have to rely on my own wits.
- **The Key:** I'm always guided.
- **The Practice:** Ask with playfulness, and then notice what happens. Keep asking.

THE WISDOM OF A NEVER-LOST LITTLE GIRL

I was around Eleven-years-old when my family took one of our adventures to North Africa, to the city of Marrakesh, one of

Morocco's imperial cities known as The Red City, for its red (actually pinkish-red) sandstone structures. We were already living in Spain, so it was an easy trip to see a land we thought we would never see again. (We didn't know then that our Dad's next assignment would be Morocco.) On our agenda was a visit the medina, the open-air marketplace. The medina is a vast, bustling place, full of noise, color, chaos, shoppers, entertainers, and vendors. It was perfumed by strong scents wafting off piles of intestines, eyeballs, fish, spices, and other strange delicacies resting in baskets on tables, or hanging on display. There was the scent of thick strands of wet wool in vibrant colors, secured on long poles high above the marketplace stretching from one building to another, drying in the hot desert sun. Oh, all those smells! My father made us hold our handkerchief up to our nose, rather than pinch our nose with our fingers, since doing so would be rude.

The snake charmers holding court on large vibrant red Moroccan rugs enchanted me. They played their flutes to entice the snake to arise from its basket and sway to the flute's melody. There were tall, stately male Bedouin dancers, jumping high into the air with prowess and precision. The Bedouin, my Dad told us, were great dancers and a very well respected tribe of desert dwellers.

Off the central square was a maze of narrow streets, cobwebbing out to parts unknown. A person could easily get lost there. As young children we were repeatedly instructed that if we were ever lost, we must stop immediately and stand perfectly still. My father said he would be able to backtrack to where we'd been, and he would find us. That was our travel protocol. There was only one occasion we ever needed to employ his injunction.

In this busy marketplace, with its many fascinations, I somehow found myself separated from my family. I couldn't see my parents anywhere. I felt a rising panic with the dawning awareness that I was lost. I'd been left behind. I immediately did as I was told. Faith and trust made me stand perfectly still, right where I was. Several male faces bent down, speaking a language I didn't understand, trying to communicate with me in their native Arabic. I sensed they were concerned for me, but I had to stand still, right here. I was scared but trusted in my father's instructions. I stood perfectly still. Very soon, one of the tall Bedouin dancers I had seen earlier came over and took a position behind me, crossing his strong arms with absolute authority. He became my tall protector. I felt strangely calm and safe in his majestic presence as my eyes continuously scanned the masses. There were no tears allowed in faith.

It seemed like forever until my Bedouin gently nudged my shoulder and pointed to an older Moroccan man careening through the crowd, his white robe flying like wings, shouting and pointing toward us. Following in his wake was my sprinting family. Still, I stood firmly as instructed until they arrived. We were, thankfully, reunited.

My father knelt down and asked me if I was all right. I nodded. "Were you hurt?" I shook my head, no. He told me he was proud that I followed his orders to stand still. There were no hugs or happy reunions, but I knew I was safe. With an upward glance toward my Bedouin protector, I put my hand to my heart and slightly bowed my head respectfully, silently saying thank you, heart to heart. He slightly nodded with understanding, and my family and I left the Medina. It wasn't until later, four years prior to my father's passing, that we finally talked about this incident and I got the untold back-story.

Let us not pray to be sheltered from dangers
but to be fearless when facing them.
- **Rabindranath Tagore**

There's always a juicy back-story to the miracles of Guidance making them truly magical after the fact. My father brought up the topic of my being lost in Morocco one day on the phone. He aguishly admitted that at that time he was frantic and nearly out of his mind with the thought of losing me to the vast unknown of the Medina. He said that experience had haunted him to this day. He aguishly asked me again if they had hurt me, to which I replied no, just the opposite. They protected me. He confessed that he had absolutely no clue where to look for me. None. He told me that just when he felt all hope of finding me was lost, an elderly Arabic man dressed in white caught my dad's attention, gesturing wildly for my dad to follow him. He began gesturing at my younger sister's height, and letting his hand move up from her head to my height. He pointed his finger to his chest, meaning that he knew where this daughter was. With that, my family took off running, hopeful that they were running toward me, and against all odds, a needle in a proverbial haystack, I was found.

We Are Never Alone

Please know that in the midst of any situation or any size of fear, if we put our hand in the hand of our inner guidance, we will never, and I mean never, be alone or lost or without protection or direction. I know there are "Yes, but's…" We don't know what events we put in our Blueprint because we didn't want to remember—that would spoil the adventure. In this Key, it's important to remember that when we won the lottery for admittance to Earth's Mastery Academy, it included a free, unlimited, never expiring, frequent-flyer-status, top-of-the line Guidance bonus package. Free Will says we can use it or not. It is up to us. The byproduct of using our Guidance is that our life is lived at a much higher level than the habitual, safe life the little mind can offer.

There's no rational way to think about intuition, guidance, or higher knowing because it's a higher vibrational frequency than we normally use. It's quantum in nature; meaning, it's non-linear and non-logical. It is beyond our mental bandwidth. That's why we call it extra-sensory. We can have one main delivery system or we can have several delivery systems for this super power. All delivery systems can be developed, because they are all available to us.

> *Trust your own inner guidance. Have faith that*
> *your steps are carrying you toward your dreams. Keep*
> *your eyes on the heavens and believe that your feet will carry you well.*
> —**Jonathan Lockwood Huie**, Author of self-awareness books and
> Daily Inspiration at www.jlhuie.com

Our factory installed Guidance System is hard-wired into our nervous system as firmly as our belly button. We can jump up and down, do cartwheels, and never accidentally lose our belly button. Like our belly button, Guidance travels with us even if we forget about it. Our bodies were already equipped with a G.P.S. (**G**uidance **P**lus **S**upport) feature. Like the GPS in our car—once we set its direction, we have to have faith in the turn-by-turn directions it gives. It will continue to reroute us until we get to our destination. We may go down roads we never knew about only to be surprised how perfect they were for us. It's synchronicity, we say. Nothing we could have done ourselves, we say. Guidance, like Wholeness, is non-linear. It isn't logical and it doesn't work in step-by-step messages. Free Will says we can always override Guidance, if we want.

∾

Spotlight Tip: What you may not know is that your inner G.P.S. is hard-wired to the specific frequency of your Blueprint for this life. Your G.P.S. is not set to the frequency of my Blueprint; it's set to your Blueprint. It is not set to anyone else's Blueprint, either. It's not a religious Blueprint, either. It is calibrated specifically to your objectives for this life, in this body, and it will continue to re-route you toward your life's objectives.

When You Trust Your Guidance

- You are less distracted and more purposeful
- You're more easily delighted
- You get accustomed to miracles
- You save time when you have clear direction
- You have a life partner for manifestation
- You develop courage to trust the flow
- You receive your truth with simple clarity
- You have higher access than the little mind

Drop the Thinking

Genuine Guidance doesn't nag at you. It's not your parent or your spouse. It never tells you that you should or shouldn't do something. It never judges or makes wrong. It doesn't keep saying *no, you can't have that*, nor does it ignore you. It doesn't drone on and on leaving you wondering *what's the message here?* It doesn't threaten you. It doesn't test you. It doesn't make promises to you. It doesn't leave you feeling unsettled. Your little chatterbox mind does all those things just fine. Too much thinking, however, turns down the volume on intuition. That said, our thinking mind isn't the enemy, nor is it the source of our intuition. It's useful to get us up and dressed in the morning. It's useful to get us to work, to decorate our home, or to pick out our car, but it cannot protect us nor can it reveal higher truths. Step-by-step thinking is linear. Guidance is non-linear. Not from the same source.

Like any unexercised muscle, intuition slips into the background when we favor the exclusivity of our mind. Our mind was designed to serve our intuition with inspired actions. It wasn't meant to be in the driver's seat any more than you would let a Five-year-old get behind the wheel of your Ferrari.

Guidance directs us to fulfilling work. It informs us ahead of tragedy if we stay tuned to it. For example, did you know that in the weeks before the World Trade Center's Twin Towers went down in New York City on September 11, 2001, psychics, initiatives and Tarot card readers knew about it? Many card readers reported that they kept drawing The Tower card, which signals disruption and depicts an image of a crashing tower. Many reported feeling intense pressure, like they were going to split apart or explode. We may not know what a particular feeling is about until we check Facebook, hear on the radio or watch the T.V. erupt with breaking news. Then, we can put the pieces of our intuition together.

Plenty of people came forward after 9/11 with stories of how they had canceled a flight, forgot something and went back to get it, decided to take a later flight in order to finish a project and had missed the fatal experience. One gave a stranger a lift that took the driver and passenger away from the Twin Towers. These experiences are the grace of Guidance. Like any big prize worth having, we have to be present to connect with our intuition. Distracted minds won't work here. We benefit by keeping ourselves attentive, yet relaxed in the moment, so when guidance arrives, will stand out. It requires soft attentiveness to recognize its energy signature.

Spotlight Tip: If an inner energy doesn't feel right or if a voice speaks to you in ways that feel commanding, shaming, or just plain creepy, blow the whistle, put a flag on the playing field, and command: "I listen only to my Higher Self for guidance. That's not you. Your services aren't required." Be still, then say: "*I now tune to my Higher Self's frequency as my only source of Guidance. Lock in this channel of communication in as my default.*"

What if Guidance is your Chauffeur?

Guidance isn't something outside of us; it's closer than a heartbeat away. Our guides were with us before birth, at our birth, right by our side every day and they will be with us as we take our last breath. They never leave us. It's okay to refer to Guidance as your Higher Self, Archangels, an Angel, the Holy Spirit, your deceased grandmother or Inspiration. Just call on it. It's not that some have it and others don't. Like all 12 Keys, we all have power in equal measure; no one has more. Some choose to develop the power of intuition and some are skeptical. We each have our own Blueprint for this life, and for some, it includes the use of psychic abilities, while others focus on other developments. Intuition is still hard-wired into each of us to use or not. Imagine life is like a Royal invitation and our Intuition is the chauffeur who gets us to the Royal party right on time. We get to enjoy the ride (right divine flow) because the chauffeur knows where we want to go and how to get us there right on time.

> *Adventure is not outside man; it is within.*
> **—George Elliot**

Guidance isn't a gift; it's a given. Remember, we have Free Will. We get to choose to be aware of nonlinear forms of communication if we want or not. Intuition is like our Soul's song being sung to us while we go about our daily living. Earth is a no-fault zone, so we aren't penalized if we pass on the Guidance package. People often ask me if there are any prerequisites to using our Guidance. Yes, there are three pre-requisites:

1. **Ask.** Hope doesn't work here, my friend. Wishing doesn't either. Whining doesn't either.
2. **Let go** of the outcome. The outcome is not our business. Asking is our business. Receiving is our business.
3. **Record** all your experiences. Carry a small notepad and pen with you because collecting evidence of Guidance is our business. Otherwise, we may think whatever happened was just a fluke. We can't explain it. It remains in the mystery box; a one-of-a-kind experience. So strange how it just happened!

Evidence, my friend—lots of evidence will validate how exquisitely we are supported and guided in our life. Guidance is available 24/7/365, no reservation needed. There are no long lines, and no number to take before your name is called. You don't have to pre-qualify and wait for approval. You don't have to seek a guide; they are always by your side. The kicker is that unless there is a life-or-death situation at stake, *you have to ask*; hence, the pre-requisite number one is **Ask**. Your Free Will cannot be interfered with. It is a requirement in the by-laws of the Academy.

There is only the way of intuition, which is helped
by a feeling for the order lying behind the appearance.
—Albert Einstein

Hide and Seek

It's common to play a game of Hide and Seek with our Guidance until we develop a consistent partnership with it. As children, we knew we were playing a game of pretend being lost and getting found. We knew it was just a game; it wasn't the truth. After all, *we knew where we were* all along. With Guidance, we don't have to hunt, seek, and hope to find answers. You and Guidance can build a working relationship like no other you will ever have while at this Mastery Academy. If you don't know what to start with, ask: *Dear Guidance, help me know I am loved. Thanks!* Be light with it. Then, be attentive. Consulting Guidance polishes our sovereignty; it does not take away from it. Seriously, the stork didn't just drop us and fly away. We aren't alone. Never have been. Still, being alone is a choice.

The Signature of Guidance

Abraham Hicks said, *There is nothing that you're wanting to know that you do not have the capacity to understand fully. And there is nothing that you're wanting to know that the universe does not already know that you want to know and has already begun the process of answering.* — (Excerpted from Albany, NY on 10/1/2001.) That's why it can seem kind of miraculous when it happens.

Intuition can help us make more effective decisions. It is often subtle, requiring a finer degree of listening, seeing, and feeling than we normally use. We're accustomed to big and bold animated media. Guidance doesn't work that way; although it has led me to movies that helped me release emotions I didn't even know were there. Guidance helps us awaken to a more expansive version of ourselves; our Authentic Self.

Our guides can have a wonderful sense of humor, which always delights me. While Guidance can seem to come and go, there really is no off button. It is always available. I went through a lengthy period of time in my adult life, where it seemed I had lost all familiar connection to my ever-present Guidance. It was like losing my best friend and I didn't know how to get it back. I thought my Guidance-well had dried up and it was my fault. After the fact, I understood that the ways I had been receiving Guidance were no longer valid for me. I was being rerouted into a new directional system. I was being asked to know I was equal to my Guidance sources. They weren't my fairy godmother. I was one of them. On a Soul level this made sense. And, they are very playful, as Jim would find out in our next story.

Sniff, Sniff

My friend, Jim and I had a short phone call to catch up one day. Jim said he'd been setting up for a big event related to his work and had a lot on his plate. In the middle of sharing about the event he stopped mid-sentence with a moment of silence. "I smell Vicks' VapoRub," he said in a puzzling tone. He considers it unmanly to use it at all. I quietly laughed because he is such a manly man. He sniffed the air like a bloodhound for a few more minutes, swearing there was Vicks' VapoRub in the air, but he was the only one in the meeting hall. Olfactory senses never really caught his attention before. He's a man of reason and action, after all. When he repeatedly smelled Vicks' VapoRub, he wanted to know what it meant, but he had a very full and challenging day ahead once the room was set up. There had already been a series of seeming obstacles in his path for this event.

"What's going on?" he asked out loud. "I don't need this!" I tried hard not to laugh, one, because it was funny to hear him sniffing around like a bloodhound and two, because I knew the wily ways of Guidance, and I knew the smell was a greeting card for Jim. I said, "I know you'd never put that stuff on yourself; it's just not manly, but, ya gotta admit, Vicks' VapoRub does the trick when you are mentally or physically congested."

"Huh?" He can be a bit clueless at times.

"Nothing like Vicks' VapoRub to help you breathe easier and clear the congestion of what's been going on." He was flummoxed and had to get going. We ended the call after agreeing to connect back in at the end of his day. His experience is an example of the intuitive usher for the Clairolfactory channel; the Guidance channel of smell. He didn't know anything about intuitive ushers and didn't care to either, but I knew his go-to saint, Archangel Michael, was messing with him. After all, he had previously wondered out loud how he could work with Archangel Michael. Duh. Expect the unexpected when you ask! That goes for all of us.

After Jim finished closing up after the event, he called again to say that after we had talked, he felt lighter, like something in his chest had lifted. He could breathe deeply, maybe for the first time ever, he said. He was still puzzled by the Vicks' VapoRub smell, however. He said he didn't smell it again after we talked.

"You think God talks to you in a human voice? Perhaps he talks with the scent of Vicks' VapoRub. Perhaps that is how Archangel Michael got your attention. He helped you clear mental congestion when you needed it most and gave you a sign of his presence. Right?" We both laughed. Jim said he didn't know God could do that, but he definitely felt better. "Think bigger, my friend," I said with a laugh.

Set the Stage

There are no hard-and-fast rules, no mantras to repeat, and no down payment to pre-pay. We don't have to clean up our life to be worthy of Guidance. For our part, we just need to slow down, make room for a lovely conversation with a wise friend, and ask a question that offers our intent to be guided. Initially, it's useful to create a space to purposefully commune with our guides. Some examples of clear spaces can be in the shower, soaking in a tub, walking outdoors, during a massage, through our art, while tinkering with our car, or by taking a pause by the sink. It can be more formal as well. Consider sitting in the same chair or location each time you want to connect with your Guidance, because this anchors energy into the space. Returning to that space will make it easier and easier to slip into conversation with your guides if you are new to this.

> *Cease trying to figure everything out with your minds.*
> *It will get you nowhere. Live by intuition and inspiration and*
> *let your whole life be revelation.*
> **—Eileen Caddy**, Actress

When we try to figure things out before we start connecting, it's a slow crawl with a frenzied, although precious, little mind. Guidance patiently waits. I invite you to drop your expectations about *how* your Guidance shows up and engage the engines of curiosity and delight. This type of relationship requires imagination, playfulness, curiosity, wonder, listening, asking, and enjoying each other's presence. Be light with it. There's no heavy lifting to do… Guidance takes care of that. There are many ways in which intuition presents itself. My Nine-year-old-self experienced Guidance through Clairvoyance (mental images; a mental movie) as a past life scene played out in the kiva. One time it showed up as the face of a smart-ass, ancient Native American male, making fun of my green clay facial mask, pretending to be afraid of me. That experience was so funny that my face mask cracked from laughing at the absurdity of the situation!

Later, my Guidance showed up as an English butler in a dark suit with a white cloth carefully draped over his arm, ready to serve me. I blinked and the vision expanded. There was an unending line of butlers in dark suits with white cloths over their arms, each waiting for my instructions. I loved that one, yet it scared me a bit. I was still busy trying to stay safe. Did I even have that many desires or questions? I didn't think so, but there they were. Guidance can also show up in the form of an animal that gives a message or warns us of upcoming danger or perhaps a song that plays on the radio at the moment we need to hear it's lyrics. It can even come in the form of a dump truck, as Carol shares in her story.

Mega Dump Trucks

Carol wanted to release old relationship habits, which her husband had recently pointed out to her. She agreed that was she was constantly picking at him. If he wasn't being attentive, she would find something she could find fault with.

"Sounds like you're trying to get his attention. What do you hope that will fulfill within you?" She hoped he would eventually come around and start appreciating her. (No one said the methodology of the little mind was actually logical.) I asked what she was *really* hoping for by getting his attention.

"I want to know he finds me sexy; that he wants me like he used to." She was afraid she had become invisible. "I feel inadequate as a lover. No wonder he doesn't see the real me; I haven't been being the real me. I've been being a poor, invisible 'look-at-poor-me-whiner'. I need help," Carol said. Like many of us, we turn to blaming someone else to cover up her own apparent inadequacy. Blaming can be a push strategy to get recognition. Admittedly, it was not the best strategy, but she really wanted to know that he found her sexy.

"Note to Self: Blaming is never sexy," she said. We both laughed at the thought, releasing her tension. She wanted to clear out all her un-sexy ways, freeing herself up to be the sexy woman he had married. For homework, she wanted to release all blaming habits; just empty them all out for good. She was through with being a blamer and a whiner. Our session finished, and she left with a lighter heart. Carol left a message on my office phone as she was driving back to her office.

"You'll never guess what is happening this very minute. You know those big green dump trucks, the Mega Dump trucks? There are two of them, one in front of me and one following me. Wait, another one just passed me, so I take this as a helping hand from my angels. I'm filling them up. No more dumping on Ted." She laughed. Carol called back again to say they had literally followed her to her office, and as she turned into the parking lot, they kept going. In her session the following week, she said her new mantra was: "I'm becoming aware and divinely guided in ways I couldn't possibly dream up. Thanks! More, please." More, please, signals our willingness to play with Guidance. It's an open invitation; not a hungry begging.

~

Spotlight Tip: Ask once. Your guides aren't hard of hearing. They aren't deaf like old Uncle Fred. They get it the first time. You don't have to do your chores before they will talk to you. They are not withholding, the way your parents might have been. Patience, Grasshopper; they are always at work. Our task is to be *willing* to receive. Receiving is not a passive act. It's a welcoming; a softening of the 'shoulds.' It is a willingness to build a working partnership.

Let Me Introduce You to The Ushers

Years ago, I learned there were actually names for how I received information. I can't tell you how much comfort that gave me, given all my experiences had been random and I had no friendly witnesses to name what I had experienced. I learned from a new friend about the Clairs. The different channels of Guidance all start with the word Clair, which means *clear receiving*. The Clairs are the ushers of intuitive Guidance. They usher us into new thought, new direction, and new understandings. They are also like radio stations we can tune into. The mind would have us set up mantras, read our goals out loud every morning and evening, or berate ourselves when we fall short and swear to act differently tomorrow. Intuition is not a taskmaster. Our intuition, thankfully, doesn't operate in that manner. For those already using your Guidance, this will be a refresher.

- **Clair-voyance** – we intuit *visual* scenes, such as images or a movie. You see. You may have vivid dreams, pointing you in the right direction with a story line that reveals how to be successful. The images can include knowing and feeling as well, but it is the visual Clair.
- **Clair-sentience** – we intuit through our *body sensations*. We literally feel what others feel. Our body links through an empathic bond with the body of another. This type of intuition is Empathic awareness. Our body senses the world and is a conduit of information unknown to the reasoning mind.
- **Clair-audience** – we intuit though *hearing*, sounds, words, or lyrics. Telepathy is also a word associated with this channel; we hear the thoughts of others, including trees and rocks and animals. We can also be Clairaudient without utilizing Telepathy—to send and receive mind messages.
- **Clair-cognizance** – we intuit by *simply knowing*. We can't explain how we know. Pre-cognition is often associated with this channel of information. We know what's coming. We know what's going on. We just know.

Sometimes it's delivered through packets of information then stops when the information is complete.

- **Clair-olfactory** – we intuit though *smell*, foul vibes or the scent a person used to wear. Something doesn't smell right. That deal smells sour. A spirit, who hasn't quite crossed over may carry an old-person's body scent to signal their presence.

- **Clair-gustatory** – we intuit though our *taste* buds. We may actually *taste* the individual notes of a fine wine. We eat something and can sense who made it and if it was made with love or not. However, if we *smell* the notes, that's the Clair-olfactory channel.

- **Psychometry** – we intuit through *touch*, either by touching a person or an object a person has touched. Holding something reveals information about the owner. The information then can come through any or all the above channels.

Our ushers of information are not bound by time or space. We must set aside the predictability of our analytical thinking in favor of partnering with intuitive wisdom.

At times you have to leave the city of your comfort and go into the wilderness of your intuition. What you'll discover will be wonderful. What you'll discover is yourself. —**Alan Alda**, Actor

Some folks have asked me if these ushers of information are from God. Yes, my friend, very much so. Still, I recommend that you require only Guidance that matches the frequency of pure love or higher. When we head into Guidance territory, it helps to have a good map. In our next story, Karl shows us how he mapped his Guidance.

Mapping Guidance

Karl is well respected among his peers, but not so much at home, according to him. Admittedly, Karl is conflicted about his emotionally unsupportive wife. He doesn't know what to do. She is always busy; too busy to notice him. She offers nothing back to him, in his opinion. He had a really good story worked up about how she ignores him. He's just a ghost that brings in the money. He said sometimes he wants to retaliate, but that doesn't feel right. "Roommates. That's all we are," he'd concluded. He was all out of options. I invited him, to consult his inner hunches for some guidance.

"What does that have to do with anything? Hunches just happen. I don't have any control over them!"

"Perhaps, it might be useful to tap into the wise hunch-giver part of yourself to see what he has to say." Karl needed a kinder inner voice to counterbalance his pre-recorded voice of resignation. He nodded and said it couldn't hurt.

"Where do you feel the most inspired and open? Where are you when you typically get your hunches?" I asked. It's very helpful to map our already present Guidance successes so we can go through that door without a passkey. Karl took a moment to discover how his hunches come to him.

"I get a lot of ideas when I'm out gardening or when I'm in the shower," he offered.

"Great, and what do you feel just before you get a hunch?" I asked thoughtfully.

"Things get kinda quiet, like a big bubble of silence, even if I'm outside in the garden. Like, time stops, and then a hunch comes in. My hunches are simple, easy to understand, and easy to do. I follow those hunches," he said. I probed deeper.

"And how did you hear, feel, or see those hunches?"

"Oh." He was quiet for a moment. "I hear them like there's a kind old man beside me giving me ideas. I hear a kind of neutral voice, and sometimes I also see an image of me doing what the voice of the kind old man was suggesting," he reported.

"Okay. Does this feel like a consistent and reliable method of receiving hunches, or do you have other ways to receive them?" I asked.

"Well, sometimes I get them while I'm driving but, yeah, they all come with this bubble of silence first," he said.

"And when you took that voice to heart, and took purposeful actions, what happened?" I asked. Karl gave several examples; enough for me to know this was a reliable channel of Guidance. I asked him if he would be willing to take his relationship concerns to his wise hunch-giver. He scratched his head, a bit skeptical of this novel idea.

"Okay, why not take an Ask to the garden first, since it's a trusted space for your hunches to visit you? The Ask and the Listening are completely portable and apparently flora friendly."

"You mean *initiate* hunches?" he asked quizzically. Randomly occurring hunches appear to have a mind of their own. I was asking him to harness and direct them purposefully.

"Yes, in a way. You initiate with a question or the Ask. Doing so provides a container for your hunches to fill up for you, just like you dig a hole, prep it, and then plant something beautiful in it. What about it? Do you want to give it a try regarding your wife?" I asked.

"Hunches don't know about relationship advice!" he blustered.

"Maybe more than you think. Maybe you just haven't used your hunches with what you considered to be unsolvable problems. Maybe you don't know the breadth of your hunches' capacity to guide you. Would you like to have an experiment this week?" I asked. He agreed but there was one contingency during this test period.

"Keep your ask simple, Karl, such as this: *How can I honor and support my wife?* Keep your experiment pure. No matter what you are guided to do, do it, and no matter how happily she responds—

and this is important: Make no attempt afterward to have sex. No sex at all. None. Deal? Sex will happen naturally once *she* is ready to reconnect. Then you can trust this connection. Just keep it out of this experiment. Just receive your guide's information, and for now, don't expect anything from your wife. Deal?"

This instruction was enough for now, and he agreed. We cannot control other's behaviors, but we can ask to be guided to be a more loving partner. Karl had forgotten to cherish and provide love for his wife. Providing doesn't always mean bringing home the bacon. It also means providing a safe, loving, and supportive environment.

The following week Karl returned with his homework report. He had followed his plan exactly and had lots to report. The hunches he received helped him remember how to court his wife all over again. He had a hunch to bring his wife two red roses with a short poem, like the poems he used to write for her when they first met. He left them on her home desk, so she would see them when she put her things down.

He had a hunch to ask his wife, "What can I do today that will make your life easier?" We had talked about keeping it simple, about respecting and following his wife's *literal* words, so if he asked that question, he was to do *exactly* what she asked, *no variations*. He shared a couple of examples of how he had literally followed her words and didn't deviate. He didn't know it would be so easy to make her happy. He thought he had to come up with ways on his own.

Karl reported how pleased she was, and he faithfully kept the sexual vibes turned off and his love vibes turned up. He said he had never been good at reading her mind, but his hunches seemed to know what to do. He reported feeling young again, free to show her love like he used to. For inquiring minds, his wife initiated intimacy when she was ready for it. Once Karl mapped out *how* he received hunches, he could replicate the situation and gain more insight through intuition. Keep it simple, like Karl did.

Intuition will tell the thinking mind where to look next.
—Jonas Salk

∾

Spotlight Tip: It's good to loosen our grip on how guidance has to show up. Guidance can't be controlled, but it doesn't play hard to get either. We need to be willing to receive it and then allow it to teach us. We can ask: "How can I improve my ability to connect with you?" To that we add, "I'm listening, my friend."

Guidance Envy

Albert Einstein said, *The only real valuable thing is intuition.* There was a time as an adult when, at intuitive workshops, I couldn't see what others described when inquiring about a topic. I had Guidance envy. I wasn't in the frame of mind to acknowledge that I actually had consistent Guidance, which always seemed to showed up on its own time. I couldn't force it. Guidance was such a natural part of me that I didn't question it. It was the water I swam in. Perhaps this is true for you, too. I seldom shared it with anyone. Psychics were clearly people who are really good at this psychic business, I told myself. Much later, I learned I am a Direct Channel, meaning I don't know until someone directly asks and the information is ready, or not, to download for delivery. I was not in charge. Sometimes we think our Guidance needs to come in a certain way just because our teacher, guru, mentor, or friend receives his/her Guidance in that particular way. Nope. Discover your own channels of delivery. Our guides can be flirtatious and playful if we invite it.

Trish, in our next story, decided she would play with her Guidance.

Play Money

Trish was skeptical about the notion of intuitive Guidance. She considered herself a pragmatist. She hadn't exercised her intuition muscle, but was curious if it would benefit her to investigate it. I asked her what she would need to see, hear or feel that would absolutely confirm the presence of her intuitive Guidance. Trish impatiently, yet humorously said, "Hey, I'll know it's real if I get loads of one dollar bills delivered to my hot little hands. I've decided to collect them so I'll have spending money on my ski trip with my girlfriends in December." This is March, so she had plenty of time.

"Okay. Why not some have fun with this? Who knows what can happen?"

Her fieldwork was to invite her Guidance to participate in her everyday life with a dollar bill. Simple. Playful. No hard work on her part. The next week Trish was so excited she didn't even greet me or sit down before she launched straight into reporting her fieldwork results. Every time she bought something for cash, the salesperson said she only had One-dollar bills for change. A friend who owed her One Hundred dollars had paid her back the full amount—all in Ones. She paid cash for lunch with a friend and the waitress apologized for having only Ones for her change. Another time she found a small wad of bills secured by a rubber band while she was out walking in the woods near her home. No one was around for miles, so she picked it up just to see what was there. Fifty dollars, all in One-dollar bills! At her next pause to take a breath, I asked Trish how she thought this had happened. She became thoughtful. Guidance was delivering information for her.

"I guess I was open to receiving only small amounts before. It seems my intuition saw to it that I had more than enough spending money for my trip. Heck, I can almost pay for half my trip with all the Ones that came my way. In fact, I might raise that to collecting only Five-dollar bills," she replied with a whoop and a holler.

"Great idea, Trish. Hmm. I wonder what the larger message is from this fieldwork experiment. What does your intuition want you to really understand?" I asked. Trish was quiet. Her cheeks flushed with emotion.

"I don't have to figure out how or where the money will come from. I just need to ask, notice, and say thank you."

Always in the Right Place at the Right Time

We will learn more about 'My Rules For Me' in our next Key, but for this Key's theme, I'll demonstrate how our Operational Rules pair nicely with our Guidance. One of my operational rules is: *I'm always in the right place at the right time.* These rules are my intended structure for inspired living. More times than I can count, I was led to be somewhere at just the right moment. Let me share an example of how My Rules for Me works.

I felt a strong need for coffee one Friday morning about 9:30. Without question, I headed out to my neighborhood coffee house. As I neared the steps leading up to the retail stores next to the coffee house, my body headed itself into the stationary store next door first. It wasn't a conscious decision. I didn't know why I was going, but I trusted the process. When I opened the door and walked inside, I paused and scanned the store. It was empty except for a young woman behind the counter. She had her back to me, and I saw she was on her cell phone. I could hear her crying. She turned and saw me come in and ended her call, wiping her tears. She attempted to be professional, but couldn't stop the tears or wipe them away fast enough as she softly asked, "How may I help you?" More tears.

I reversed our roles and asked, "How can I support you, love? Would you like a mother's hug?" I asked because I felt and saw that her mother had deceased and was standing near her. Not quite ready to hug, she blurted through her sobs that her sister had just called to say their brother was in the hospital after a very, very bad car accident and the doctor had rushed him into surgery. She was upset because she was the only one available to work the store that day, so she couldn't leave. She said she prayed for him, but it still left her feeling helpless. She wanted to be there for him. With that thought, she leaned into my motherly arms and cried it out. After a few moments she stepped back, took a centering breath, and thanked me.

I asked her if she would like to join me and send her brother some heartfelt healing love. "Oh, yes, please," she said. I asked her to envision, with me, a soft golden energy blanket of pure healing love, and to imagine softly wrapping it around her brother so he could feel her healing love. After we finished, she said she liked that experience a lot and was positive that he'd actually felt her love. Is this real? she asked. I told her it is very real. I asked if she still felt helpless.

"No," she replied emphatically. She said she could send healing love that way as many times as she wanted and knew he would welcome her healing love even if he was unconscious. She was helping him. She remarked what a blessing it was that I showed up when I did. She wouldn't have been able to make it through the day without worry.

"You're so welcome. I seem to be in the right place at the right time today." She thanked me with a warm hug and I left. I thought about coffee, but honestly, the coffee was just a spiritual ruse to get me to her. I headed back to my car and returned home. "That's just the way it is in my world," I said out loud to my Guidance friends.

"I love it. I'm always in the right place at the right time. How wondrous!"

I Wonder...

I wonder... What an innocent musing. As a leading question, it invites lightness, experimentation, and curiosity. It invites participation with a larger source of information than our every-day understanding. Nothing has to be wrong before we invite our Angelic guides to play. I was in Mt. Shasta one weekend, and wanted to hike up to a high meadow on this sacred mountain. I had my backpack, water, snacks, lunch, and I was ready. I hadn't been on this particular trail before. Apparently, I was also the only one on the trail this particular day. A Ranger had given me vague directions, but there were no clear signs on the path once I left the starting point. I found myself being guided about which turn in the path to take. I love this Guidance, I thought to myself. It was a lengthy trail, and I was getting tired and heated with all the uphill climbing. As I stopped to rest, on a whim I said, "I wonder what it would feel like to have my indwelling spirit walk this path with me." When I finished my snack, re-hydrated and was rested, I got up to continue to my destination.

No sooner than I had taken a few steps, I noticed how unusually light I felt. I couldn't feel my backpack. My feet seemed to literally glide, as if on air, and I swear, the air had somehow grown softer and cooler. I was effortlessly walking, and it was so much fun. My body was literally as light as a feather. I'd never felt such effortlessness and lightness. What a joy! After a while, having a scientific-type mind, I wondered out loud, "Hmm, just to test reality here. What would it feel like if I was mere mortal and on my own?"

Bad idea. Really bad idea. What was I thinking? Don't ever do

that again! I dropped like a two-ton anvil back into planetary grav-
ity. Every movement of my legs felt like I was walking through
waist-high sludge. My pack felt like it weighed One Hundred
pounds, and I was gasping for breath and sweating just to keep
going. It was worse than before I had asked for spirit to walk with
me. Ugg, I did ask to know what it was like to walk on my own.
Dumb idea. I sensed and saw my spirit guides having hearty belly
laughs at my expense. *Silly girl. She doesn't know when she has a good
thing going.* Lots of knee slapping laughter was going on in Guid-
ance land. "Not funny," I said to them, and I heard and felt them
laughing even harder at my expense. It didn't occur to me to
request to walk with spirit again. Lesson learned. No need to be
so dense.

There's real potency in the 'I wonder' statements. Use them wisely!
'I wonder' is a great springboard for your intuition to engage. Here
are a few engaging 'I wonder' statements you might like to play
with—one at a time please:

- I wonder what guidance I'll be receiving today?
- I wonder how easily I handle what comes up today?
- I wonder how I will be inspired on my project?
- I wonder what it feels like to be fully present?
- I wonder what it feels like to partner with intuition?
- I wonder what will further my success today?
- I wonder what it will feel like to really love myself?

After you offered your *I wonder* question, go about your busi-
ness and simply notice what feels different during the day. Perhaps
the air is softer, or did things just seem to move along effortlessly.
Perhaps the coffee tasted exceptional. Noticing small, subtle differ-
ences builds intuitive evidence.

If these statements are a bit of a stretch for you, why not start with a Q. and A. mini-session with your Guidance? Keep it simple: use the same set of questions listed below to start a conversation with your intuitive Guidance, a bit like Karl did when he asked his garden for advice. Write the questions in your journal, one page per day, same set of questions, in the same order. Let your Guidance answer these same questions, every single day for one week. You can ask for a different guide each day, if you like. This exercises our inner ears; we ask, then we simply take dictation. You'll get a different answer every day, I promise you, but they will gather into a coherent message by the end of the week. Write down what you receive, then say thank you and move to the next question. It's really eye opening. Perhaps you might take a current challenge as the theme for your session and you will be amazed.

- **What do I need to know about_____?**
- **What am I ready to let go of?**
- **What quality am I underutilizing?**
- **What will support my_____ today?**

The Spontaneous Intention Springboard

Setting an intention is also an enjoyable way to invite our Guidance to play. Intention is not the same as willing or controlling something. We don't have to try as hard when an intention is handy. One Saturday morning I was on the freeway, headed from Sacramento to San Francisco to be with my daughter for some fun. I had the thought that the trip could be difficult; I could get lost again, and I'd arrive at her new place frazzled, as usual. I pushed the Stop button on my habitual mind. Well, that's unattractive, I thought. Why would I do that to myself?

These days, I see this kind of thinking as my guide *inviting* me to create a fresh viewpoint, one worthy of my best life. After I entered the freeway and was settled in my lane, I spontaneously visualized a fresh experience as I robustly said out loud: "I intend to have an easy and safe drive. I'm comfortable in my car, and it's a smooth ride across the bridge, and it's easy how I just instinctively know where to turn. How great it is to have a parking spot right near her building, one I couldn't miss even if I tried! I arrive relaxed and centered in my body. That will be great! Thanks in advance." I then let the thoughts go and rocked out to some tunes on the radio.

Sidebar: In my early Twenties, I had agoraphobia. It was my little secret. It took many years to overcome the fear of being lost and unable to find my way. I didn't seek therapeutic help in those days. I was terrified to leave the house for a place I hadn't been to before. I developed a lot of coping mechanisms for sure. Many years later, I was no longer agoraphobic, but I realized that I had habitually settled for uncomfortable outcomes as my norm. This realization was delivered by my Guidance, like a breath of fresh spring air. I could have a different outcome.

Thanks to my spontaneous intention, my driving experience that Saturday was indeed calm and enjoyable. I felt supported. My body was actually very comfortable, and everything happened as I had intended. I magically turned onto the right streets, at the right time. I was unusually calm. My parking space was clearly visible on a street full of parked cars. I didn't notice the parking space at first, but what caught my eye was a tall 'statue' of beer bottles stacked four tiers high, right in the center of the San Francisco sidewalk! Never before or after have I ever seen such a sight. People were walking around it like it belonged there! I saw the beer bottles a split second before I saw the parking space, which was the only parking space open, and it was right next to the beer bottle sculpture. I couldn't miss it if I tried! There was no traffic waiting behind me, either, which was unusual for this time of day. I pulled up, and without a thought, parallel parked with ease and perfection the first time I tried! Not a fan of parallel parking at all. Just saying.

Arriving doesn't have to be difficult when we intend ease and we partner with our unseen pranksta-helpers. I laughed at how they caught my attention using the four-tiered beer bottle statue. Brilliant! Like my long line of butler guides, I am well supported. As Archangel Michael once told me, "Life's too serious to be taken seriously." That's good because my Guides love to play with me!

I had been too serious for too long. I welcomed the refreshing sense of play from my Guidance partners. They don't care what you call them or how you ask for what you want to know. There is nothing too small, too frivolous, too big, or too important for your intuitive guidance partners. Just ask! You don't have to figure out your life, dear ones. Even if you already utilize your intuitive guidance, how can you expand the scope of what's possible for you this week? Which of the Clair's would you like to experiment with this week? Are you ready to make this Key REAL?

Playful Embodiment Experiments

Pick one or two experiments to embody your power. You can also design your own experiment.

1. If I have always known that *I'm always guided*, what would I want to experience today?
2. Gift yourself a quiet space for fifteen minutes. Relax. Simply say, "I'm listening." Perhaps you are prepared to write down messages that may come. Be patience with the process. It takes time to trust.
3. Which Clair would you like to experiment with this week?
4. Map out how your own intuition works.
5. Keep a journal specifically for notating each time you are guided. This practice collects evidence. It can also be

used to ask the four questions and record the answers you receive. What is their cumulative message?

6. It's safe for me to be powerful because I have a great support team.

My Weekly Mantra: I am *always* guided in delightful ways.

I AM ALREADY ABUNDANT

KEY ELEVEN

When you are grateful, fear disappears and abundance appears. —**Anthony Robbins**

- **The Universal Law of Vibration** states that everything in our universe, seen or unseen is an energetic pattern of vibration.
- **The Myth:** I have to make things happen.
- **The Key:** I align with my ever-present abundance.
- **The Practice:** I see my abundance in every situation.

THE WISDOM OF NO GLASS

A well-known proverb says "An optimist would say a glass is half full, while a pessimist would say it is half empty." We all have our preferred way to address this proverb. A Congressman might say the budget could be balanced if the other party would get on board and pass a decent bill in Congress. A scientist might say it's inconsequential, because the method of measuring progress keeps changing. The philosopher might say that if no one had language to name "a glass," we would still get our liquid any way we could. A psychiatrist might ask, "What would your mother say about the glass?" A mystic might say, "The glass is a window into all possibilities." A parent might say, "Who broke the damn glass?" That is the nature of perspective. There's always some explanation that can be attributed to something.

Really, what's all the fuss about whether the glass is half full or half empty? It's just a glass. It isn't a true measure of our abundance, success, or love. Does a glass hold infinite potential? Yes, everything does. Mother Nature doesn't measure her abundance by how many leaves are on her trees or how brilliant her sunsets are or how spectacular her sunrises are. I seriously doubt she pins her worth on a half-empty or half-full anything. The river never thinks, *I don't have enough water. Something's is wrong with me. OMG! I need to manifest more water with the law of attraction and pray it works. It's shameful for a river such as I not to have an abundant flow of water.*

I seriously doubt Mother Nature works hard, struggling to manifest the beauties of our world, everything from expansive arid deserts to majestic snowcapped peaks and everything in between. Mother Nature is always creating, having and releasing—spring, summer, fall, winter, rain, snow, wind, blooming, decay and sprouting. Mother Nature never once doubts her abundance. Our half-full or half-empty metaphor is the measurement our socially conditioned minds uses to determine our worth, as if it even knows how grand we really are! How much do I have? How can I get more? What if I'm just money cursed? My friends, we need a new measuring stick. This one makes us sick.

In this KEY we'll look at abundance from a perspective of

Having rather than earning, getting, losing or being lucky or ruthless. Abundance has always been available, free to everyone, in equal measure since the inception of this Academy. No one has more right to abundance than another. There's no abundance shortage. Free Will is *always* at play, and while some lifetimes aren't focused around money, some are.

Life only asks for the best we can be. We are joyful creators and great actors, writing our own story as we go. We are always in right divine flow. We were already Pre-Approved for this Academy. We harmonize with the frequency of abundance when we *have* rather than need, want or envy. We get to personalize our life our way, because Life is for us. Being unique is the name of the game here. But what about the poor and starving people? Perhaps this population provides stimulus for human kindness and this *is* their elected spiritual purpose to serve humanity's advancement. Our value is not determined by what we have; but by who we are and how we direct our creative energy.

Releasing

When I'm out photographing, I feel a sense of awe every time I witness life springing forth through tiny cracks in big rocks or flowers holding their own in a dry desert riverbed or a beetle surviving just fine in an arid desert. Nature isn't worried about survival. Nature is about thriving through cycles. Nature does not judge worth. Life expresses itself non-stop because that's the nature of nature. Life is everywhere! Sometimes, a seedling doesn't manifest for reasons of its own. Nature doesn't beat itself up about a failed attempt. Only humans do that.

Releasing is a natural and important phase of the manifestation cycle. If we can't let go, we can't take advantage of new potentials. Life is always changing and evolving, and that's a constant we can count on. Stay the course and be creative with what you have. Yes, but I can do that *so* much more if I have more abundance, says the human. Here's the deal: Creators create. That's what we do, so start where you are by releasing the stress-mess of lack in any form. It goes against your magnificent grain.

Two Kinds of Stress

We know there are two kinds of stress:

#1. <u>Unhealthy stress.</u> The most talked about is the unhealthy worry-and-anxiety version. This kind robs our vitality and breaks down our health. There's something about *not having* that makes our little minds go nuts, thereby stressing our nervous and immune system to the max. How many times have you lost your car keys or cell phone, a ring, or a favorite pocket knife, and you can't find it to save your life? The stress of *not having* kidnaps our focus from the abundance of the present moment. Oh, little mind; look around; there is abundance all around us.

#2. <u>Healthy stress.</u> This stress rises from taking on an invigorating challenge, accomplishing something we had envisioned, or making a plan and following it to fruition, against all odds, to do what we didn't think we could do. This kind of stress actually releases endorphins. Both types of stress involve imagination. One builds the muscles of having, and one excretes stress-messes. (Pick door #2 to win the prize).

Stress Termites

We often tell ourselves to just push through discomfort, be brave, make a better tomorrow, and this strategy is initially a useful one for growth. The seed, after all, needs to break through the hard seedpod of doubts and fears, if it is to bloom. Don't allow the

Harpies to be disrespectful; otherwise we will give up our quest too soon. Let's expose these familiar pesky habits.

- **Not appreciating** the life you currently live creates *envy stress*. We resist change and shy away from the unknown. We dissatisfy ourselves with what we don't have. Dissatisfaction jams the abundance wheel. Gratitude for what we have lubricates the wheel.
- **Not owning** our own choices creates *second-guess stress*. It erodes our authenticity. Comparison erodes our dreams. Not respecting our choices jams the abundance wheel. Developing self-respect lubricates the abundance wheel.
- **Not attending** to what doesn't feel right leads us to create *blindness stress*. "Whatever. It's all good," shoves healthy discomfort underground. Saying it's 'all good' when it isn't jams the wheel of abundance. Leaning toward our joy is what enlivens us and lubricates the abundance wheel.

Tiny Thimble

Here's what we know: We are not here by accident. We are Whole, Perfect, and Complete, and we continually re-write our life story. This is our life. We personalize it with our style. We are always supported and guided. Life is for us, so why do we *still* choose perspectives of struggle, lack, or strife? *Simply because we can.* Poverty is not the opposite of prosperity. Enough is the opposite of poverty. We each authored our Blueprint for this life. Some lifetimes, we want to take abundance out of the equation so we can work on compassion. We can use a small thimble to contain our abundance or we can say, "Bring it on, baby!"

Abundance loves it when we develop worthy projects for it to fill. I want more money doesn't provide sufficient direction. Spirit and Guidance want to know: Where do you want to *direct* the flow of money? We don't need to stockpile money and resources because the universal supply has already done that for us. We direct the flow of abundance when we say, for example, "Money loves me and I love to build homes for those who have none. Thank you. We're a great team, Money and Me." From here, let Guidance lead the way and give it your attention.

Abundance doesn't put conditions or limits on what we can withdraw from the divine warehouse. It isn't our banker. It isn't our parent; it doesn't withhold our allowance because we left a towel on the bathroom floor. We are not handicapped just because there are wealth hoarders. The universal warehouse is *always full* for whatever project we want to apply it to. It never runs a special sale to bring in more customers. There are no penalties for frequent withdrawals, and interest is never charged on what you take out. We have the freedom to choose how much we want to use, but it's *not* a measure of our worth.

> *Life has got to be lived—that's all there is to it.*
> **—Eleanor Roosevelt**

Smash the Belief Ceiling

Most of us know the familiar refrain from the movie *Jerry Maguire*, where Jerry yells, *Show me the money!* That line made the movie memorable for many people. We can all relate to wanting more money. The flaw is that we tend to make abundance synonymous with money, as if money gives us a free pass and cures our boredom stress.

Someone once asked Maharishi where the money would come

from for the building of a much-needed ashram. "From wherever it is when we are ready for it," he responded. Do we have that kind of faith? I don't think worthiness ever entered the mind of the Maharishi.

Can we trust that there's already something powerful within us which is destined to bloom riotously in the same way an acorn is destined to become a majestic oak tree? Earth's Mastery Academy already planned for each of our successes in this Academy. What we're really looking for is the freedom we think more money will bring. My friends, we already have the freedom to choose what will fuel our dreams. We are the ones who limit what we can have. In the next story, Shawn demonstrates how the issue of worth propelled him into prosperity.

Spotlight Tip: Money is often measured based on a salary or a contract, so we think we work for others or we get our money from others. Dear one, you work for yourself, even if your company pays you a salary. The Divine Source is the *only* source of your abundance. We lose if we think someone or something else is the source of our abundance.

The Crack of Dissatisfaction

Shawn chose to answer a strong inner call. He felt his current salary didn't match the amount of work he was doing. He loved his work in counseling. He loved helping people find themselves, but he didn't love the red tape, disreputable bosses, dysfunctional system, low pay, and being taken for granted. Tired of complaining, he chose to take advantage of this crack of dissatisfaction before it became a deep crevice that swallowed him whole. Shawn decided to start a private practice. He said once he made that decision, his path became crystal clear and his peripheral vision softened any distracting issues. He became sharply focused. He was *having* what his heart and spirit wanted, and that was that. He developed a transition plan, and he got to work cultivating his private and group practice. Today he has a full and lucrative practice and is well respected in his industry. Shawn chose to water the seeds of his dream. *Low-value-itis* was only a springboard. Desire and focused action seeded a new reality.

> *The greatest achievement was at first and for a time*
> *a dream. The oak sleeps in the acorn; the bird waits*
> *in the egg; and in the highest vision of the soul a*
> *waking angel stirs. Dreams are the seedlings*
> *of realities.* —**James Allen**

Here's the thing; we don't know enough about what's really possible for us. Maybe our job is to reach through the cracks in our life and see what wants to bloom and then to engage our Guidance to follow that idea. We are, after all, bold and audacious creators. The truth is, abundance is always available. We can tap into abundance and drink fully or we can get by, or we can put up with drought. Those are decisions, not fate.

How can I tap into my abundance, you may ask? The *how* is the concern of your Higher Self. What do you want to use it for is your business. Do you have a worthwhile goal? Remember, there is no eternal judgment waiting for you if you pass up the abundance package this time around. Even if you think you passed up that package, it doesn't mean you don't already have abundance, so let's talk about our part in the abundance equation.

Having-ness as a Practice

As with each preceding Key, the practice of *having* involves gathering evidence of an ever-present abundance in our lives. Evidence is practical. Wanting, hoping, comparing, and wishing are but impotent beggars. Abundance runs on the four wheels of these Universal Operating Laws:

1. The Law of Attraction
2. The Law of Abundance
3. The Law of Non-resistance
4. The Law of Manifestation

Allowing the first three laws to work together in partnership will lead us to realize law Four, the Law of Manifestation, or actually *having* and seeing our desire manifest in real time. These four Universal Operating Laws form the core transport system for *having* what we really want. Let's take a *brief* look at these laws and make some key distinctions of how each contributes. I'll share a story to demonstrate each Operating Law.

• **The Law of Attraction** The Law of Attraction is about noticing what we align with. The Law of Attraction is an exquisite feedback system. It is like looking in the mirror to see if there's spinach in your teeth before a hot date. The world's mirror will always show us *what* we still believe to be true, based on *what* shows up in our day. There is no failure; only feedback, as Susan discovered in the following story.

Susan was ready to figure out why she couldn't attract a partner. Everyone she met was, according to her, not ready for a relationship. After we talked about the law of the mirror and alignment, I asked her, "If they're all showing up as unavailable, and if they are a mirror of *your* thinking, then what's the wisdom here for you?"

"Gosh, I hadn't really thought about it with respect to me. I thought it was just my bad luck. Ugh. I guess it means...well... It must mean that *I'm* not available for a relationship. Wow! I think that might actually be true. I thought I had to have a relationship, but maybe I don't really want one just now," she said with amazement. "I feel lighter; relieved, even. I mean, I really want to pursue other things right now that would make me happy. I'd put them off because I thought I needed a relationship to be happy and complete, so I'd fit in with my friends and their mates." She smiled, aware of her sovereignty. Her outer mirror offered her neutral feedback—nudging her toward the adventures she really wanted to experience. On one of her adventures, she actually met the love of her life, and they are happily traveling the world.

Spotlight Tip: The time wasn't right for a relationship because otherwise she would *have* a relationship. Susan was not flawed.

• **The Law of Abundance** The Law of Abundance says every adventure in the Academy is fully funded. We wrote our life's Blueprint before we were born, and we have all the resources we need to fulfill our plan. This law says that *nothing* is withheld from us in the pursuit of our creations. When we welcome our *having*, I'm sure our Higher Self gives us a high-five. There is no failure in this Academy. There is only feedback and redirection of our focus.

The Law of Abundance is hard to grasp because we have such a fascination for circumstances and outward appearances. We may think that someone, other than us, holds the purse strings or perhaps it's just the luck or the un-luck of the draw.

Instead, Abundance is Grace in action. It is not earned, my friend. There is no judgment whether we chose hardship, struggle, poverty, middle class, or massive wealth. One isn't better than another. Each offers a different focus of abundance. We selected what would serve our focus for this life. Still, we are fascinated with the idea of the have and have-not drama of competition. True abundance means there are multiple outcomes within every single choice we make. We are not flawed. We are funded. Casey demonstrates how he re-aligned using both The Law of Attraction and The Law of Abundance.

Where's My Abundance?

Casey was grumbling about what he didn't have. He said he felt poor. "Where is all the abundance everyone is talking about? I asked to have a really great job that pays well, and nothing has happened. I think the Law of Attraction is broken," he said, with a half-smile. I laughingly reminded him he wasn't yet aligned with *having-ness*. I challenged him to take a break from the stress of *not* having and play a different game for a full week. He was ready for a new approach. His homework was to produce a written record of everything he already has in his apartment *in excess*, meaning more than two of something. He gave me a deer-in-the-head-lights-glazed-over stare. Yes, this assignment can seem daunting.

"Look, you don't have what you want, so you assume abundance is freezing your dance card, but the truth is that you are already abundant. You have more abundance than you think you have, things like excess toilet paper, for example, so what do you *already* have in excess of what you need? Leave nothing out. Inventory *exactly* how many you have of each item and record the amount in a journal. Do one room or one space at a time. This can't be done in one day because it would blow your circuits! Be mindful of your energy. Stay hydrated. Ask to be guided to the right timing to approach each task. You will be guided, and that will take much of the stress off you. Ok? Bring your journal record with you next week," I requested. Sometimes it takes focused awareness for us to catch how we are already abundant. I got him started, and he finished his inventory as homework. Don't gloss over this list; I'll ask you a question about it in a few minutes. Here's Casey's partial list in answer to this coaching challenge:

Pencils – everywhere – 38
Pens, in all different colors, mostly black ink – 30
Small cases of pencil lead – 7
Paper pads of paper – 22
Small portable notebooks – 9
Spiral notebooks, 8 x 10 – pack of 6
A case of copy paper, all but one ream – 5 packs
A big bag of toilet paper – 24 rolls
A big bag of paper towels – 11 rolls
Books – four large bookcases full of books (too many to count)
A medium-sized packing box full of papers to shred
Big stacks of papers to file – 6 stacks
Running shoes – 5 pairs
Dress shoes – 2 pair
Suits – 1, well worn
iPhone with ear buds + more than 3,000 songs
Workout gear – 10 bottoms, 16 tops , 3 pair of gloves
Sports gear – all kinds, fills a quarter of my garage in open tubs
Fitness DVDs – 23
DVD movies – 78
Sports magazines – 3 banker boxes full, and 7 on my table
Fitness magazines – 2 banker boxes and 10 on my table
Old clothes I never wear – most of my closet, actually

Casey had filled Thirteen pages in one of his many notebooks citing actual evidence of his ever-present abundance. He said he was surprised, even shocked. He took all these things for granted; after all, it was just his "stuff." I asked him what he had discovered in the midst of all this abundance. He still felt overwhelmed with what he had discovered, so it took him a few minutes to respond. As he searched deeper, he had a light-bulb moment.

Casey realized his list held the answer to what he had always wanted to do more than anything else. He could never seem to figure out what he wanted to do, he told himself, but it had been right in front of him all along. (Can you sleuths see his discovery based on what he listed? If you want that challenge, go back to the list and see what is there before you read further.) He laughed out loud. He now has a very profitable and enjoyable business with a swanky loft to call home. His *having* attitude triggered a new attraction frequency which highlighted his joyful career path. Now, he could give his career his full attention and take action.

Casey admitted he always wanted to write articles for sports and fitness magazines. This desire energizes and fulfills him. He is often sought after for his sports commentary abilities as well. Abundance is not about *having* more. It's more about appreciating what we have. We ignite our abundance as we acknowledge what we already *have*. The sense of lack belongs to the little mind.

• **The Law of Non-Resistance** The Law of Non-Resistance states: What you resist persists. The more we push against something, the more it eludes us. When we move into the Grace of non-resistance, we can accept that our life is abundant by nature. There's a quiet joy about accepting this truth. If we resist, it might be because we forgot our three life's companions—faith, trust, and alignment. First comes faith in the existence of our inherent abundance system. Second, we ask for Guidance, then trust in right divine timing. Third, like Casey, we make sure we are in vibrational alignment with our intention. Cumulatively, these three life's companions function as a whole system.

If we knew there was no such thing as failure, would there be any need for resistance? Not necessarily. Sometimes resistance is about right timing or re-routing, as we learned. Perhaps, being stuck is only a pause, so the universe can line things up for us. Perhaps a pause is a gift to reset our vibrational *having* frequency. Fifty percent of humans are actually designed to reach a plateau, or a place to rest a bit while the things we asked for have a chance to catch up to our present. Alignment is the new normal, as Kaitlin founds out in our example story.

Don't Should On Yourself

Even adults need a time out. Kaitlin's long list of *should's* had wrestled her to the floor and she was exhausted. She should be out drumming up more business, but what her body really wanted was a much-needed rest. She should try harder instead of wanting to quit. She worried if she took time off she would lose the big clients she had cultivated and not find any new clients. She couldn't find a time-off switch that didn't lead to loss of income. She'd been working seven days straight and her body was screaming for downtime.

"Kaitlin, you're *body is begging you to rest*. Don't *should* on yourself. Your Soul is calling you to rest. I wonder what it wants for you," I asked in playful admonishment.

"I don't think it wants me to stop. Maybe just get more sleep and eat better, you know," she said lamely.

"What if your stressed body and your *shoulds* are your Soul's way of bringing you what you really want?"

"That's just dreaming. I can't afford that now. I have to work while I can," she said. I knew she was financially able to take time off because she had a healthy reserve of money.

"What if destiny and joy are the ones calling you—not stopping you? It seems inspiration is tugging on your shirtsleeves. Not listening and not honoring an inner call might be the real stress you've been feeling." She slowly took this in with small nods of her head.

"What would make your heart sing right now? For real. Notice only the call of your heart for the moment."

"Well, what would make my heart sing would be to take a charitable service vacation, maybe something physical, such as clearing land or building houses for the less fortunate. I've always wanted to do that; help others to feel safe and cared for because their basic needs were met through my efforts."

"Stay with it and let it become a movie you just love. Let it be real right now. Feel yourself there. Notice the camaraderie. Feel the air. Listen to the hum of the work force. Move through a whole month of this joyful experience....."

As her awareness came back into the room, she said this felt so right. To deny what was calling to her now didn't feel good at all. She settled on a plan to begin with Habitat for Humanity as a service sabbatical. As part of her homework, she contacted them and found workable openings and signed on.

Kaitlin then shared her upcoming service sabbatical with her clients, along with her passion and vision. They loved what she was doing and welcomed taking a purposeful pause for themselves as well. In fact, her clients scheduled advance appointments for when she returned. In the end, she took three months off. Kaitlin made new connections that actually boosted her business in ways that excited her. She now has a nonprofit organization which supports the health and success of impoverished women, another call that tugged at her heartstrings.

Everything is energy and that is all there is to it.
Match the frequency of the reality you want and
you cannot help but get that reality. It can be no
other way. This is not philosophy. This is physics.
—Albert Einstein

• **The Law of Manifestation** This Law states that the universe makes real whatever *we* choose to focus on, intend, give our attention to, and energetically align with. We are the Boss of our energy and the director of our lives. The good news is we've already successfully manifested every single thing in our life right now, even if we don't like it. This Law means that the timing and the how are not up to us. What *is* up to us is the Why, the What, and pure Expectancy. Blood, sweat, and tears are optional. Success is not a measure of your efforts; it is a measure of intent, alignment and expectancy. For our next story, I'd like to share one of my experiences about the ease of delivery.

Ask And Ye Shall Receive

I was getting ready to head out to my office. I was looking for my water bottle with the straw I loved so much, but I couldn't find it. I like the straw because I can hydrate myself without losing visual connection with my clients. I searched all the bottles I have, pulling them all out onto the kitchen floor, and I didn't have time to put them all back in the cupboard before I had to leave for work. Grrr. None interested me. In my haste to get to the office on time, I said out loud, "I would like to have a beautiful straw-sipping water bottle, thank you." I let it go and I went to work sans a water bottle.

My second client of the day arrived with the most magical water bottle in my favorite color. It sported a plastic straw the same color, which was delightfully embossed from tip to end in glorious stars. I fell in love with it immediately. My client said that something just told him to buy it for me when he had stopped to get his coffee on the way to my office. He was thrilled by my reception of his gift and felt like a hero as I shared my earlier frustration. He got to be the answer to my request. This is the power of playful manifestation at work. We have *no idea how or when* our request will arrive. It's not our business to know how our requests will be manifested, my friend. Keep it simple. Ask and trust in delightful surprises.

We are fond of saying: You'd better be careful what you wish for! My son wisely counters that thought. "You never have failure. If you think you won't get what you wanted and it doesn't happen, that's a success. When you want something and you get what you wanted, that's a success. Everything leads to you being successful." Quantum physics says *everything* is possible, so Ask Big and have some fun with it, my friend.

Lock and Load your Having-ness

Clients always ask how can we make abundance real if we don't know *how* to make it happen? What they don't know is that once they intend something positive out loud, the right actions will happen if they follow their intuition and leave the driving to Guidance. That's why the Guidance Key comes before we talk about abundance.

Having-ness is about the expectancy that things will turn out the best for all. This was the perspective Shawn chose. I'll have a lucrative private practice, thank you! Susan chose to have her single adventurous life, thank you. Casey chose to already have abundance, thank you. Kaitlin chose to have a bigger dream, thank you. I chose to have a new bottle with a star-studded straw, thank you.

None of these manifestations required self-confidence. Don't use that as an excuse for not *having*. Self-confidence is nothing more than the expectancy of positive outcomes, meaning multiple outcomes we may not even be aware of.

*The law of harvest is to reap more than you sow. Sow
an act, and you reap a habit. Sow a habit and you reap
a character. Sow a character and you reap a destiny.*
—**James Allen**

Expectancy vs. Expectation

We have talked about releasing the expectation that things have to happen a certain way. Remember, the *how* and the *when* are not our business; it's the business of our intuitive Guidance. Expectation—expecting specific results *limits* the possibilities of something even better from happening. Expectancy leaves space for something even better than we could have hoped for to happen.

My expectancy is that "My Rules for Me" will be fulfilled, even if I don't know how. That's the way it is in my world, I say. There's no resistance with expectancy, but rather a curiosity and sense of wonder for how it will show up. Expectancy is based on a working partnership with the quantum field of all possibilities.

When my son and his wife wanted to increase their business, all they had to do was focus on the clients they love—which was all of them—and ask for more, please. "More, please" recognizes we *already* have what we love; we'd just like another serving because it's so delicious. My son and his wife have the *expectancy* that their phone will ring with new clients, and it always does. They have clients when they want them. When they first started the expectancy experiment, the results took days. Soon, the manifestation of their intention took half an hour at best.

When I talked with him on the phone one day, he said as soon as they decided to have a big work project, his phone literally rang *at that very moment*. His favorite client was calling to ask if they could take on a new big project for him. In our next story, Richard shows us another example of expectancy. Here is a map of expectancy:

Envisioning + Having-ness + Expectancy of positive outcomes + Gathering evidence = Abundance on call.

Start your Stopwatch

Richard Bach, author of *Jonathan Livingston Seagull*, tells a story in his book about learning how to work with the idea of manifestation. I am roughly paraphrasing from his book. He lived in a small, rural town away from the big city. He decided to test the universe to see how quickly he could manifest his desires. He started with something he thought was utterly impossible.

He wanted to see a Rolls Royce in town. He'd never seen one before so he figured it would be a really good test. At that very moment, he started his stopwatch. If I remember the story correctly, he said just shy of a week later he saw a Rolls Royce parked in front of the general store. He clicked the STOP button on his stopwatch and noted the amount of time it took for the car to arrive. Then, he asked to see two Rolls Royce cars, since that would *really, really* be impossible. Again he started his stopwatch. That afternoon he did indeed see two Rolls Royce cars driving one behind the other, passing through his town. He stopped his stopwatch and noted the time it took to manifest.

Spotlight Tip: The point is that Richard was actually expecting to see a Rolls Royce, something so far out of his experience that he would immediately notice it as different. Then, he timed its arrival. He wasn't fretting about seeing one; he wasn't pushing to see one. He wasn't obsessing about it. He was training his mind to have the impossible. He was keeping it light with expectancy.

What you do for yourself—any gesture of kindness, any gesture of gentleness, any gesture of honesty and clear seeing towards yourself—will affect how you experience your world. In fact, it will transform how you experience the world. What you do for yourself, you are doing for others and what you do for others, you are doing for yourself. — **Pema Chödrön, Comfortable with Uncertainty:** 108 Teachings on Cultivating Fearlessness and Compassion.

You Rule!

We had lots of rules growing up, but they were seldom chosen by us. How we *wish* our life could be holds no power. That's why I enjoy the structure my chosen rules provides. No matter the circumstance, "My Rules for Me" are always in operation. Rules, in this case, are expectancy culverts. They are Big-picture rules about how I choose to experience my world. And, to this day they have always been delivered in the most amazing ways. I offered a taste of this in the previous Key.

My rules, as culverts, serve to organize my energy for manifestation. I don't expect others to follow my rules because they are *my* Operational Rules, after all. This is how I call into being a higher quality of living my life. They hold hands with goal setting. By inviting Divine's participation, I'm always surprised.

If we could have only one rule, it might be attributed to Hippocrates, the father of medicine. He coined, *"Primum non nocere,"* which means, "First, do no harm." I like that as my rule of all rules. From playing with "My Rules For Me," I soon discovered my *Three Steps to Having*©2004, Spirit's Wisdom, as a result of putting my rules into action. Let share these with you.

Step One: Declaring our personal rules for *how* we want to experience our life is the first step of an abundance framework. These rules are electives I selected because *clearly*, I did not have them. They are not affirmations. They are set in stone, a given; that's just the way it is in my world. Playfully, I decided I would take the exact opposite of my not-having experiences. Like a queen, with a flourish of my magic scepter, I boldly declared, "These are My Rules for Me!" It was a bold step for a woman who had followed the rules of the patriarchy *well* into her adult life. And, it had to be fun for me. Here are a few of my *having* rules to inspire the creation of your own My Rules for Me, should you decide to play. They shape how I aspire to experience life. They offer a structure for my Guidance's active participation.

My Rules for Me

- I am always guided in my speaking.
- I always get great service everywhere I am.
- I'm always in the right place at the right time.
- I am an answer to people's heartfelt prayers.
- Miracles happen wherever I am.
- Healing happens wherever I am.
- I am always safe.
- I am joyful prosperity in action.
- I live a magical life.
- I unconditionally love myself.
- I love money, and money loves me.
- My money makes money babies while I play.

We create our world by verbally directing our energy. These are invitations for participation with the Divine. Usually we focus on what we want, then try to figure out how to get it. That's okay too, but it's really fun when we focus on *how* we'd like to experience life and leave it up to Divine to bring it. This makes the journey a surprise and a delight. Our rules direct our energy in any circumstance. Thinking and imagining are great, but what helped me materialize what I wanted faster was speaking my Rule out loud. Nobody needed to listen except my body cells. Mostly, I assumed the Divine would follow through—you know, "Let there be light, and there was light" kind of thinking. The Divine set a good example and I chose to make it my own methodology.

Step Two: You've decided on the quality of life you want and you've created your own list entitled: My Rules for Me and recorded it in your journal. Now, your job in the second part of *having* abundance is to collect evidence of its presence everywhere, no matter how insignificant or how grand the evidence appears, as Casey did and as Richard did. I'm BIG on the evidential part. *I always get great service everywhere I am* is a good example. I was in New Zealand on a spiritual-tour vacation. Our tour group was having dinner together early one evening, as was our custom. The server told us we could order one main dish and one side dish for our meal. Okay, I thought, but I'm *really* hungry. I wanted a small side salad with my meal in addition to the cooked vegetable side I selected. I asked our server for a small side salad and said I would be happy to pay extra for it. The server took my order.

She soon brought out our orders, serving everyone. No side salad. Hmm. I didn't say anything. I trust my manifesting universe. While we were eating and talking, the server brought me a HUGE bowl, filled to the brim with salad. Seriously, there was enough salad to feed the entire restaurant, even the entire town!

"Here you are, love. Here's your salad," she said as she set this MASSIVE bowl on the table in front of me. This seriously was supersized! Wow! I didn't know what to think or say, so I said, thank you. Everyone was looking at me with wide eyes. What just happened? And, a footnote— the salad did not appear on the group bill!

Note to Self: Often, there is a pause before what we asked for comes, as if to check in: "Are you sure you want that _____?" (Fill in the blank.) I could have easily slipped into, 'Oh well, that was just wishful thinking' when the salad was not yet delivered, but then I remembered my Rule: *I always get great service wherever I am.* And, I'm relaxed about the *how* of delivery. In Step Two, my job is to collect evidence that my Rules are working for me. Oh, yes they are, and that salad was a whole lotta evidence!

We can frequently claim evidence for more than one of our Rules at the same time. Did you happen to look back at My Rules for Me list to see what other Rules this experience also fulfilled? If so, congratulations! You are well under way in collecting evidence of your abundance. We already know how to collect evidence; we do it all the time. Sometimes we collect evidence for why we don't have what we want, right? Whether we collect *having* evidence or *lacking* evidence, the Law of Manifestation makes it real. Diamonds or coal? Same process. Just saying.

Step Three: Let's say you have your list of My Rules for Me, and you've started collecting evidence of their validity. Now, you get to claim *having* as your norm. Step Three is about affirming that *this is just the way it works in my world.* This step acts like bookends for manifesting. It will solidify your Rules as your norm. Some folks believe it's too arrogant to say, *This is just the way it works in my world*; It's just offensively arrogant. Nope. Keep it light, my friend. It strengthens the My Rules for Me muscle, as our way of experiencing the world. Remember, Ask, and ye shall receive? It didn't specify how it would come to you, so be prepared to be pleasantly surprised. Expectancy in action is really fun. No pushing or begging is needed.

Back to the dinner table. With all eyes on me, I shrugged my shoulders as if to imply, *what can I say?* I gathered my wits about me in the face of this miracle and said to the group, "That's just the way it is in my world. I always get great service. Who'd like some salad?" It was still too soon in this having-experiment for me to know that when someone calls me love, honey, or hon, it is definitely code for Angelic helpers and my right divine flow at work. Another important point to note in manifestation is that my idea of small and the universe's idea of **SMALL** were two very different things.

My abundant universe couldn't help but fulfill my order with a bit of humor. We never know how or when an order will be delivered, only that it will. We decide what makes a high-quality life for us; that's the purpose of the Rules. Without Step Three, however, what we manifest can seem like a fluke. Random. Weird. An anomaly. I want us to feel like *this is our normal* way of walking in this world. The statement: *That's just the way it is in my world* directs our expectancy. It will actually pave our neural pathways for even more miracles of *having*.

Naysayers

Some folks aren't sure they like this boldness business, but I favor it, since I know my real power. I am a joyful chooser. I assume that's the way it is for me because I have lots and lots of evidence of partnering with Infinite Intelligence. Some folks don't like this approach because it isn't humble. It can seem like a miracle and we can't take credit for miracles. That's God's domain. It doesn't seem like I'm thankful for what I received, they say. Humbleness may be someone else's idea for keeping us from holding too much Light, too much happiness, or from having too much fun. Abundance doesn't need a middleman before it gives us more. It only needs our clear direction and a sense of playfulness.

This process of living from the heart of our power doesn't require a divine middleman to whom we should be thankful, because the Divine lives within us and loves to play with us every time we allow it, especially when we set aside the middleman of religion, parental beliefs, social norms, selfishness, shyness, etc. Religion, family beliefs, and social norms aren't bad, but honestly, when it's just you and Divine in the deal, what's so bad about that? I like to think the Divine loves to have fun through me.

That's just the way it is in my world engages the engine of delivery, just like Richard using his stopwatch. When he clicked it off, it was because his Rolls Royce had arrived, and he was stamping synchronicity as his norm. I'm still a fan of saying it out loud, even if I'm in my car, in the parking lot, or by myself. My cells are always listening.

~

Spotlight Tip: When we get into the habit of speaking our Rules out loud to ourselves, we actually strengthen our connection with our inner Guidance system. Life is enjoyable once we celebrate what's already working perfectly in our world.

St. Thomas Aquinas said, *It is the nature of goodness to pour itself out.* It's silly to think the Divine withholds anything from us. It's our joy and responsibility to direct our energy toward a desired end, then to collect evidence which affirms that abundance *is* our norm. My *Three Steps to Having*©2004, Spirit's Wisdom, invites a playful approach to manifesting. Life is joyous when our operating system sponsors our Divine partnership and our inherent abundance.

Struggle is not a requirement nor is it a hall pass back into heaven. It's not a merit badge of honor. Struggle is a choice, just like loneliness or happiness are simply choices. You, dear one, are a joyful chooser, so be that! If we choose to struggle, let's make sure it is for something actually worth having, maybe then it will be more about effort and focus than about struggle.

We were not meant to go without unless we wanted that particular experience for our own growth and put it in our Blueprint. We are fully equipped with everything we need to excel in this Academy. Ask and then playfully start your stopwatch. Be bold; you're already abundant. Save effort and sweating for the gym, okay. Are you ready to make this Key REAL?

Playful Embodiment Experiments
Pick one or two experiments to embody your power. You can also design your own experiment.

1. If I have always known that *I am already abundant and cannot fail*, what choices would I make today?
2. Today, when you think you don't have something you need, pause and remind yourself that nothing *for* us is ever withheld from us: "I'd like *this*, please." Then, feel the delight of having it and set your timer.
3. If you feel bold and daring, make a list of your existing abundance. It got there because you called it into being. These are the areas in which you are already a successful Manifestor. Don't complain; celebrate!
4. What miracles of synchronicity have you experienced, but hadn't related it to abundance? Write them down or share them as a story with a good friend.
5. What are your My Rules for Me? Write them down and start collecting evidence until you have repeatable results.
6. It's safe for me to be powerful and abundant. I say what and why; the universe does the how and when, and I faithfully collect evidence of my success.

My Weekly Mantra: I am already abundantly successful. That's just the way I roll.

I AM DIVINE LOVE IN ACTION

KEY TWELVE

Start at the place where your own feet stand.
—Zen saying

- **The Universal Law of Unconditional Love:** When we say yes to being unconditional love, we open to the expression of harmony in the world.
- **The Myth:** Love is something I have to find.
- **The Key:** Love loves through me.
- **The Practice:** I am what Love is doing today.

THE WISDOM OF THE HOLY SHADOW

There is a Sufi story about a man who is so good that the angels ask God to give him the gift of miracles. God wisely tells them to ask him if that is what he would wish, so the angels visit this good man and offer him first the gift of healing by hands and then the gift of conversion of souls and lastly the gift of virtue. He refuses them all. They insist that he choose a gift or they will choose one for him.

"Very well," he replies. "I ask that I may do a great deal of good without ever knowing it." The angels are perplexed. They take counsel and resolve the issue with the following plan: Every time the saint's shadow falls behind him it has the power to cure disease, soothe pain, and comfort sorrow. As he walks, behind him his shadow makes arid paths green, causes withered plants to bloom, and gives clear water to dried-up brooks, fresh color to pale children, and joy to unhappy men and women. The saint simply goes about his daily life diffusing virtue as the stars diffuse light and the flowers scent, without ever being aware of it.

Rachel Naomi Remen, M.D., shared this story in her sweet book, *Kitchen Table Wisdom*. By rooting ourselves in a larger perspective—just being our natural selves—Love loves through us as it was with the good man. What opens next is a natural way of living. This is what Wholeness in action looks like.

Being Love in Action encompasses both emotional and spiritual mastery. This is the hallmark of a sovereign being. Spiritual mastery is when our awakened, unguarded heart effuses pure Love and joy for all life, without even thinking about it, like the good man in our story. He is at peace in his life. Love attends to its expression through each of us, as it did with the good man. We trust we are whole, fully funded, and supported. Now, as a Pearl of Wisdom, we are fully Alive. We are about our business, living and enjoying life. We naturally effuse joy as we go through our day.

This moment is where Love lives. One of My Rules for Me is: *I am what Love is doing today.* This Love has no opposite and no opponents. It flows freely. We're here to contribute our Light to a new evolving world. Each action can advance loving kindness and seed peace. As we inhale and exhale Oneness, hate ends. Separation ends. Corruption ends. Loneliness ends. Harmony reigns.

We can start simply, but powerfully by synchronizing our breath. Inhale, and intend in your mind: *Every breath I take is a breath of peace. Make it so.* Hold the breath, then intend as you exhale: *Every exhale is a blessing of peace for the world. Make it so.* Rest. Repeat. Breath is the movement of Divine Love sustaining us. The truth is, we don't breathe; we are breathed. Breath is the gift of Life. It centers us and brings us home to ourselves. Notice that as you inhale … the breath will naturally pause on its own. As you exhale, if you trust, it will also end on its own. When we exhale in this manner, we surrender everything. Receiving a breath is the first thing we did when we came into the world. Our exhale is the last thing we surrender as we leave our body. Breath is life. Breath is love. If you breathe, you are being loved. When you die, you are still being loved. No matter what you do, you are being Love.

We are Divine Love's creation. When the call went out that Earth's Mastery Academy was ready to graduate to a higher octave of planetary Love, we all raised our hands. Pick me, we said, jumping up and down. You are here now *because* of your great Love and Light. Please know, this doesn't require you to do anything special. Just be about your business like the Saint. Every Key before this one has been about laying ground for us to remember the heart of our power: We are Divine Agents of Love in action, bringing our Light and Love to everyday activities.

Love Is The Glue

Lovers, poets and songwriters know that "Love makes the world go around." Scientists and physicists, being evidentially focused, have always been enamored with how the world was made and what makes it go around. It turns out that science discovered what our songwriters, lovers and poets already knew. In the early 1970s,

Frank Wilczek, a theoretical physicist, discovered what he called *gluons*, which are smaller than quarks, and which act like glue holding mass together (congealed matter). That's the glue he proposed, that holds the world together. While he didn't call it God, he knew that *something* held all things together. Proof is in the teeny, tiny invisible particles. It wouldn't be until 2012 when the tiniest particle would finally reveal itself to technology.

In 1993, Physicist, Leon Lederman wrote the book, *The God Particle: If the Universe Is the Answer, What Is the Question?* He named his book this because the particle apparently provides mass to the most basic building blocks of matter. Without it, all the fundamental forces and particles of the universe would have collapsed. Quantum physicists, needless to say, weren't too happy about that title. Nevertheless, we can agree that something connects us and holds this Mastery Academy together. Therefore, if you are here, you are evidence of Love's glue in action.

There are only two ways to live your life. One is as though nothing is a miracle. The other one is as through everything is a miracle.
—Albert Einstein

Speak Your Peace

The real truth of your heart is that the world doesn't hold Power. You do. Peace doesn't mean life is going well. Peace is our natural state of being. You can't force yourself to love or not love, like or not like. Love is the absence of judgment. When your actions originate from compassion, your destiny will blossom. This wisdom requires a deep connection with yourself and what you want to create in your life. Deborah shows how she pivoted to became the power of peace in action.

Deborah definitely had conflicting emotions about her niece's wedding. Her aunt Thelma, on her father's side, would certainly be there. Aunt Thelma was old and bitter, full of blame and always ready to shower the family with shame. Deborah wanted to celebrate her niece's big day peacefully, but she could only see trouble brewing, like the thick black thunderclouds around her aunt. Deborah, like many of us, unintentionally carried unhappy futures in her back pocket. We're so accustomed to fighting predictable battles because, well, it's been that way forever and it'll continue to be this way, because that's just the way it is. The adult in her needed to know how to safely detour around Aunt Thelma's diminishment's with loving-kindness. Deborah said she feels her power drain out when it comes to confrontation of any kind. That's how she lets herself down, she said.

No matter how much power we feel, family has a way of pushing our buttons. Deborah wanted to avoid this family member because it would just be easier. But more than that, she really wanted to walk into the celebration, relaxed in her power and without a disruptive scene. I asked if she would like a statement she could use before her aunt did what she usually did. She was relieved. "Yes, please."

"What if you walk into the gathering with peaceful power wafting like a subtle perfume? Lovely, yes. (I paused) Truthfully, you already know how to recognize the moment just before she's about to say something, right?" Deborah nodded.

"What if, in that moment, just before she can say anything ugly, you put a firm, but loving hand on her arm. When she stops, gaze into her eyes and say with the peaceful power of your loving heart, 'Aunt Thelma, I'm here to celebrate a special wedding, and I'm glad you're here, too.' Give her arm a little squeeze, smile as you gracefully turn and walk away. You can always circle back when she moves on."

Deborah had never considered she could be that bold or that peaceful around her aunt. I knew it was less about being bold than it was about being in her peaceful heart with malice toward no one.

"And, what if she keeps trying to drag you down?" I asked, to test the system. Deborah felt clueless. "Deborah, how about inviting love and grace in first, okay? Will you allow yourself to be in the company of Divine Mother?" She nodded. She knew that loving energy by heart.

"Will you ask Divine Mother to embrace your aunt with grace and love? Just let Divine Mother do all the work. This depth of Love is Divine's business, not yours. Notice how you feel, knowing Divine Mother loves through you?"

"I feel relieved and positive. Should I ask Her to do this every time I look at my aunt?" she asked.

"Do you have to remind Divine Mother to make sure the sun rises every day?" She shook her head no and laughed. "Can you trust her to do her business once you ask? She's never once failed to deliver the sunrise, right?" She nodded with a wry smile. She really liked the feel of it.

"How much of your peaceful power color has returned," I asked as a test of the emergency broadcast system.

"Sixty percent." she said, a bit puzzled. I knew. A little one was holding Deborah's happy future hostage. I asked her if there was a little one in her who had become accustomed to being the 'forever brunt' of other people's upsets.

"Oh, yes there is!" Deborah emphatically said. As we continued, she asked the little one who had expectations of unhappy futures to come forward. We asked her what she would need to be able to bring her loving self to the party, and to enjoy Life as the grand party of all parties? Deborah softly reported that her inner little girl said: "I only need an invitation!" With that, she felt peace where there had once been protection and rejection. Deborah felt the power of her self-loving even stronger.

I suggested a mantra for her: *"I am the power of Divine Grace in action."* Peaceful power took hold. With that, she future-cast her peaceful actions to the day of the wedding. Deborah said she felt calm and centered. She discovered that others don't have to be any different for her to live in her peaceful power. Before we enter any room, let us take a moment to decide what energy we contribute by our presence. We are responsible for the energy we bring. We have Free Will to decide how we use our energy. We are also responsible for who and what we allow in our presence.

There is nowhere that Love is not; it is in all things. It is the creation of all life. Love is not a platitude, but rather an energetic frequency; the Divine's heartbeat in all Life. It is wordlessly felt when in the presence of a revered Master.

Truth: Love judges nothing. No one takes Love away from us. No one is the boss of our life but us. There is no need to get love; we *are* Love in action. Our energy field is fueled by LOVE. Love isn't a sensation, emotion or a feeling; it is the heartbeat of Life. As we breathe we are being loved. When we stop breathing we are still being loved. Even hate and evil are but dimly lit bulbs of Love, for we are all made of Divine Love and Free Will. Love is the melody of all hearts. Putting our heart into everything we do is Self-loving. In our next story, Donna invites us to consider the practical power of love over the power of fight.

Ever since happiness heard your name, it has been
running through the streets trying to find you.
—**Hafiz**, Sufi poet

Pink Blanket Love

Before our news went electronic, my dear friend Donna expressed to me how upset she was that her newspaper delivery person could never seem to get her newspaper *on* her doorstep. She said she always had to go traipsing in the snow to retrieve the paper, and the cold was hard on her bones. The newspaper's customer service wouldn't do anything when she had repeatedly called. I silently smiled to myself. I adore my friend and she is lovely even when she gets distressed. I asked her if she would like to try an experiment from the comfort of her sofa. She knows how I love to play on the edge of what's possible, so she readily accepted the challenge.

"Let's see how quickly this works," I said. "Here's what you do. Imagine the paper delivery person in your mind's eye. See him? Got it?" She nodded, with a hint of disdain smirking on her lips.

"Now imagine him surrounded in the softest, most unconditionally loving energy, like a soft, comfy, pink blanket. Let the same love you have for your sweet granddaughter flow to him for a moment or two. Soft, pink love energy." I then brought her back from this image. I didn't want her overworking the simple image because it would dilute its transformative power. She said she felt more relaxed.

"Now," I said, "leave the image alone and go about your business. Repeat this image briefly, only once, every other morning for one week. Don't add anything to it, and don't linger. Feel love, send love, and go about your day." She was happy there was something she could do. I knew the power of her loving energy would only need a few seconds to work its magic. Love knows its business like nobody's business! She didn't really need to repeat the exercise daily, but it gave her little mind something to do. We humans can over-exert effort, not trusting that it will be done the moment we direct our energy.

The very next morning, and every morning thereafter, rain, wind, snow, or sunshine, her paper was laid neatly on her front porch, leaning eagerly against the door. She didn't even have to step outside; it literally fell into her home the moment the door opened. She only needed to find the innocent Love already residing within her and offer it to the delivery person. Love does the rest. This is a peaceful heart in action. If you feel like you have to do all the heavy lifting to keep your life on track, head on over to the gym and lift those weights. But know that Divine Love always handles the *how* with way better results.

Love Has Us

We don't need to do anything to have Love. Love has us. This Love is not an emotion; it is a state of Being, the pure vibrational energy of Creation. Our job is to cultivate trust. Cultivating trust, by partnering with the Divine, is the function of <u>My Rules for Me</u>. It develops practical trust in directing *how* we experience our life. In 1854, Chief Seattle said, *Humankind has not woven the web of life. We are but one thread within it. Whatever we do to the web, we do to ourselves. All things are bound together. All things connect. The kindnesses we offer ripples the web.*

It takes great courage to shed the assumption that we have to make life happen or we'll be left behind. It takes great courage to admit we aren't defective, wounded or refuges from Paradise. To engage this Love, we only need to say *yes* to what inspires us, and then trust that we are guided, supported, resourced and sustained. No need to push. Our Guidance and synchronicity will set the pace of delivery if we partner with it.

Love loves through us. Evidence of this was at our birth. We don't take our first breath; we are breathed into life. We've trusted that fact since birth. Every day, Love still breathes us. That's why focusing on softening into relaxed, attentive breathing always resets our nervous system.

There's a Zen story about a fellow who is going off to war and is in such a hurry making ready that he neglected to see to his spiritual well being before he leaves. The closer he gets to battle, the more anxious he becomes about his unanswered questions. Finally, he's in such a state that one of the other soldiers tells him of a Zen Master living nearby and suggests that the fellow go visit.

He rides over and asks for an interview and when it's granted, he asks the Master if he knows the secret to life. The Master nods. The soldier pleads, "Will you tell me? I am off to war and cannot know if I will survive." The Master says simply, "Pay attention." (Story quoted from, *That Which You Are Seeking is Causing You To Seek*, copyright 1990 by A Center for the Practice of Zen Buddhist Meditation.)

Love asks that we pay attention to its nudges and not dismiss our deep desires and dreams. This Academy is the place to remember we are Divine Love in action 24/7. The Sufi, whose gift was never to be aware of his impact, was just minding his business, with no drama, no self-doubt, and without having to control anything or to expect others to give to him. The advice for the young soldier, to pay attention, invites us to stay attentive to the quality of our life and to its subtleness. Love is all there is. Love moves in practical ways. When we ask, it is given.

Love Moves Mountains

I find joy in partnering with Divine Love. After this thought, I happened to walk past my home office and noticed it was a mess. I mumbled, that's just a mountain I can't climb right now. It had been the repository for everything that didn't seem to have a place since I moved in my house just a year ago. I had forgotten that a few weeks ago I asked my guides to help me get that room cleaned and ordered. I had no idea what that would look like, but I knew that if I asked, I would have an answer in its own time. I didn't worry; I just went about my normal activities. The next week I found myself heading into the office with no thought about it. I felt my body moving me toward a box. My mind must have been out to lunch because my thinking was radio silent. I was simply moved.

Everything flowed with a ballet-kind of efficiency. Every move was peacefully orchestrated. I wasn't hungry or tired. Instead, I had a sensation of peaceful pleasure and ease. When I felt finished I said to the room, thank you for energizing me. And, I truly was energized in a very quiet, productive way. Only two hours had passed, according to my clock, yet 20% of my room had been organized. I knew the room would call me again when it was the right time to continue the clean-up and organization of my office.

I made a commitment to partner with my Higher Self for all my projects. When I forget, I get cranky, agitated, physically and mentally exhausted when I try to force things. Those are good clues to stop, drop, and connect with Divine timing and say, "I'm stopping. I recognize this might not be the right time for this to happen. Please inspire me when the time is right. I'm listening." I put forth my intent, and then I let Love move me. There's no need to push life to meet our agenda. Love moves everyday mountains.

There is a soul force in the universe, which, if we permit it, will flow through us and produce miraculous results.
—Mahatma Gandhi

This is the opening quote for this book because it represents the core truth that fuels our success in life. Love produces miracles. When I was growing up, I thought only God was Love. I wasn't taught that I was Divine Love and Light. I thought that I had to be baptized to make myself clean so God would love me and I could get back to Heaven. Now I know Love is what breathes me and I am in good hands.

When I had my first major automobile accident in 1984, as I shared in Key 11, I had no injuries or bruises, but I totaled my Mercedes. Moments before the accident, as I later learned from my Guides, I was lifted out of my car and was taken on a spirit journey with a lovely angel. Apparently, they forgot to stop the car before they took me out! Nevertheless, I was lifted up and was shown how we are all inter-woven by the same thread of scintillating, Intelligent Love and Light. It was a breathtaking Light show! I saw individual bodies on earth as brilliant, spectacular, luminous energy, intertwined one with another in a magical dance of creation.

I understood without words, that we are the very Essence of Love. We are scintillating energy, continually expanding as one collective body. I knew instantly that we had never left home, yet we get to experience the idea of separation as 'real' for the purposes of this Academy. When we believe we are just our bodies, our thinking or our experiences, then we understand the root of all existential suffering: I am separate from my Source. Oh, little mind ... if you only knew the truth. We never left our Divine Home of Light.

Love Animates Us

During the car crash event, I understood my body/Soul relationship. Here, at the Academy, we have a body, so we think we are someone. That's the persona talking. We are a choreographed dance of Radiant Beings of Light. I was never the same after I slipped unharmed back into my car on the day of the accident. There was literally a new Self, still me, but more brilliant, now occupying my body and, who *literally* did not know how to cook! Yep, fun and games around the dinner table.

We are more spectacular than we can imagine. We'll never find this kind of beauty in the bathroom mirror or even in another's kind eyes. Love sustains us whether we open our heart or not. We are *already* the fabric of the Love we seek. Love isn't something to get; it is literally the fabric of the Academy. We are all literally

Living Love in Action. The Sufi, whose gift was never to be aware of his impact, minded his business without controlling anything. He was happily centered in his life as he defused healing and blessings in his wake.

~

Spotlight Tip: What would our life be like if, for one day, we let Love do our listening and our speaking? If we don't know how to kindly respond, we could pause, just for a breath and inwardly ask, what would Love say?

I Love Because I Can

We are humans with amnesia. We suffer from the B.S. Virus (Belief Systems). I love this simple affirmation because it cuts through all the B.S. *I am what Divine Love is doing today.* I continue to be amazed by where Love leads me. When we let Love be our only compass, we become gentled. Mike, in our next story, discovered that love is a personal decision.

Mike is the CEO at his company. He revels in that role, and his company is blossoming. His new love life, not so much. When I arrived at Mike's office, instead of business, he wanted to find out what he needed to do to make his girlfriend of ten months happy. His business acumen didn't cover matters of the heart.

"I can't do anything right. I can't be myself, or she gets upset and criticizes me," he said. Mike is, as he says, a normally outgoing, fun-loving and adventurous guy; however, around his girlfriend he becomes instantly defensive, no matter what she says. He suffers from double vision. He says he splits himself into two different people—the one he knows and the one he becomes around his girlfriend. I quizzed him further.

"What if you are being you *all the time?* What if you just lose connection with yourself when you feel you have to defend yourself?" I asked.

Mike nodded his head as he felt the truth of that. He didn't want to lose his core, and he didn't want to argue either. I asked him point blank, "Truth. Do you love her?" The answer was congruent and surprising to him—"Yes!"

"Truth, do you see a future with her?" I inquired.

"Yes. Wow, I really do."

"Okay, then," I said. "Would you be willing to have an experiment for a week?"

Mike was up for that but a bit unsure of what I might ask of him. "What if, for one week, you accepted her exactly as she is, really accepted her as she is; uniquely one of a kind? And can you love her anyway, even in those moments where she needs something to be upset with, even when she's bossy? [Pause] What if you love her, *just because you can? Just because you do?* [Pause] What if she doesn't have to be any different than she is, for you to be a loving man. Being a loving man is your decision. It's not dependent on your girlfriend's behavior." I suggested.

"What if I forget? What if I can't hold that feeling all the time? It seems like a lot to ask," he fretfully said.

"It seems that way at the moment. If you look back on your life you will find many, many times you have been loving in all kinds of circumstances, true?" He nodded and I asked, "What will help you to remember that *loving is a choice I make?*" Mike thought about this question for a bit. He knew he needed a practical resolve to help him.

"What would help me...would be to notice when I get frustrated and see it like a red flag, red for my heart, telling me to pause, take a breath. I can tell her she is perfect for me, exactly as she is. And, maybe I'll even give her a kiss on the cheek and then go about my business." Mike had something he could do.

We ran through past and future scenarios with his resolve to be loving using his red flag symbology. The next week, Mike was happy to report that he was 85% successful with his decision to love and wanted to do it again for another week. He happily decided to love her, simply because he can. Simply because he does.

Spotlight Tip: We think withholding our love somehow diminishes our vulnerability to others' bad behavior. It doesn't, right? You know that. It only diminishes you. Give Love in Action a try. Just because you can.

Give What You Appear to Lack

A Course in Miracles says, "What you find lacking anywhere, is what you aren't giving." Love is *being* the very quality of what we hope to receive. It's not about holding others hostage to respond in an accepted manner. That would be transactional, right. Like Mike remembered, I don't need to *be loved*, I get to *give* love to my wife because I decided to love her. It was his joy. There were no contingencies. Now, let's visit Jean and Barney as they discovered how to *give* what they thought was lacking in the other.

On our first meeting, Jean immediately launched and set the context of their work. She loved Barney, but she had admittedly replaced a large portion of that love with criticism, which left Barney and Jean both feeling unloved and defended. Jean said she wanted peace in her relationship. I wanted to hear from Barney.

Barney said she was always overreacting to every little thing he does or doesn't do. Nothing is good enough for Jean, he grumbled. He just felt unappreciated. Jean stepped in and pointed out how Barney had disappointed her, yet again. He ignored that comment, took a breath, then relayed that Jean always has an opinion about what he should have done differently, and she wasn't shy about sharing it, he said. She was sticking to her story, and Barney was in the doghouse. Realistically, he wasn't intentionally giving her the silent treatment. He said he just didn't know any way he could ever be heard or appreciated, much less respected. Jean said she wanted peace, but she wasn't being the experience of peace. She expected Barney to man-up, and she missed the obvious.

"If you want peace, Jean, it's already in you. Take a moment now to feel the peace you have when you look at your sweet, little sleeping child." As she imagined her little one, she physically softened, her body shedding the tension of the fight. She enjoyed the moment, but she was still reluctant to accept Barney's disappointing behavior. Jean said those were two different things—baby love and Barney's behavior. Two *very* different different things.

"Do you want peace or not?" There was a big pause in the room. She finally deflated her righteous balloon and said yes, she really did want peace. Now that her internal system had been primed with her love for her child, her inner GPS could begin to move toward peaceful love.

I asked, "Truth. Have you ever been able to change Barney?"

"No," she said with a comic grunt.

"Do you know why you haven't been able to change him?" I asked.

"Honestly, I don't know why. I've tried everything," she said, looking over to Barney for some kind of answer to mitigate her inner fight.

"Well, what if this isn't about Barney? What if there is something stuck in your heart and you keep trying to avoid feeling it again? What if Barney is just the catalyst that triggered an earlier hurt? Would you be willing to look at what feeling you might be resisting? Clearly you have no control over Barney, but what you do have is control over is finding out what is really scaring you."

Jean really was tired of being the boss of Barney. We already know we can't solve what doesn't belong to us, right? Barney's behavior doesn't belong to her; therefore she couldn't change him. Barney's behavior belongs to himself. We talked about what feeling she was avoiding by attempting to control Barney's actions. Thoughtfully, she spoke in a child-like hushed tone.

"I'm afraid we will divorce like my parents did. It was ugly, and I cried a lot. I was just Five-years-old when they argued their way to divorce. My dad left us anyway. I guess I'm still a scared Five-year-old. I guess I'm bossing Barney so he won't leave me." This was an eye-opening revelation.

I asked her how she knew Barney was different from her father. She said Barney didn't yell at her; he wasn't abusive like her father. Also, he never yells like like her mom did either. He didn't ignore her like her parents did when they were fighting. He is still here. She seemed surprised at this realization and sat up taller.

"How can I accept that he really is different from my parents? How can I feel the love I know he has for me?"

"Perhaps it isn't Barney you needed to accept. Perhaps it's your terrified little Five-year-old," I suggested.

"Can you give the younger you the same kind of love you give to your little daughter?" I softly asked. Jean nodded.

"And will you, her Future Self, pop in on that younger self, in your imagination, and reassure her that one day, she will marry a wonderful man who really loves and cherishes her. Let her know she will bring a beautiful child into the world; a child birthed in love. [Pause] Will you let your younger self know that you, her Future Self, completely loves and accepts her and her fighting parents?" When her eyes opened, she said she felt lighter; she felt peace in her whole body. Now she could forgive her father for leaving her. Barney seemed to relax as well.

Jean turned her soft, open-hearted face toward Barney, and gently shifted her body to align with his. She held Barney's hand. Her softness, openness, and honesty filled the room. She softly asked for Barney's forgiveness. Barney didn't say anything; he was blissed out with the shift he'd felt.

I asked Barney what he was aware of. He said, "A wall inside me melted. I desperately wanted to feel like her hero, like she really respects and loves me. I needed to know what that felt like as well," he said with a grin on his face, reaching for her hand again. They agreed to put peace and love at the center of their marriage, right where it belongs.

The Mystical Heart of Your Power

The heart I speak of here is not the heart organ. It is the Sacred Heart that carries the very pulse of Life, Love, and Light animating all Life. Love's illusive secret is that within our Mystical Heart, we are One with the Divine. All sense of separation has burned off, leaving only an undefended heart—as we were when we were a little babe fresh to this Earth. When in our Mystical Heart, we are Love in Action. That is why I say *"I am what the Divine is doing today,"* as one of My Rules for Me. I acknowledge we are One, working together as One to bring healing Love to this evolving Earth.

> *Everyone gets to take as long as they want before waking up*
> *to the realization that life is a love game.*
> *Game on. The universe.*
> —©**Mike Dooley**, www.tut.com

Living our Signature Soul Color opens our Mystical Heart.

When we want centered power, we stay in our Authority Circle 24/7. What if our purpose is not a destination but rather releasing everything that has no heart? What if it's about offering our kindness, compassion and listening heart whether we think others deserve it or not? We came here to build a new world as the last vestiges of fear, manipulation and control are leaving our planet. Let's let Rena show us how her compassion saved the hearts of two people.

What Does Love Want Me to Know?

Rena was upset. She plopped herself down and shrugged in the chair. She said last night, her husband told her, in a firm and clear manner, that she was *manipulating* him. "What? Me? No way," she said, hands gesturing in the air.

"Oh, he was calm on the outside as he called me out, and while I appreciated his straightforward complaint, I felt unfairly judged."

"What was important enough to you that you would become so upset?" Rena thought a moment.

"I wanted to be right. I *am* right! I'm a loving person, right? I mean, you know me, right? I'm a loving wife."

"True, but what did you hope to gain by messing in his business?" Rena was pensive.

"To be quite honest, I do feel like I need to manipulate things so I can get our love connection back on track. Sometimes he just disappears in his man cave room without a word. I feel completely cut off and unable to connect. It's so lonely. I guess I get scared. Nothing I do seems to restore the love connection we had. I hate feeling helpless; you know that." I invited her to take a calming breath. This was an opportunity to help discover her real superpower here. The power of unconditional love awaited her honesty and clarity.

"What was the vow you made when you married George?"

"I promised to keep my heart open and loving," she softly remembered. Her marriage vow would lead to a new level of love she could not yet see.

"If you invited Divine Love to show you the truth about *why* you need to manipulate, for his own good, of course, what does Love want you to know? The situation didn't start with George, but he is the current placeholder in order for you to make room for sovereignty."

"I can see I do manipulate him, just like he said. When I sense him moving away from me, I get scared and try to pull him back. I feel a painful loss that feels so real. Crazy, because I *know* he loves me." She paused, listening inwardly, and I waited. She continued, "Love just showed me all the times I needed my dad, and he wasn't there for me. He pushed me away. He was my security, but he really wasn't there for me. He expected me to figure everything out on my own. I would feel scared when he turned and walked away as if I didn't exist. Wow, no wonder I get scared when George pulls away!" She ended with a question. "Why does he pull away, anyway?"

"Great noticing, Rena. George is highly creative, right?" I asked, and she nodded her head. "Often creative types need to go into their Cave of Inspiration. It can feel like he doesn't care about you, but that's not what's happening. Creative types actually need time to get back to basics about why they make their art, what their values are, who they are, what they want to leave as a legacy. This alone time is life-blood for them." Rena seemed to be surprised at this perspective.

"Knowing this, what can you do next time you feel George pulling away?" I asked Rena.

"I didn't realize he needed his inspiration time. I think I can... I can get his attention and let the Divine Love you taught me about lead the way. I can let him know I love him and he is free to have his private space. He needs to know I support him. I will love him while he takes all the time he needs. I can ask him if he would come and give me a hug and kiss when he's done, no matter how many days it takes. I can tell him I know this isn't about me, because I know he loves me. Wow! I really do know that!" Now she is in her compassionate, loving power.

When we walk in the power of a Loving heart, we see with new eyes. I invited Rena to remind herself that: "*I am what Love is doing today. I am Love in action!*" Rena, in her next month's session, shared how she had asked George to give her a heads up when he knew it was time to disappear into his Cave of Inspiration. This was the first time he had heard about this creative need. In truth, George didn't know why he needed to disappear, either. He just needed time to himself. He felt guilty for pulling away and really didn't know how to reconnect when he was done. Her loving acceptance freed him of guilt and shame of pulling away. He began to need less time in his Cave of Inspiration. Rena discovered her creative passion as well. Both felt loved and supported. Allowing Love to be the first responder acknowledges our Mystical Heart.

Spotlight Tip: When a challenging opportunity presents itself, remind yourself, *I am what Divine Love is doing today. Inspire my actions today, blessed Love.*

It is only in softening the grip of our story of wrongs that we can come to know we are Divine Love in action.

Love is that condition in which the happiness of another person is essential to your own. —**Robert A. Heinlein**, author of a **Stranger in a Strange Land**

First Responder

When we aren't in our loving nature we are in our pain or we're preoccupied with circumstances. We may set aside our loving nature because there is so much going on. We can get lazy and forget the power of our love, even in the smallest gestures. In the heart of our peaceful power, we know when we don't offer our best. We know when we blamed, we had weak boundaries, and when we were saving face. With hindsight, we might wish we had given ourselves a pause before we launched. Until we decide to live authentically, we will keep plastering the cracks of our authenticity with self-doubt or self-righteousness.

Allowing Love to be the first responder restores kindness in caring for ourself and insures honest accountability. We are the ones to restore our good nature, to speak from our quite truth and to restore our balance. This is living sovereignly—with full agency. In our last story, I will share a brief insight of how I was healed with my father and from abuse. Love would lead the way. It was time for me to notice all the perfect cherry blossoms.

Spotlight Tip: When a challenging opportunity presents itself, remind yourself, *I am what Divine Love is doing today. Inspire me.* You'll be in good hands!

The End of Struggle

At the end of any struggle, we realize that all we really experience is ourselves. Remember the opening story–Mirror, Mirror? We are how we see ourselves. Divine Love asks if we would like to see ourselves as Benevolent Presence sees us. That's the only mirror to look in if we want the truth. Aelethia reminded me, *"You didn't come here to fight. You came here to bring your Love embrace to the world."* Her love for me invited me to remember that every step on my journey had been absolutely perfect. Our power and wisdom comes from surrendering hurt and entering a peaceful heart, not from wishing things were different.

Only when I developed my sovereignty through mastering these Twelve Keys, could I authentically heal my relationship with my father and with all men everywhere. After all, my father was the first place I learned what to expect from men. I had a hard time feeling loved by my partners until I learned that these supposed deficiencies I felt, were what I came to offer to the world. I thought I had to get love first; I didn't know I came here because I Am LOVE. I learned that my Inner Being flows LOVE through me even if I'm totally out of sorts. Love is not about how we look; it's how we see Life. It's not about what we do; it's how we hold our sovereign power. Divine Love would lead the way to my final exit from the Abuse Template I had taken on with great love.

> *Only in love are unity and duality not in conflict.*
> —**Rabindranath Tagore**

The Healed Heart

As a mature adult, I had healed so much, but I didn't know how to set the fight down once and for all. I asked my Archangel colleagues, what it would take to set this fight down for good. I knew they would guide me. One day as I was walking my favorite trail, I was given a vision of the world between lives. I had to sit down off the trail to be with this revelation.

I knew in Tibetan Buddhism, the bardo is the intermediate state between death and the next rebirth. In this bardo vision, I saw a group of people gathered around a big round table, discussing their contributions to my life plan, and I to theirs. I knew these Beings as friends. We had been together before. We were designing what part they would play in my life, and what part I would play in their lives. We even developed back-up contingency plans, including for when we die. This Academy is very well organized, even if it doesn't feel like it.

I said to my friends that I wanted to free my cache of unconscious memories of terror, evil, abuse, and control by others as my contribution to the world. I wanted to transcend all that and offer my Love embrace to the world. I wanted to bring the balance of masculine and feminine energy to the planet by balancing it peacefully in myself.

My soon-to-be-Earth Dad was sitting on my left, and he spoke. "I'll take you around the world so your Love touches many people. I'll also abuse and entrap you as you asked. In return, I have never experienced unconditional love, so will you show me what it feels like." We struck a bargain. Each of us around the table laid out plans and contingency plans to assist each other. My human self didn't know we did this. Clearly, we are brilliant planners and creators! We planned this whole thing out ahead of time with great Love for one another!

> When all your desires are distilled,
> you will cast just two votes. To love more.
> And be happy. —**Hafiz**, "The Gift"

The Beauty of Gathering Pearls

Soon after I had this vision, I visited my father, who was now in his late Sixties. He was out working on his car when I arrived. I greeted him and asked if we could take a walk; I would like to share something with him. He parked his tools and we headed out.

As we walked, he held my hand. In that moment I had the choice to feel fear, knowing what had been done to me under the guise of friendly walks, but after my vision, I only felt Love. I trusted Love's planning. I sweetly shared my vision with him.

He nodded pensively. He said it felt right to him. We walked on wordlessly, holding hands. Now, I felt a different kind of father-daughter handholding. This time it was comfortably firm, conveying *I'm here for you and so happy to be with you.* It felt like we were great companions and there was beautiful clear energy between us. I no longer saw him as my abuser. We healed each other in the light of our pre-birth agreements.

The Pearl-maker in me finally saw him as someone who had never known unconditional love. Later on, when he was wheel-chair bound, my brother, sister and I took him out to the grave of his parents. After sitting in deep thought in front of their grave-stones, he finally said he could never understand why his father had beaten him during the Great Depression. I checked in with his Soul.

"Dad," I said, "if he hadn't beaten you, you never would have sought refuge in the meadow. You laid in the meadow looking up at the sky, watching the clouds and air planes. It was in that meadow, on your back, that you decided you were going to fly airplanes. If you had never found your way to cry out the beat-ings, you would have never discovered your career path. You would have never joined the Army Air Corps and traveled the world so your children could discover their place as world citi-zens." He had never considered how his beatings led to his greatest love, flying and traveling the world. He would have to chew on that a bit more. My brother and sister said this felt true to them as well.

After that day, as he allowed, I began gently teaching him, in natural moments, how to show love to a daughter. He just didn't know how, and he was pleased. In the last years of his life we both experienced a comfortable and genuine love for each another. I remembered—every little girl just wants to love her father. But this wasn't full circle just yet.

And now abide faith, hope, love, these three; but the greatest of these is love—**First Corinthians**, 13:3 (NKJV)

Let me fast forward to his emanate transition from this life. Everyone had said their good-bye's at the nursing home, and my Dad had slipped into a coma. With family going home for the night, we kept a sacred vigil—my sister sitting in a chair near the end of his bed, I was sitting in a chair closer to his torso, while my brother was taking his turn sitting in another chair. We rotated these positions throughout the evening.

The silence was soft and sacred, as it always is as this transition approaches. We could feel the presence of our deceased Mother with us. Although my Dad was in a coma, we noticed that he was trying hard to get his hands to move. I felt and saw that his Soul wanted to communicate something. I marveled how the body could be comatose, yet the Soul could still animate it at will. He was reaching for my hand with both of his. I softly moved my hand closer to his and let my hand gently rest in his palm, as his fingers closed firmly around my hand, his upper torso actually leaning toward me, wanting to communicate. I was surprised by his strong grip. Then, I began to feel an embrace of pure Love emanating from his nearby Soul.

Tears of love cascaded down my cheeks as I waited for his next move. He was in the driver's seat here, and clearly wanted to communicate. Amazingly, he positioned his head closer so he could kiss my hand. In that moment, I felt his Soul flooding me with deep appreciation and unbelievable Love.

The mental image his Soul sent me was that of a faithful Knight, kneeling at the feet of his Queen, kissing her hand for blessing him with unconditional love. I silently spoke to his Soul. *Thank you*, I silently said, *for so faithfully keeping our promise. It has been my joy to offer you unconditional Love. I now release us both with great Love.* His hands instantly slacked and his head glided down back onto his pillow. The animation from his Soul had completed and he resumed his inanimate coma. I felt a spacious peace for us both. Two hearts open and free.

Love always knows the way. Never in a million years would I have predicted this kind of ending to our story together. Edwin McCain's song, *I Could Not Ask For More* came to mind. He peacefully passed away early the next morning.

Someday, after mastering winds, waves, tides and gravity, we shall harness the energy of love; and for the second time in history of the world, man will have discovered fire. —**Pierre Teilhard de Chardin**

Who Do You Think You Are?

This is where we began our time together. Who do you think you are? Who would you be if you were to see yourself as Divine Love sees you? The truth for any of us is, *I am how I see myself.* Powerless or Powerful. I hope you have an even greater appreciation and love for yourself now. I hope your heart is lighter. You are innocent LOVE in action. You were Pre-Approved for Earth's Mastery Academy. Everything you would need was already hard-wired within your Blueprint. You came to contribute your bright Light and great Love. You have never failed. Not ever. You are sufficient for your life. You are enough.

Our Soul inspires every aspect of our Being with Unconditional Love. We come Alive as we liberate our heart and remember the power within us is Love. We have polished our priceless Pearl: our compassionate heart. We have awakened our Spirit's guiding wisdom. Each Key has led us to remember that we are, above all, Divine Love in Action. Being Love in Action as our beginning point for every day will awaken our Pearl of Wisdom.

The humorous truth behind life is that this is a grand costume party Love throws just for us. Love is always shining through our costumes. Isn't it time we remember that we are manKind and womanKind, with the emphasis on *kind*. We are Love and we are Loved.

We live in turbulent times, yet we are awakening to a higher Love frequency. The world needs our peaceful power to reshape a loving world where we care for one another. A world where there is enough for all and where kind regard guides our thinking, speaking and our actions. We are authoring a new Love story for our beloved Earth's Mastery Academy.

As we become peaceful, it is because, no matter what we experience, we can surrender to the Greater Love within us. A free and loving heart, walking in its peaceful power, can literally change the world. Respect yourself and others, dear one, because we are all Divine Love, disguised as mortals, remembering what it is to embody Unconditional Love. Together, let us envision a world where peace, respect, and kind compassion abound; one where everyone is safe, cared for, heard, known, supported, encouraged and loved. Together, this is our greatest gift to the world.

Meanwhile, unbeknownst to us, all hearts will open everywhere we are. Love in Action is the greatest Alchemist. It is our greatest strength. Love is who we are. Love is why we came here. May we, like the saint, simply go about our daily life, diffusing virtue as the stars diffuse light and the flowers scent, without ever being aware of it.

Let us be about the business of living and let it be done in a good way, a way of peace and love, without ever being aware of the miracles our Holy Shadow arranges for the world. Are you ready to make this Key REAL?

Playful Embodiment Experiments
Pick one or two experiments to embody your power. You can also design your own experiment.

1. If I have always known that *I am Divine Love in action, and so is everyone else,* how will I walk in the world today?
2. Choose to let every action today stem from this question: *How would love respond?*
3. For today, how will you *let* Divine Love guide your actions? At the end of the day, notice how this influenced the quality of your day.
4. In those situations, where you want to duck, hide or divert attention, why not ask: *Love, how can I open my heart a little more in this moment? How can I be more fully present in my peaceful power?*
5. See everyone you meet today as another face of Love no matter what they do or say. Notice how this changes your experience with others and your relationship with life itself.
6. It's safe to be Love in Action. As I walk in my Sovereignty, my shadow blesses wherever I am.

My Weekly Mantra: I am Compassionate Love in action. And so it is.

CONCLUSION

We've shared quite a journey together, dear one, and your journey will continue forward, as mine will. I hope you found inspiration from my book. I hope you used the stories of others as a compass for your Pearl-gathering. I hope your heart has taken on a new luster after reading this book. If I could softly take your hands in mine, gaze into your beautiful eyes, and feel your tender heart, I would softly say to you, I love you. I love your Light. You are a peaceful and a powerful influence, even if you never utter a word or lift a finger. Your presence is enough.

I can feel your innocent heart and spirit, and I deeply love and honor you. It's not always easy here, but you hold great power for peace and love. The more sovereign you become, the greater your Light. Don't be afraid to be your magnificent Self. This is why you came here now. You are loved. Blessings on your journey, my friend until we meet again.

"And above all...have a good time."
—Julia Child

YOUR VOICE MATTERS

Thank you. I greatly appreciate your taking the time to read *The Heart of Your Power*. I thrive when I'm able to share what I learned on my journey so your journey can be lighter.

I would love to hear what you experienced from reading this book. Your stories inspire me and make me a better writer. How did this book inspire you? What were your challenges? What are your triumphs? I would love to celebrate them all with you! And, if you discovered any typos, I also welcome your loving eyes so email me, please.

Others may be searching for help, wanting to feel powerful, too. They can benefit from your experience as well. By taking a moment to leave an honest review using the *Review this book* link on Amazon, you may be the one to change another person's life. Someone else might step into his or her power because of what you shared.

SUMMARY OF THE TWELVE KEYS TO THE HEART OF YOUR POWER

We do not earn power. It is remembered.
The World does not hold power. We do.

ONE—I Am a Joyful Chooser

The beauty of being an adult is that you can sort through the beliefs you grew up with and decide which ones enliven your life. We are serial creators. We either choose/decide on purpose or we default to other's whims. It is possible to be a joyful chooser. We can't fix what doesn't belong to us, but we can choose *how* we respond, based on the kind of life we want to live. Be a joyful chooser in all your decisions. You've got this!

My Weekly Mantra: I create from my joy, and my best self is assured.

TWO— I Am the Author of My Own Story

We change our stories through experiences that are out of our comfort zone. All stories have one thing in common. Sovereign power comes when we recognize that our worst moments are what seeded our greatest contributions. The fact that you have designer genes shows your capacity to author a different outcome. Like an oyster, you're here to make priceless pearls out of irritants. Your power lies in being the author. You've got this!

My Weekly Mantra: I write more joyful stories every time I speak.

THREE—I Am Already Whole, Perfect, and Complete

We remember our Wholeness best when we have a beginner's mind. We aren't here by mistake. All the tools we needed for sovereign power were hard-wired in us from birth. Therefore, we are perfect and complete. We are not imperfect creatures. We are great Souls, sporting very cool bodies and personas, with a specific focus which will contribute to all life. We always express the Whole. We don't have to show up perfect; we can simply come together being relaxed in ourselves. You've got this!

My Weekly Mantra: I am Whole, Perfect and Complete in action and in deed.

FOUR—I Am Always in Right Divine Flow

There is an energetic current of Wholeness that carries us along and ushers each of us into our destiny. No matter what experiences look like; we are always in *our* right divine flow. Nothing can kick us out of our right flow, because we are always being rerouted to our desired future. We are amazing creators, bold and adventurous. We planned this Academy to advance self-loving, which leads to self-respect which leads us to a reunion with our peaceful power. You've got this!

My Weekly Mantra: I am always in my right divine flow. Thank you!

FIVE—I Am Already Pre-approved

We lose touch with the heart of our power when we seek validation outside ourselves. If we think anything we've ever done is a failure, we divest ourselves of a joyful future filled with our best dreams. Seeking approval is anything but sovereign. We don't need permission to be ourselves. We received the green light even before we were born. Mission approved. Our worth was never questioned. Please take your unique place in the world. You belong here. You've got this!

My Weekly Mantra: I am Pre-Approved for life. I have a seat at the table. I belong here.

SIX—I Am the Actor Who Plays Many Roles

We are all great actors in this Academy. The best way to be successful is to perfect the parts we play in daily life. When we distort or confuse our role with the role of another actor, we create drama and upset on the stage of life. When our role is clean, and we play our part with mutual respect, there's less resistance for all. Our roles function best when they are contextually appropriate. We are more than any role we may play, but clear, clean, healthy roles actually advance our peaceful power. You've got this!

My Weekly Mantra: I am a wise Soul, shining brightly through my many roles.

SEVEN—I Am Empowered

No one does anything *to* us. Our life is ours, and we can take any experience and decide how we want to play it out. Life happens, we say. Yes, and we get to decide how we meet it. We are sovereign beings. All of us carry a backpack full of old emotions that weigh our heart down. The backdrop for the stage of life is as neutral as our ever-present Blue Sky. Events and circumstances come and go like clouds. Sovereign power is unaffected by changing weather. Nothing is personal. You've got this!

My Weekly Mantra: I am empowered when I am faithful to my own life.

EIGHT—I Am Always Supported

Is this a friendly world or an unfriendly world? It's just a decision we make. From this decision, life will deliver us our experiences. When we understand that life has our back every step of the way, we realize how deeply we are loved and supported. Knowing this, we can relax our pushing and posturing. When we break up with fear, we discover life really is totally for us. We may need to change our starting point for a happier life. You've got this!

My Weekly Mantra: Life is for me in every way, every day. I am totally supported.

NINE—I Am Irreplaceable; One of a Kind

We diminish ourselves by wearing social masks to fit in and be safe. We learned to protect our core self in the face of trouble. There's a Magnificent Being inside each of us that does not need our protection. Identifying and living from our values gives luster to our actions and creates our legacy. Asking *Big* opens up the aperture of vitality. It demonstrates how well we are always supported 24/7/365. Our destiny is assured, so go for it. No masks needed. You've got this!

My Weekly Mantra: I am Irreplaceable; One of a Kind, and I respect myself.

TEN—I Am Always Guided

We weren't just dropped here by a stork. We weren't put here just to fend for ourselves. We were hard-wired with all the support we need to be successful. All we have to do is ask, connect, listen, and then do. Repeat. We have an awesome Guidance system built in. Our particular Guidance delivery can be mapped. The *My Rules for Me* creates a container through which our Guidance can function in all situations. I decide the quality of my life. Guidance has a sense of humor if we are willing to play. You've got this!

My Weekly Mantra: I am *always* guided in delightful ways.

ELEVEN—I Am Already Abundant

The truth is that we are already abundant. A *Having-ness* attitude is key. Nothing that supports our purpose for this life is ever withheld. There's a structure to abundance. Expectancy trumps expectations. We ask, then start our stopwatch and collect evidence. What we feel as lack is really what we are here to offer to the world.

My Weekly Mantra: I am already abundantly successful. That's just the way I roll.

TWELVE—I Am Divine Love in Action

When we strip everything away, what remains is Divine Love. Love is the best energy source on the planet. We are all Love in action. There are many false beliefs about what Love is. Love is what animates us. We forget we *are* the Love we seek. Everyone is a face of Love in action. No exception. As we realize we are Love in Action, we become the force for good we came here to be.

My Weekly Mantra: I am Compassionate Love in action, through and through. And so it is.

ABOUT THE AUTHOR

 Linda Nichole Carrington, Ph.D. has been in the Personal Transformation and Spiritual Awakening industry since 1984. She is a storyteller, an energetic healer of body, mind, and spirit, and a psychic medium.

Nichole coaches around organizational values for personal, professional and team Leadership. She holds degrees in Graphoanalysis, Clinical Hypnotherapy, Organizational Behavior and NLP, where she created, trained and led a 360-degree training room. She loves helping people turn on their radiant power. She currently lives in Northern California.

Staying in Touch

If you would like to receive my blog, please contact me at Nichole@Spiritswisdom.com and sign up.

f

Made in the USA
San Bernardino, CA
11 November 2018